Sacred Vows

A TRUE STORY OF FORBIDDEN LOVE

CÁNDIDA R. DEVITO

Printed in the United States of America.

Library of Congress Control Number: 2012907379

| ISBN | Paperback | 978-1-64803-058-1 |
| | eBook | 978-1-64803-059-8 |

Westwood Books Publishing LLC
11416 SW Aventino Drive
Port Saint Lucie, FL 34987

www.westwoodbookspublishing.com

DEDICATION

I dedicate this book to the two men I have most loved
and who had the greatest influence in my life:
my husband, **Frank Ralph DeVito**, and
my father, **José Méndez Guillén**,
both of whom are now in heaven.

I also dedicate this book to my dear mother,
María Martínez Chávez,
who did the best she could to raise me
and with whom I have a loving relationship today.

Acknowledgments

Writing a book is an enormous task, both challenging and rewarding, that requires a team effort. I am very fortunate to have had an angelic host of collaborators who assisted and encouraged me every step of the way.

First and foremost, I wish to thank my amazing husband, **Paul Bennett**, whose love and support were essential in giving birth to this project.

I am deeply grateful to my wonderful children: **Francis, Anthony, Marie**, and **Andrew** for their help and support in so many ways. From reading early drafts to coming up with creative ideas for the title, carefully revising the manuscript and courageously providing insightful feedback. My gratitude is extended to **Yolany DeVito** and **Todd Culhane**, who are more like my own children than my in-laws.

I owe very special thanks to all of my **family and friends in Honduras**, who have encouraged and supported me from a distance. I especially wish to mention my beautiful sister, **Alma Méndez**, and my dear brother, **Mario Méndez**, who inspired me to pursue my dreams by their unwavering confidence in me.

I also wish to express my heartfelt gratitude and admiration to my wonderful cousin, **Vilma Doris Méndez,** for loving and inspiring me my entire life.

I am eternally grateful to my dear friend, **Carol Ann D'Arcangelo**, whose editorial help, enthusiasm and ongoing support were essential to bring my stories to life in addition to writing that heartfelt and amusing afterword. I just hope that God sees me the same way she does.

I am endlessly indebted to "mi amiga del alma" (my soul friend), **Liz Guzmán,** for sharing her expertise when proofreading the manuscript and helping me with translations, which conveyed what I wanted to say. I owe her special gratitude as well for writing the fantastic foreword.

I am forever grateful to my cherished friends, **Marty, Candace and Richard Macdonald** for providing me with constant inspiration and support. I also wish to express my deepest appreciation to **Richard** for helping me translate the introductory analogy and also for developing my biography page.

I owe special thanks to **Candace McCall**, a book lover, for sharing her keen insight and for providing me with valuable feedback.

I wish to thank my very talented "paisano" (countryman), **William Reyes**, a film producer, for his great review and for considering my book as film material.

I humbly extend my heartfelt thanks to **Dr. José Santos Ardón Ordoñez and his family** for writing such an incredible review describing my book as "A gift from heaven."

I would like to acknowledge with deepest gratitude the passionate encouragement and support of my dear friend **Reyna Machado Romero** and her brother, **Alonso Machado Romero**. It was through their efforts that my book was discovered by a film director.

I offer a most profound thanks to my coworkers at Pearson, a group of remarkable ladies, who make work fun and constantly provide me with inspiration and support: **Linda Sasso, Karolina Mierzewski, Araceli Adams, Andrea Tarczynski** and **Nancy Dipilato.**

I cannot express enough gratitude to my treasured friends **Brigitte, Mario, Sara and Sandro Corsaro** for making such a beautiful difference in my life with their constant love and support throughout many years.

From the bottom of my heart I wish to thank my amazing and long-time friend **Joyce Foss** for helping me understand the meaning of true friendship.

There are other relatives and friends that, in one way or another, have provided me with encouragement and support. I wish to thank them as well.

To **Westwood Books Publishing**, I am deeply grateful for their interest in publishing my new book. I especially wish to thank **the designer** for working so hard to please me with the cover and to **Jane Miles** for her assistance and professionalism.

A very special thanks to **all the readers**, who have graciously stated that my story has inspired them to follow their dreams with courage and perseverance.

With deepest love, I want to acknowledge my **beautiful grandchildren**, who fill my heart with so much love and endless joy. I especially wish to praise and thank my grandson, **Sean Culhane**, for his editorial help and love of books.

Lastly, but most importantly, **I wish to thank God** for His boundless love and for richly blessing me by putting such marvelous people in my life.

FOREWORD

*I*t is my pleasure to introduce **Cándida DeVito** to all of you, and to express my feelings about her and her wonderful book, **Sacred Vows**.

Cándida and I share the same native language and culture. We are both from Latin America, and we met in the United States in the 1980s. One of the hardships of leaving one's country of origin is to miss one's family and friends. So when I heard that a church was having a seminar for people of different cultures, I decided to attend.

The seminar was very interesting, and several people talked about their personal experiences of coming to the United States. I was especially impressed by one of the speakers, who was dressed in a becoming and flowery dress, with beautiful tanned skin, a pink rose positioned on the side of her jet-black hair, and a nice and friendly smile. The way she was dressed was certainly an attention-getter in itself, but when she started speaking and I could hear her heavy Spanish-laced accent, I became spellbound. The most amazing thing was that in just a few words, this person had been able to explain that as long as you were open to new thoughts and ideas and were willing to change, you eventually would be successful in adjusting to life in the United States. Her name was Cándida.

My newfound friend and I exchanged telephone numbers, and we talked almost nonstop during those first days after meeting the other. I could not believe that I had finally found the kind of friend I had been searching for ever since arriving in the United States. She has now become more like a sister and best friend, someone I can always count on.

Many times I have called her, thinking that I was at the end of my rope, that there was no solution to whatever anguish I was going through; and all it always takes is Cándida's smile and her soothing words: "Liz, don't worry about it. I understand how you feel. It seems as if there will never be a resolution to your problems, but you will see how in time everything will be resolved." She is always unfailingly positive and always gives me the courage to continue the struggles of life.

Time and time again, Cándida has helped me as she has helped so many people, with the same friendship, love and respect. Cándida is one of the most wonderful women I have ever known, and I feel honored to be not only her friend but also the person writing this foreword on her behalf.

This book that Cándida has written, with such determination and motivation, *is* her life story; and it is a story told wearing her heart on her sleeve. What I have learned about Cándida is that she is true to her word and tells you how it is without embellishing anything.

I thought I knew all there was to know about Cándida, but after reading her book, I realize that I needed to learn about her past to appreciate all that she is and all that she has had to overcome—not an easy task, especially considering all the hardships she went through: child abuse, discrimination, low self-esteem, and persecution for marrying the man of her dreams.

Cándida could have become cynical and world-weary because of those difficult experiences, but it seems as if they have done the exact opposite. They have turned her into a more giving, loving, down-to-earth, understanding and compassionate woman.

Cándida's life story is more than a beautiful and romantic story of forbidden love. This is a story of love and forgiveness in several dimensions; but it is also the story of a courageous woman who flourished and thrived in spite of such difficult and humble beginnings.

In her book, Cándida opens up about a very painful past that must have brought difficult memories to the surface as she was remembering experiences and writing about them. And yet Cándida felt the need to write this book so that perhaps others could benefit from the lessons she learned. I have no doubt that you will enjoy Cándida's book as much as I have.

I wish all the best to Cándida with her book. May it be the first of many more—she still has much inspiration and wisdom to impart! I am so proud to consider her as my best friend and sister of the heart!

Liz Guzmán

CHAPTER 1

*M*y life is like that of a wildflower which sprouted in a tropical forest, but was torn from its native soil, and was transplanted to another place where the harsh cold freezes the earth. But despite the shock of adaptation to its new environment, the fragile flower not only managed to survive, but also to bloom, leaving a beautiful array of color and vibrancy that captivated all who saw it.

I was born in the late 1940s in one of the most remote corners of the world, a village called Las Limas, which is located in the town of San Esteban, province of Olancho in Honduras, Central America. I am the illegitimate child of parents who came from two extreme educational levels and social classes. Being the product of these two opposite poles in a society where machismo prevailed and social classes were deeply divided, my life was destined to be extremely difficult and stormy.

My father, Don José Méndez Guillén, was also born in Honduras but had European roots. He was well respected and highly educated, and he enjoyed the prestige that comes from being a member of what was considered the wealthy and upper-class society.

His parents, Don Jaime Méndez and Doña Antonia Guillén de Méndez, were descendants of an aristocratic family from the North of Spain, who immigrated to Honduras in pursuit of a better life. Due to the political and economic instability in their own country, they had lost some of their fortune and Honduras had a thriving cattle industry which was very appealing to them.

Unlike most of the people in Las Limas who are *ladinos* (non-indigenous, a combination of Spanish and native Honduran) and

1

who have dark skin like mine, my father had a very light complexion, blondish hair, and hazel eyes. He was six feet tall, robust and soft-spoken. Because of his European-like features, he was considered in his society as the epitome of great looks. In addition to his many physical attributes, my father was very kind, generous to a fault, extremely intelligent and an accomplished poet. He was also blessed, or maybe cursed, with a charisma that women found irresistible.

My father's parents were highly educated, well-known beyond the province where they lived and well respected. Besides working as a judge, my grandfather Don Jaime was a landholder, cattle owner, and considered wealthy by the standards of his time. I was about five years old when I met my grandfather, Don Jaime. By that time, his hair was all white, his tall and slim body hunched over, his snow-white skin all wrinkled, and he walked with a cane. He used his cane not only for balancing himself, but also to scare animals and children as well. When I was a little girl, I kept my distance from him because he frightened me, and it was public knowledge in the village that my grandfather was not interested in getting to know his dark-skinned granddaughter.

I never met my grandmother Doña Antonia, but I was told that she was a very kind and strikingly beautiful woman. She was tall, slender, with a light complexion, and wore her abundant auburn hair in a French braid. She wore fancy clothes and walked with her head held high and with the grace of a ballerina. "Everything about Doña Antonia had an air of elegance and sophistication," commented someone who knew her well.

Having been blessed with loving parents, my father had an idyllic childhood in the first few years of his life. Unfortunately, everything in his young life drastically changed when his mother died, leaving five small children. My father, the third child in his family, was barely five years old.

The loss of his young wife left my grandfather completely devastated and grief-stricken. His emotional pain and feelings of guilt were so intense that he became uncaring and emotionally distant from his children. People said that even years later after her death, they could

2

still hear my grandfather sobbing and lamenting, "I killed her! I killed her!" He blamed himself for his wife's death because she had been sick for a few days, and he had refused to call the only doctor in town. "She is so beautiful," he exclaimed when relatives suggested that he should call the doctor, "I cannot stand the idea of another man looking at my wife!" Consequently, she died, and my father and his siblings ended up almost as complete orphans because my grandfather was never able to recover from the loss of the only woman he had ever loved and considered worthy of being his wife.

His children were not able to recover either from the very premature loss of their mother. Six decades later, my father was still lamenting their misfortune, and he often said, "The servants were able to care for us and feed us, but the loss of our mother left a hole in our hearts that nothing and no one was able to fill." He also shared that the servants did not have any authority or money to buy any clothes for him and his siblings. So when they ran out of clothes after their mother died, their only recourse was to wear their father's clothes, including the fancy sports jackets he used to wear for work.

During the time that my father, his three brothers, and sister were growing up, there were no schools in Las Limas. Rich people would often send their children to the nearest city to be educated, and poor people had to remain completely illiterate for the rest of their lives. Of course, my grandfather had the means of providing an education for his children, but he was too devastated to even think about that. Fortunately for them, through the kindness of some caring relatives who lived in Tegucigalpa, the capital city of Honduras, my father and his siblings were able to obtain an education. My father and his oldest brother, Pablo, even had the opportunity of going to college. My father majored in philosophy and literature, and he continued to acquire knowledge throughout his life and to cultivate his talent for writing poetry.

On the contrary, my mother, María Martínez Chávez, came from a good, honest, and hardworking family; but they were painfully poor, uneducated, and the family was very large. My mother was a petite young girl, with dark complexion and vivacious black eyes, a small waistline, a big bust, and long and straight black hair. She was about 5'5" inches tall and weighed 105 pounds.

During the time when my mother was young, being slim was not considered attractive because it was associated with illness and poverty. Therefore, even though my mother was attractive in her own way, she was always negatively self-conscious of her weight and embarrassed by her skinny legs.

I assume that when my mother was a girl, she was able to hide her inferiority complex rather well. I was told she was a kind and sweet girl with an outgoing personality. Unfortunately, by the time I had my first memories of her, her sweetness had turned into rage and her kindness into cruelty.

My maternal grandparents, Don Lino Martínez and Doña Mercedes Chávez, had almost a dozen children, and my mother was their third child. My grandfather Don Lino was 6'6" inches tall, but because he was so slim from hard work, he seemed to me as tall as a coconut tree. Besides being a farmer, my grandfather Don Lino used to make *tejas* (clay roofing tiles) to make ends meet to support his many children. He was so tall that whenever the *tejas* were ready to be installed on the roof, he would not need a stepladder as other men did. My grandfather would simply hand the *tejas* to the man who was on the roof placing them. Everyone in the village used to call my grandfather "Don Lino," and it was unusual for a poor person to be given the title of "Don." However, my grandfather earned that title of honor by being very honest, hardworking, and dignified.

It has been said that opposites attract, and that certainly was the case with my maternal grandparents. My grandmother Mencha, as people used to call her, was as short and stocky as her husband was tall and skinny. Being chubby at that time was considered to be a sign of good health; so people would always tell my grandmother, "Mencha, you are so healthy!" Her reply to that comment was always the same, "This is not a good fat. This is not a healthy fat."

Unfortunately, her hunch turned out to be absolutely correct. However, in spite of being sick most of the time and swollen with fluid, not fat, my grandmother Mencha was a very gentle, kind, and peaceful soul. Unlike other women of her time, my grandmother Mencha did not use corporal punishment to discipline her children. She taught her children good values, mostly by example. She shared what little she had with other needy families, and she spent a great deal of time leading novenas for the dead or for honoring saints on their feast day. (A novena is a Roman Catholic service that lasts for nine consecutive days.)

I have no idea how it came about, but my grandmother Mencha knew how to read. I heard her read when she was leading the novenas, but she could not write at all. She recognized all the letters of the alphabet and knew all their sounds, but she could not write them. She was fully aware of the value of an education, and the only thing that she seemed to regret about being poor was not being able to provide an education for her children.

Unlike my father and his siblings, who had the opportunity of going to the city to be educated, my mother and most of her brothers and sisters remained completely illiterate because obtaining an education was beyond their means. Only the youngest three of my mother's siblings were able to attend a couple of years of grammar school. When the first public school opened in Las Limas, my youngest two aunts and uncle were already teenagers, but my grandparents made sure to send them to school in spite of their age. Their education was very limited, but at least they learned how to read and write.

By the time my father laid eyes on my mother, he was 33 years old, already had countless conquests and even two illegitimate children with one of his father's servants. While my father refused to give these children his last name or to be a father to them, he volunteered to accept the financial responsibility for their support. He kept his promise of supplying financial assistance, but completely lost interest in the mother of his children. As most men in my father's culture, he was more interested in the chase; after a successful conquest, he would completely lose interest in the woman.

My mother knew my father's history only too well, but she was an innocent peasant girl, not quite 18 years old with big dreams. She was also aware of the social and intellectual abyss that separated them, but she believed in fairy tales and felt like Cinderella. Her oldest sister, Elvia, warned her, "Do not believe everything Don José is telling you because he is just looking for another conquest." But my mother only became angry and accused her sister of being jealous of her good luck. Other relatives warned my mother as well, but their advice fell on deaf ears. She was so infatuated with my father that no human power could ever convince her that her Prince Charming would eventually end up giving her one heartbreak after another throughout her whole life.

Being a known *Don Juan* (a legendary Spanish nobleman, famous for his many seductions), leaving countless women heartbroken and disgraced because they had lost their virginity, did not make people respect and admire my father any less. The fact that he had fathered two illegitimate children did not make any difference either. As a matter of fact, he was applauded for taking the financial responsibility for his children because that was more than most men did.

At that time in Honduras, there was no social pressure or laws in place that would compel a man to take any kind of responsibility toward his illegitimate children. All of the responsibility to raise and support them fell on the women. The men were not considered responsible for any affairs or for getting a woman pregnant. It was always considered the woman's fault for having seduced the man or for allowing the man to seduce her.

I have never forgotten the lyrics of a song that was very popular while I was growing up. The song is titled, "A Man is always a Man." Following are the verses for the central theme of the song:

> "Un hombre siempre es un hombre.
> Si resbala, cae parado.
> Pero si una mujer resbala,
> siempre cae mal parada."

Which translated means:

A man is always a man.
If he falls, he lands on his feet.
But if a woman falls,
she will never get up again.

The lyrics of this song summarize the attitude of the people in the village toward men and women during my younger years. I probably made up my mind even then that I was not going to be one of those women who fell flat on their behind and stayed down by having sex before marriage. I remember that as many women as men belted out the lyrics of that song and both sexes internalized its message. Unfortunately, this attitude in some ways still prevails even today.

A few years ago, during one of my trips back to Honduras, I met a professional midwife, and I learned there was a different fee involving the delivery of a baby boy than that of a baby girl. The midwife explained to me that it was a much higher fee for helping with the birth of a baby boy. I asked her, "Why? Are baby boys harder to deliver?"

Her answer was not only surprising but shocking to me. "Not necessarily," she said, "we charge more to help with the delivery of a baby boy because boys are worth more than girls."

That statement left me extremely sad and very disappointed because it made me realize that in the last fifty years, things had not changed that much in the village, as far as discrimination and machismo were concerned. Fortunately, the beauty of the country stayed the same.

CHAPTER 2

My birthplace, Las Limas, has been described by foreign visitors as one of the most beautiful places in the world. The village is located in the Department of Olancho, which is one of the eighteen departments in which the Republic of Honduras is divided into. It is the largest department in the country, and it borders with Nicaragua in Central America.

The village is situated in a beautiful green valley, surrounded by mountains with a heavily wooded forest. Nature in its entire splendor can be found here. The forest is thick with majestic pine trees, and the sweet scent of pine and wildflowers permeate the air. Wild animals, such as leopards, deer, wild pigs, armadillos and iguanas are abundant within the forest, along with flocks of parrots and other exotic birds.

At the foot of the closest mountain there is a hot water stream which is considered by the villagers as a wonder of nature with healing powers. Some people go there out of curiosity and others to seek out a cure for different ailments. Actual cures have been affirmed by a few of the natives.

The valley is enormous; it can be seen from a great distance and it is covered with a carpet of green grass for most of the year. Because of its tropical climate, flowers in bloom can always be found there. The poinsettia, which is a small plant in the United States that blooms only during Christmas time, grows in the valley like a tree. It is taller than houses, and it blooms two times a year, during Easter and Christmas. Roses and hibiscus of different colors can be found in almost every house, but gardenias are everyone's favorite flowers because of their magnificent fragrance.

Surprisingly, the climate in the valley is very dry because of its elevation. The temperature ranges between 70- and 80-degrees Fahrenheit all year round. When I was a little girl, I used to think, "Thank God He made my country nice and warm because clothing is kind of scarce here." As the daughter of Don José Méndez, I did not really lack for anything, but people around me did, and my child's heart used to ache for them.

Not lacking for anything meant that I had the basic necessities, such as food, clothes and shelter. I did not have any luxury by any means; however, compared to other people, who did not even have basic necessities, I was considered lucky and a member of a wealthy family on my father's side.

My father was thought of as wealthy because he was a landholder, a cattle owner and also his last name, Méndez, carried much prestige. But in actual cash money, he did not have that much. Nevertheless, when he needed money, all he had to do was to sell a cow or two, while a poor man had to work hard all day long in the fields to make a single *Lempira* (the Honduran currency, worth half a dollar, or fifty cents, at that time).

I was born in the beginning of the year 1949, in my maternal grandparents' huge but humble ranch. The old, sprawling ranch included a huge, ancient house which had a kitchen, a large living room, one bedroom, and two enormous corridors. It was an adobe ranch with a tiled roof and a dirt floor. It was the biggest house around and accommodated several families of the Martínez Chávez family. This included the parents, all the adult children, their spouses and their children as well. The crowded atmosphere was like people stacked on top of one another, with couples fighting, children screaming, and animals running all over the place such as: chickens, pigs and dogs.

The kitchen had a very long table, which extended from one end of the wall to the other. The women fed the men and the children, but they never sat down at the table to eat. As a matter of fact, I never saw them eating when I was little, and I was under the impression that women did not eat. The living room was huge; it had the square footage of a school gym. However, it was divided into partitions made out of a very heavy cloth called *canceles* in order to give each family a little privacy. The only bedroom in the house was occupied by my grandparents and their single daughters.

The ranch did not have any running water or electricity. Women used to go to the river to wash clothes, bathe and to get drinking water. There was no outhouse; people had to go to the nearby woods to do their necessities. Wooden stoves made out of clay were used for cooking and pinewood or candles provided lighting. Almost every night, all the families would sit around a bonfire. Some of my uncles played a guitar and sang while the children played games with pebbles or sticks. None of us had any store-bought toys. My father bought me a plastic doll once, but my joy of having a doll was short-lived. Only a couple days after receiving this big and beautiful plastic doll, I stood it up near the fire. She fell forward into the fire and her face became completely disfigured. I was devastated of course, but I preferred to have no doll than an ugly one. I do not remember ever getting other toys.

My grandparents were very religious and had very high moral values. However, by the time I came into the world, they had accepted the fact that their favorite daughter had become pregnant out of wedlock. I always felt loved and welcomed by them and by my extended family. I recall my grandmother Mencha telling me often, "Tú eres una estrellita que Dios mandó para alegrar a nuestra familia" (You are a little star sent by God to bring happiness to our family).

I was told that I was a beautiful baby, but some people expressed pity for me because I had inherited my mother's dark skin color. Throughout my childhood, I heard over and over again the same comment from different people, "Too bad you don't look anything like your father. You don't have his nice white skin or his beautiful blue eyes." One woman also added, "I hope that at least you got some of his brains. Everyone knows that Don José is very smart."

At the time I was born, it was required by law to register the birth of every child within seven days after birth. The registration had to take place in the town hall of the nearest town, which was San Esteban in my case. This town is about thirteen miles away from Las Limas, and the only means of transportation at that time was either by foot or horseback.

It was also required by law for an illegitimate child to be registered with his/her mother's last name, unless given permission by the father to use his last name. My father volunteered to name me, and he called me Cándida Rosa. However, he did not volunteer to give me his last name; therefore, in my first birth certificate, I appear as Cándida Rosa Martínez, which is my mother's last name.

My mother was extremely hurt when my father refused to give me his last name. However, she felt somewhat happy that at least he had come to see me and had given me my first and middle names. But that spark of joy rapidly disappeared and turned into a towering rage when a few days later my mother discovered that my father had named me after one of his many girlfriends (someone he was still involved with at the time).

After learning the reason why my father had named me Cándida Rosa, my mother rushed to San Esteban with every intention of changing my name. My new name was going to be Beatriz María. However, when she went to the town hall, she was told that her child had already been registered. Even though my mother pleaded with them to change my name, they flatly refused to change the registration.

Regretfully, some public officials in my country refuse to do something they could very easily do because they want to be bribed into doing it. Since my mother did not have any money to bribe anyone, I was stuck with a name that constantly reminded her of my father's unfaithfulness.

Once my mother cooled off about the name incident, my father returned to see me a second time when something unexpected happened. His fatherly instinct was awakened when he saw me! After that, he came to see me often and brought me presents. During my father's first visits, my mother allowed him to see me, but refused to talk to him. The ice around her heart melted, according to her, when she witnessed a very touching scene between my father and me.

She told me about that incident many years later. "You were about three months old, and as usual your father came to see you. He was not aware that someone was watching because he was alone with you, but I was watching him through an open window. Your father lifted you up in the air, looked at you adoringly and said to you with his softest and sweetest voice: 'You are so beautiful, so strong, and so smart! I bet you are going to be the first woman pilot or maybe a poet like me.' After seeing that side of José for the first time, I started talking to him again," my mother concluded.

The next time my father came to visit me, my mother's attitude was different. She answered his greeting for the first time and even asked him how things were going. "Things are terrible at home," he answered, "because my father and I do not get along. I feel more at home in your house than in my own," he added.

My mother thought for a while and after a rather long pause, she said in a convincing voice, "If you are that unhappy at home, why don't you come over and stay here for a few days? My parents like you, and I do not think they would mind if you stayed with us for a while."

My father thanked my mother for her kind offer and reassured her that he would think about it. After consulting with my maternal grandparents because they were the owners of the ranch, my father accepted to move in with us. Soon after that, my parents resumed their love relationship.

Things were fine for a while and the new arrangement seemed to be very beneficial for all parties involved. My father was well-cared for by my mother, and he felt the warmth of the family he never had. My mother's advantage, besides being with the man she loved, was financial security and food for the entire family since my father could always supply beef and dairy products.

I was probably the main beneficiary of the whole arrangement because I had the privilege of having a full-time father. However, he did not want to be called daddy or father. He taught me to call him José. Since I was taught to call my father by his first name, I ended up calling my mother by her first name as well.

At a very young age I realized that my parents had the same name as the parents of Jesus Christ: Mary and Joseph. Regrettably, their resemblance to the holy family ended with the names, especially in my mother's case. Many years later I found out the reason why my father wanted his children to call him by his first name. "I was sure that the woman of my dreams would show up at any time," he explained to me one day, "and I didn't want any children going around calling me dad for fear of scaring her away."

The period of peace that we enjoyed for a while when my father first moved in with us, was unfortunately short-lived. Soon after, my mother started hearing rumors about a young woman from another village which my father had brought to live in his father's house. The rumors were that this young lady was my father's girlfriend and that my father was trying to get away from her. According to the rumors, that was the reason he had agreed to live with us.

When my mother confronted my father about the rumor she had heard about the young woman, he could not deny it. Then he went on trying to explain to her, "Understand woman!" That is how he used to call my mother when he was angry. "I didn't have the heart to throw that girl out, but I am hoping she leaves on her own because she is lazy." Then my father continued to give examples of the reasons why he considered this young woman lazy. "She doesn't do anything around the house, and I have to go to San Esteban with wrinkled shirts because she is too lazy to press my clothes."

Call it wishful thinking or being naive, but after my father's explanation about the lazy young woman, my mother began to think that he had brought this woman to be a servant in his father's house. That made sense to my mother because the servant of my grandfather, Don Jaime, was already advanced in years. "That poor old lady! She certainly could use some help with the cooking and caring of that big house," my mother thought.

A few days after this discussion took place, the young woman left my grandfather's house and went back to her village. My father was relieved, and my mother's anger subsided. The fights between them had stopped for a little while until my mother found out that the young woman my father had brought supposedly to be a servant in his father's house, according to my mother's wishful thinking, was now pregnant with my father's child.

Needless to say, upon learning of this new betrayal, my mother's rage returned with the force of a hurricane. Surprisingly, she did not make my father move out. However, she made his life a living hell; but not only did my father take the brunt of the storm, I did as well.

Ever since I can remember, my mother was in a constant rage. I never experienced the loving care of a mother during my childhood from my mother. My first vivid memory of her, as most of my memories, is a very painful one. I remember being between three and four years old when my mother first beat me with an *azote* (a long stick made out of wood with a stiff leather strap attached to it, used mainly to discipline pigs).

I was in the living room of my grandparents' ranch that morning, happily playing with a cloth doll one of my aunts had made for me. My mother came into the room holding the *azote*. She was obviously in a fury, and I became terrified. She commanded me to kneel, and I obeyed. Then she started beating me with the *azote*, until the leather strap broke the skin on my back and my skinny legs.

I had no idea why I was being severely punished. I screamed for help, but no one came to my rescue. Everyone was in the kitchen which was far away from the living room, and they could not hear my screams. When my mother saw the blood running down my legs, she finally stopped and said in a very angry voice, "This will teach you never to pee on the bed again."

After that, my mother put the *azote* aside and proceeded to clean my blood with a wet cloth. I could not stop crying because the cuts on my broken skin really hurt. But then trembling and terrified I had to hold my tears when I heard my mother say, "If you don't stop crying, you will get the *azote* again."

Receiving this type of punishment from my mother became a way of life. It was not unusual for me to be cruelly beaten from time to time, finding out the reasons why much later. I remember that another time, in addition to getting beaten up with the *azote*, my mother threw a burning log from the stove at me. Fortunately, I ran fast and only the tip of the log reached my back. But that was enough to cause me severe pain and get a big blister.

Almost after each beating, my mother would end up cleaning the blood and putting peroxide on my cuts. I used to think she did that because she felt sorry for me; but looking back, I now know there was another reason. She was trying to cover the evidence of her abuse from my father and grandparents. Her cruel treatment to me caused major fights between her and them, and she would only punish me when they were not around to protect me.

I do remember one time when my mother's brutality was exposed, but I did not know all the details until later in life when one of my aunts, who had witnessed the incident, filled me in on the story. My mother was caught beating me by my grandfather Don Lino, her father. Although he was a very peaceful man, he gave my mother a taste of her own medicine. This happened after my mother had locked me up in a storage room that was detached from the big ranch. She was punishing me with the *azote* as usual, because I had accidentally broken a coffee cup. While she was beating me, I was screaming, "Papa, Papa!" I called my grandfather Don Lino because I knew he was nearby unloading some sugar cane.

My grandfather heard my screams for help and came rushing to my rescue. He kicked the door open and quickly took the *azote* away from my mother. He was about to use it on her, but she started running. He chased her for a while until he caught up with her on the bank of a brook near the ranch. He then gave my mother a few lashes with the *azote* and told her very angrily, "Now you know how it feels! Stop beating your child!"

But even after having experienced the pain inflicted by the *azote* herself, my mother did not stop abusing me. Whenever she became enraged, which was very often, she would lose control of herself and would punish me as if everything that was wrong in her life was my fault.

The physical abuse that I had to endure at the hands of my mother was really bad, but the emotional abuse was even worse. It was not uncommon for her to curse me during her rages. She would call me names such as *tonta* (stupid), or *diablo* (devil or evil one), and wish me to experience horrible things, "I hope you get struck by lightning," was one of her common curses. Another one was, "I will be very happy the day I get rid of this devil."

The combination of the physical and mental abuse that I endured, caused me to develop a severe inferiority complex. As a little girl, I considered myself a very bad child because I got punished so often and also because I hated my own mother. "Good children do not have such evil feelings," I used to tell myself.

It took me years to understand that feeling hatred toward my mother because of her abuse was absolutely normal. It also took me a very long time to understand that her constant rage had more to do with her relationship with my father than with me. I was already on my early 30s when I was able to finally forgive her, forgive myself and make peace with the past.

Ever since I can remember, I experienced extremes of both hate and love. My father was as loving as my mother was cruel. I always felt loved, cared for and protected by him. One of my first and most vivid memories of my father's loving kindness took place when I was about four years old. I remember that I was trying to mold a ball of clay into a flower vase. I had seen my aunts making beautiful vases and pots out of clay, and I was trying to imitate them. I kneaded the clay with my small hands until it was very soft; then I was trying very hard to shape the clay into a vase. But after trying many times and failing, I became very frustrated. It was then that my father came to the corridor where I was working. He was wearing a brown suit, white shirt, and a pretty necktie with red and white stripes. His hair was carefully combed, and he smelled of Tabu, his favorite perfume. Obviously, he was on his way to a meeting or maybe to a party. He was all dressed up, and his horse was saddled and ready to go.

My father could sense my frustration and with his soft and caring voice, asked me, "What are you doing, Cándida?"

I responded crying, "I am trying to make a vase, but I can't do it." Placing his hand over mine: he reassured me. "You can do it. Do not cry, little one." At that moment, in the grip of my father's hands, I knew that I could shape the vase, and with his help I did it. "Look at the beautiful vase you just made," my father said, and a smile from ear to ear came over my face.

My father then went to the kitchen to wash his dirty hands. But there was no running water in the ranch, and the *tinaja* (a huge clay pot, where we kept the water from the river) was empty. I was afraid that he would get angry at me. I felt responsible for getting his hands dirty. But rather than getting upset or annoyed with me, my father found an old rag and cleaned his hands as best as he could.

Making things out of clay was one of the few joys I had in my childhood. But my greatest thrill during my youngest years was watching a small plane land or take off in the village three times a week. That was the only modern means of transportation from the country to the city. There were hardly any passengers traveling, but the plane came on a regular basis to pick up meat to export to other countries. Besides being thrilled watching this small plane, I developed a strong fascination for flying. I used to tell people, "I want to be a pilot when I grow up." But soon that dream was crushed when I was told by different people, "Only men can be pilots." One old lady also added, "Don't you know that, you foolish girl?"

Children in my village did not have much fun during our growing up years. It was a corner of the world that seemed as if Santa Claus had completely forgotten and neglected to visit. Most of the children did not have any toys. Their only form of entertainment were the games children created by themselves. My favorite game was called *zapateros* (shoemakers), which was played with pebbles. The aim of the game was to throw a bunch of pebbles into the air and try to catch as many as one could with the back of the hand. The child that caught the most pebbles was the winner of the game. My cousins and I used to play this game every night near the campfire, after all of our chores had been done.

Besides having no toys, many of the children in the village hardly had any clothes or enough food to eat. I remember that some families did not light their *fogones* (a clay stove similar to the old-fashioned wood cooking stove) some days because they had nothing to cook. Their children would walk with bare feet because they had no shoes. And when the first school opened in the village, some of these families could not send their children to school because they could not afford to buy pencils or paper. Regrettably, the government at that time, did not provide any school supplies.

I was one of the fortunate children who had the privilege of attending school. I was three years old when the first school was established in Las Limas. My youngest aunts and uncles were already teenagers, and they were attending school for the first time. I would go to school along with them. Since the teacher was one of my cousins on my father's side of the family, she allowed me to attend her classes. We were all on the First Grade.

I did well in school; I found the letters of the alphabet fairly easy to write with the exception of the letter "P." One of my aunts had informed my mother that I was having a problem writing the letter P. She then came up with a way she thought would help me. My mother would give me a piece of paper and would ask me to write the letter P several times. Since she was not able to read or write, she would take the piece of paper and would ask someone who knew how to write, "Has this stupid girl made the letter P correctly?" When she would find out that it had been done incorrectly, she would take the *azote* and give me several lashes while yelling, "This will teach you to write the letter P correctly." Needless to say, I had to put extra effort into learning how to write the letter P to avoid added punishment. I continued to attend that particular school for the next two years, and by the age of five years, I had learned to read and write.

A couple of big events happened in my life between the ages of four and five that changed the course of my life. The first was a very happy one. My brother, Mario, was born! My father proudly named his son, Mario Napoleón Méndez. He gave my brother the name Napoleón as his middle name in honor of the great Napoleón Bonaparte, and gladly gave him his last name Méndez because of my brother's gender. I remember that my brother was a very big baby. He probably weighed at least ten pounds when he was born. Even though my mother nursed him, he still needed all the milk of one cow to satisfy his huge appetite. So, my parents set aside the best milking cow especially to provide milk for him.

My brother and I have the same skin complexion and hair color, but I do not remember anyone expressing any pity for him because of his looks. Even though he did not inherit my father's most desirable features according to the people of Las Limas, he always received preferential treatment because of his gender. I noticed that my mother treated my brother with the loving care she never gave me, but I never felt jealous of my brother. I loved him very much, and I gladly accepted the added responsibility of caring for him.

The other significant event that occurred around this time was the death of my beloved grandmother Mencha. She had been sick for a while, but no one had realized she was dying. Her bed had been moved from the bedroom to the living room to provide more space for people to visit her. One day, she called all the members of the family to her bedside. Once everyone arrived, she blessed the whole family and said her goodbyes. Then she turned to her husband, my grandfather, Don Lino, and requested with her last dying breath, "Please, Lino, come and hold me. I want to die in your arms." My grandfather rushed to sit at her bedside and held her tenderly. She fixed her eyes on him with a look of love and quickly died in his arms.

The whole room broke into hysterics. Everyone was crying and wailing! During this whole heartbreaking scene, I was standing at the foot of my grandmother's bed. I cried and cried along with the rest of the crowd; God knows for how long! I thought that nothing could hurt me more than the beatings with the *azote,* but the loss of my grandmother did. Even though she had many grandchildren, I had been her favorite granddaughter. She even wanted me to sleep with her from the time I was a few months old until she got very sick. I called her Mama rather than grandmother, and as mentioned I called my grandfather Papa.

After my grandmother's death, nothing was the same in the big ranch. In addition to feeling the intense sadness due to her absence, there was more turmoil than ever in our home. Not only did my parents and the other couples continued fighting with each other, but my mother's brothers and sisters started fighting amongst themselves as well.

Another particular incident that made a big impression on me was the death of Antonio, who was the significant other of one of my aunts. They already had two children and they were fighting all of the time. I do not know why, but I can guess since infidelity was the main cause of most arguments. Antonio was a young man, maybe on his early 30s, when he suddenly became very sick and died. I was surprised that there were no novenas for him because that was the custom. But when one of the family members asked my aunt, "Are we going to have a novena for Antonio?" She quickly replied. "NO! That devil should go straight to hell!"

Even at five years old, I felt really bad that Antonio did not get a novena as was the custom. He was the only person I knew for whom no one said a novena for; nor was he given a dignified burial.

At this point, my parents decided to move out in order to get away from the chaotic environment of the big ranch. There was a small house for sale about half a mile away from the ranch and my father bought it. Soon after, we moved into our own place, which further complicated things in my young life.

Chapter 3

Moving away from my grandparents' big ranch was a traumatic experience for me for many reasons. The main reason was that I had no one to save me from my mother's rage when my father was not at home, which was often. Being a cattleman, he often needed to be away tending the cattle or supervising the men he had working on his corn field or coffee plantation.

However, I remember an incident that happened when even my father's presence did not help me from getting abused. It happened just a few days after moving away from the big ranch. I was probably a little over five years old. My crime was that I had asked my father an intelligent question, and before he could even respond, my mother kicked me really hard on the forehead with her muddy shoes. I was sitting on a small stool; consequently, her powerful kick caused me to make a backwards somersault leaving the imprint of her muddy shoes on my small forehead.

What did I do to deserve that type of punishment? First let me explain that there is a concentration of indigenous people called the *Pech*, previously known as the *Payas*, who live in a town of Olancho called *Santa María del Carbón*, about twenty-five miles from Las Limas. The Spanish conquerors named this group of Indians *Payas*, which means savages. That derogative name was later changed to *Pech* by the Indians themselves. Their new name means "People" in their own language. The *Pech* are short stocky people characterized by a non-contagious skin condition which causes a discoloration of the skin. Because of that, most people in the village shunned them. However, my father treated them differently. He always welcomed them in our house and shared with them whatever food or items he had available. As an expression of their gratitude, all the *Pech* used to call my father *Pariente*, which in Spanish means relative or family member.

One day, a tall, white and strikingly good-looking man came to our house and he graciously greeted my father by saying, "Muy buenos días pariente!" (Very good morning relative!) My father answered calling him *pariente* as well; just as he did with the *Pech*. It was then that I asked my father with great curiosity. "Hey José, is this tall, handsome man a *Pech*"? That was the question that caused me to get a kick on the forehead in front of my father's great looking cousin. My father was terribly embarrassed not because of my question, but because of my mother's reaction. While trying to control his anger and hide his embarrassment, my father softly told his cousin. "Please excuse this woman's ignorance and lack of manners."

Many years later during one of my trips to Honduras, I decided to visit *Santa María del Carbón* to see the *Pech* Indians, my father's many parientes, in their own environment. I was amazed at how hospitable, kind and creative they were. But what surprised me the most was that there were some children, teenagers and even some adults named José Méndez. I even met several women and girls named Jackeline Kennedy. Among other popular names were John Kennedy and Bill Clinton. I soon learned that when the *Pech* Indians love and respect someone, they name their children with the name of that person using both their first and last names.

Besides being left somewhat unprotected, moving away from the extended family also meant that I no longer had aunts, uncles, and cousins to help me with household chores. I was not quite six years old, and some of my chores were: getting up 4:00 a.m. to help my mother grind corn for tortillas, walk about half a mile to the river several times a day to get water in jugs balanced on my head, feed the animals and get a fresh broom made out of weeds to sweep the house before going to school. And of course, since I was the oldest child in the family, I also had the responsibility of taking care of my brother, Mario. If my brother broke something around the house or hurt himself playing, I was the one who was severely punished because according to my mother, it had been my responsibility to watch over him. Furthermore, he was a boy; so in her eyes he could not possibly do anything wrong.

My love of nature made my miserable childhood somewhat more bearable. I loved to plant flowers and to watch them grow. Now that I look back, I remember doing something very creative when I was about six years old. One of the chores I detested the most was feeding pigs. I hated their foul smell and how they would rush to the pigpen, all wet and muddy, to devour large amounts of corn. Then I came up with an idea that made the task more pleasant.

I planted flowers around the pigpen, but in their rush to eat as much as they could, the pigs destroyed most of the flowers, except for one hardy flower which was able to survive, and it grew wildly around the pigpen. This particular flower is called *Amor de un Rato*, which means "momentary love." It is a moss-like plant which produces an abundance of beautiful pink flowers, similar to the Pachuca plant. It is called *Amor de un Rato* because its flowers only open up for a few hours in the morning, and then they remain closed for the rest of the day. Looking at those lovely flowers every morning distracted me from the stench and the squeals of the ravenous pigs.

By the time I was seven years old, which was the official age to attend school, the village had a new teacher, a male teacher. The teacher's gender presented a big problem for me. Both my parents believed that only a female teacher should instruct a girl. Because of this belief, my parents forced me to attend school in another village called *El Limonal* for the next four years. *El Limonal* is located a great distance from Las Limas, which meant that I had to board there and come home only for weekends one or two times per month.

My parents decided to send me to this particular village because the teacher was female, and she had a reputation of being a great teacher and also very strict. Plus, in *El Limonal* lived a very respectable and pious older lady called *Doña Josefa*, who was in charge of taking care of me and also of instructing me in the Catholic religion.

One would think that I should have been happy to attend school in another village because I would be safe from my mother's rage. However, that was not the case. I did not want to stay at *El Limonal* because I missed my brother and especially my father. I would cry profusely every time I was taken back to *El Limonal,* and a couple times my mother had to leave me there tied to a post to make sure that I would not follow her home.

Besides being sad and homesick, my life at *El Limonal* was not any easier either. *Doña Josefa* was also in charge of taking care of six other children whose parents had sent them to attend school because of the excellent reputation the teacher had. I was the oldest girl in that group; therefore, I was held responsible by *Doña Josefa* to do most of the chores around the house. Even though three of the four boys in the group were older than me, boys were not required to do what was considered woman's work.

After being in *El Limonal* for about three months, during one of my weekends at home, my father noticed that I had lost some weight. I was losing weight rapidly, even though I was not overweight by any means. My father picked me up with no effort at all and asked if I was eating enough. I did not want to worry my father; so I never told him that I was working like a horse and not eating enough because the food he was sending for me to *El Limonal* had to be shared with everyone in *Doña Josefa's* household.

There were no scales available at the time to weigh people; there were only balancing scales to weigh food. So, there was no way of knowing exactly how much weight I had lost. At that point, my father decided to supply my caretaker with larger amounts of food; but because of the large size of the household, there was never enough food to go around. I was hungry most of the time, but I never complained to my parents because I did not want to worry them.

I did get an excellent education at *El Limonal.* The teacher certainly lived up to her reputation, and since I was used to working hard, doing all these chores at *Doña Josefa's* house seemed normal to me. *Doña Josefa* was indeed a very kind and pious woman. Becoming too skinny was a small price to pay for everything she taught me. Among other things, she taught all the children to pray the rosary and to make paper flowers to decorate the altar. We all prayed the rosary every night, and I had the privilege of being the leader of the prayer group.

I had been at *El Limonal* for two years. By this time, I was nine years old when two events happened while I was home on vacation. I experienced the greatest joy in my young life and also the most terrible pain, both on the same day.

During the early hours of February 4, 1958, my mother gave birth to my beautiful baby sister. My father named her Alma América. My sister looked pretty much like my brother and myself. She did not inherit my father's fair skin color, blondish hair or blue eyes. And yet, I thought that she was the most beautiful baby in the world while considering myself an ugly duckling and the black sheep of the family. I was very happy to have a baby sister, and I was not jealous of her.

The same day that my sister was born, my maternal grandfather, Don Lino, was making brown sugar. It was a long process, and it took a lot of work to make brown sugar. First, the juice from sugar canes had to be extracted. Then, that juice had to be boiled for hours in a gigantic metal container. When the sugar cane juice became very thick, it was converted into molasses. Then the molasses was beaten up until it became hard. At that point, it was placed in containers with the shape of a huge block. The last step was to grind the blocks the following day.

Whenever my grandfather used to make brown sugar, most members of the family would ask for a little molasses, because at that point, the cane juice is the most delicious. So, the day my sister was born, I went in the afternoon to my grandfather's big ranch to get some molasses. I had brought a metal white cup with a handle to put the molasses into. While the molasses was still boiling, my grandfather had begun to distribute it to family members and even to some neighbors. When my turn came, he filled my cup half-full. I was trying to get away from the crowd to eat my hot molasses, but in the confusion my cup tipped, and some of the boiling molasses got stuck on the palm of my right hand.

I had never experienced such excruciating pain! I do not remember screaming, and no one in the crowd noticed what had happened to me. I just remember dropping the cup, holding my right hand with my left hand, and taking off like lightning to a stream nearby where the brown sugar was being made. I put my hand in the water and kept it there for a long time until it was almost dark.

My hand was still hurting very badly, but I knew I had to go home. When I got home my mother was out of bed and asked me furiously, "Where have you been all afternoon?" Before I could answer her, she noticed that I was trying to hide my right hand. She grabbed me by the arm, and I started crying. When she saw my hand completely red, she asked me screaming, "How did you do that to yourself?"

I answered her sobbing, "I burned myself with the molasses." Then my mother got angrier. The *azote* was not nearby, so she slapped me around, then grabbed me by my long hair and shook me like a rag doll. During the whole time I was yelling for help, "José! José!" Fortunately, my father was just arriving home from work, and he heard me screaming his name. My mother was still grabbing me by the hair when he came rushing into the room. He pushed her away from me and shouted to her in a fury, "What's the matter with you, stupid woman? Have you gone completely insane?"

My mother's reply was, "I am trying to teach this idiot to be more careful. The imbecile burned herself with boiling molasses."

My father took a look of my hand and exclaimed with deep sadness and compassion, "You poor, poor darling! I will take care of you." Then he took me to his bedroom and put some medicated cream on my hand. To protect me from my mother, who was still in a rage, he let me sleep in his bed that night. My mother had to sleep in another bed with the baby.

The medicated cream made my hand feel somewhat better, but nothing could have taken away the pain I was feeling in my heart and soul at having been the victim of such treatment from my own mother. She was someone who was supposed to love me and protect me. Since in my child's mind I could not understand my mother's behavior, I concluded that I probably deserved the harsh punishment.

Now that I look back, maybe being physically and mentally abused seemed normal to me because my cousins who were living in the big ranch also experienced corporal punishment. Many people at that time believed that punishing their children was the right way of bringing them up. However, I have beautiful memories of a happy and peaceful household that was very different than mine. It was the home of my cousin, Vilma, the daughter of my father's older brother, Pablo, and his wife Raquel.

I owe to this cousin some of the few happy memories that I have from my childhood. We are about the same age and we have been as close as sisters since we were little girls. She would invite me to her house for Christmas, and I was amazed at the beautiful large Nativity set her mother would create using real hay to place the infant Jesus and fresh plants for decorations. I was always treated with loving kindness by Vilma and by all of the members of her family.

My hand eventually healed, and I went back to *El Limonal* for two more years. I completed my grammar school education with above-average grades in all subjects and with impeccable behavior. I had finished grammar school one year earlier than most children of my age. When I first went to *El Limonal* at seven years of age, my mother had registered me to enter first grade, but two days later, the teacher promoted me to the second grade because of my performance.

My main motivation for excelling academically was not only to please my parents, but also to make up for what I thought were my deficiencies. I figured that since I could not be beautiful as my father, at least I could be smart like him.

When I returned home from *El Limonal*, my education came to a halt because in order to continue studying, I would had to go to the city and my parents would not have allowed that. They were extremely strict, especially my father. During all of my years in school, I had not been allowed to attend any school celebrations with the exception of Independence Day, which is on September 15. I had always felt a strong desire to learn to dance, but I had never been allowed to attend any parties, even within the family circle. I had not even been allowed to go to San Esteban, the closest town to Las Limas. I had been to that town only once, to be baptized and for my confirmation when I was a baby. Yes, I was baptized and confirmed the same day. Since it was very rare for a bishop to visit San Esteban, parents had their children confirmed whenever they had the chance.

I longed to see the ocean, which my father had described to me in vivid detail, but I had no hope of ever going there. I loved literature and I aspired to continue my education, but I was told by my parents, "A woman doesn't need to be highly educated to be a housewife." I dreamed of falling in love, like other girls my age, but I was never attracted to any of the local boys.

None of the things I aspired to seemed possible, and I felt completely stuck in a place that was considered a tropical paradise by the few tourists who had visited it. I could not see its beauty then, because I was too involved in my own loneliness and despair. In those days for me, Las Limas was nothing more than a prison from which I was hoping to escape someday.

At that particular time, I could not see any light at the end of the tunnel. I believed that my future was going to be as bleak as my past. I hardly had any happy memories, but one rather pleasant event kept on going through my mind. It was the memory of attending a Catholic mass for the first time and meeting the priest who celebrated the mass.

I was about eight years old when for the very first time a Catholic priest from the United States, named Father Andrew DeVito, came to the village to celebrate mass. I had never been to a mass nor had I seen a priest until then. Father Andrew was the first priest I saw, and the second person I met who was from the United States.

The only other foreign person I had seen was an ambassador. I was about four years old then. When I heard that this strange man was an *embajador* (ambassador), I understood that new word to mean descendent from above. So, I actually thought that the he had come down from heaven. Then my father explained the meaning of the word ambassador and that the man was from another part of the world, the United States.

I was brought up Catholic, but religion then was only practiced in people's homes because there was not a church in the village. The only priests were the missionaries from the United States. Each priest was assigned to shepherd an entire diocese, and each diocese included many towns. Consequently, the priest could only visit each town a few times a year. Father Andrew was the first priest who started visiting villages and he had come to Las Limas to celebrate mass and to perform baptisms.

The mass was celebrated in the luxurious house of Don Maximiliano Luna, who was considered the wealthiest man in the village, who had the biggest house and was the owner of most of the land in that area. He originally came from Spain and was a distant relative of my father's family.

My mother was too busy to attend the mass, but she had some of my aunts take me along. Since I was too shy to greet strangers, I was hoping to be invisible at the mass. I had received many beatings from my mother for being too shy to greet some distant relatives on my father's side of the family.

Most of the people from Las Limas and nearby villages attended the mass. The enormous living room in Don Maximiliano's house, where the mass was being held, was crowded from wall to wall. To my surprise, in a crowd of such magnitude, Father Andrew noticed me, and he said, "*Hola, muchachita!*" (Hi, little girl!) I did not respond; I was frozen. Then he gently touched my chin and asked, "*Te comieron la lengua los ratones?*" (Did mice eat your tongue?) I was even more embarrassed, and I could not bring myself to say a word.

When we returned home after mass, my mother asked my aunts, "How was the mass?" One of my oldest aunts replied, "Your daughter acted like a *tonta* (a fool) as usual. The priest said hello to her, and it was like taking to a wall. She didn't say anything."

My mother got very upset and screamed at me, "How dare you ignore the greeting of a priest?" Then she punished me with the azote again.

Even though Father Andrew had had nothing to do with the beating, in my mind he was responsible for my punishment. "If that priest had not said hello to me, I would not have been beaten," I thought. At that point, I had no interest in ever seeing Father Andrew again. Neither did I have the vaguest idea that in the future, he would play the most important role in my life.

CHAPTER 4

~

ather Andrew was born in Boston, Massachusetts, U.S.A., and was the only child of Alicia and Antonio DeVito, who were Italian immigrants. He joined the Franciscan Order immediately after graduating high school and was ordained as a priest in June of 1954. Soon after his ordination, Father Andrew was sent to the missions in Honduras to a parish in a town called Gualaco, which is about twenty-five miles from Las Limas. Even though the distance between Las Limas and Gualaco is not that great, it would usually take two days to make the trip because a mountain separated the two places, and horseback was the only means of transportation.

When Father Andrew arrived in Gualaco, he did not speak any Spanish, the language of the country; neither was he prepared for the hard life in a third world country. Since he had taken a vow of obedience, Father Andrew had to stay in the missions, and his only choice was to either sink or swim. He longed to meet someone within his diocese who spoke his native language, but he could not find anyone until months later when he met my father.

My father had been in the Honduran navy and had fought along with the United States during the Second World War. When the war was over, my father stayed in California for a couple of years and learned to speak English fluently. Father Andrew and my father became the best of friends.

After my first meeting with Father Andrew when I was eight years old, I had no contact with him for a couple of years even though he visited my father once in a while. Since I was away at school, I did not get to see him. I had been back home a couple of times when Father Andrew came to our house, but because I was still very shy, I made sure to stay away when the priest was visiting.

Father Andrew saw me from afar doing my chores, but he just assumed that I was the daughter of my father's servant and that my mother was the servant who worked for my father. The priest had every right to make that assumption because every time he visited my father, my mother had always been in the kitchen doing the cooking and serving the food. Other visitors also made the same assumption about the relationship between my parents as Father Andrew had, and my father was responsible for that. Although he and my mother were living together, my father never introduced her as his live-in partner or as a significant other. He simply would say to his guests, "This is Maria." Father Andrew finally found out that my father had a family, but several years passed before he made the connection that the little girl, he had met years earlier, was his best friend's daughter.

One day, Father Andrew announced in the village that he was looking for boys and girls with possible religious vocation, and I had been highly recommended by several older women in the village. These pious ladies believed that I had a vocation for the religious life because I was always such a good girl, and I did not show any interest in boys.

It was a custom then in the village for girls to get married young, probably because of the lack of opportunities to do anything else. The average marrying age for a girl was fifteen years old, and since I was very tall and mature for my age, people assumed that I was old enough to get married. But in reality, I was only twelve years old.

I had no idea that I had been recommended for a possible religious vocation. So I was amazed when one Saturday morning my brother, Mario, went to El Limonal to take me home for the weekend and told me, "You got a letter from Father Andrew."

Then I asked my brother, "Why is Father Andrew writing to me?"

My brother replied, "Father Andrew wants you to become a nun and go to a convent in Juticalpa." I had no intention of becoming a nun, even though I did not know what a nun was; but I liked the idea of going to Juticalpa, the capital city of Olancho. I had not even been to a small town, and the possibility of going to a city was very appealing.

As soon as I arrived home that day, I asked my father about the letter. He handed me the letter and said to me with a voice of authority, "Father Andrew already talked to me about giving you permission to study in a convent in Juticalpa, and the answer is no. You are too young. If you still want to become a nun when you are thirty years old, then you can go."

I knew my father meant what he said, and my hopes of going to a city faded away. I read Father Andrew's kind letter over and over again. A few days later, I answered his letter and informed him of my father's decision.

After that first letter, I received several letters from Father Andrew with the same message: "Please do not get discouraged, my child. Be patient! Let's hope and pray that your father changes his mind." In one of his letters, Father Andrew explained to me, "Saint Clare had the same problem with her father, but in the end, God's will always prevail in spite of any opposition." Father Andrew and I kept in touch by mail with the hope that eventually my father would change his mind and give me permission to become a nun.

Surprisingly, the postal service in Las Limas at that time was very good. The mail from all over the country was sent to an office in San Esteban. There was no mail delivery to Las Limas; so when someone from the village went to San Esteban, they would pick up the mail and deliver it to its recipients.

There were no telephones at that time, but a quick way of communicating was by telegraph. People would pay for each word to send a telegram, and there was a telegraph office in La Venta, three villages away from Las Limas. A telegraphist was on duty all day and most of the night. The telegrams were delivered immediately by a messenger on horseback.

In the telegraph office in La Venta, there was only one trained telegraphist and he came from another department in Honduras. He had very pretty green eyes and women admired him for his looks, but he was not very honest. One day, a very kind but naïve lady went to the telegraph office with a pail of baked goods that she had made for her son, who was in the Army in Juticalpa. She asked the telegraphist, "Can I send these things to my son in Juticalpa the way you send a telegram?"

Quickly he replied, "Of course! Just leave the pail here and return tomorrow to pick up the empty pail."

Then the kind lady asked, "How does that work? How do you send the pail to Juticalpa?"

The telegraphist took her outside the office, showed her the cables and explained to her, "We attach the pail to the cables; then it's carried all the way to Juticalpa."

The poor lady went back the next day to pick up her empty pail, but she never sent any more baked goods to her son by telegraph. When she found out that her son did not receive the baked goods, she exclaimed very aggravated, "Something probably went wrong with those damn wires."

Father Andrew and my father continued to be the best of friends. During one of his visits, he left a package for me after getting my father's permission. The package contained two books, one about the life of Saint Francis of Assisi, the founder of the Franciscan Order. The other book was about the life of St. Teresa (the "Little Flower," as she was nicknamed). I was thrilled to receive such a surprise! I read both books time and time again, and I began to feel somewhat curious and interested in the religious life. However, there was no sign that my father would ever change his mind. Every time I approached him about letting me go to the convent in Juticalpa, his answer was always the same, "Wait until you are thirty years old when you know what you are doing."

About two years later, Father Andrew and I were still corresponding. He used to write to me every few weeks, and I always looked forward to receiving his letters. I would write to him just as often, giving him feedback on the additional books he had sent to me about the inspiring lives of other saints, and I would ask many questions about the process of becoming a nun. He kept me posted on the progress of girls my age who had entered the convent, and he would send me photos of them and postal cards whenever he went to the United States. On the back of the cards, he would describe the different places he was visiting, and I would visit those places in my imagination.

Father Andrew also sent me many postal cards of interesting places in Honduras. He knew that I had never been anywhere, except in the village where I was born and El Limonal where I went to school. I was curious about seeing other parts of the world, and that need was somewhat fulfilled through his post cards. No one had ever given me that kind of attention before; no one had ever made me feel that special! I started developing a huge crush on this priest, but I was always very careful not to show him these feelings; at least that's what I thought. By the time I was fourteen years old, I was hopelessly in love with Father Andrew.

He was not strikingly handsome, but because of his kindness and soft manner, Father Andrew came across as very good looking, at least to me. He was about five feet nine inches tall and slightly overweight. His big hazel eyes reflected the goodness of his heart, and his black hair complemented his fair skin. Along with a dry sense of humor, his lips always had a ready smile and a kind word for everyone, including me.

In addition to the religious content and description of places in his letters, he was very complimentary of my father and me. In one letter he wrote, "You are definitely your father's daughter; you reflect his great kindness and noble spirit." Needless to say, Father Andrew's compliments were for me like a shot of self-esteem to which I soon I became addicted to. In addition to a love as deep as an ocean, great respect and admiration, I felt an enormous debt of gratitude to this priest for the way he made me feel and for giving me the kind of attention that I had never had. The feelings that began as simple gratitude ended up turning into an all-consuming love.

I tried very hard to keep my feelings for Father Andrew a secret, especially from him, but also from my parents and from all of the people in the village. There were many taboos for a woman at that time. Having a crush on a priest was probably considered one of the biggest taboos. Priests were considered holy men of God exempt from the human condition, unable to experience the most normal of human emotions, such as romantic love. If a priest broke his vow of chastity, it was always considered the woman's fault for allowing the devil to use her to make a holy man fall from grace.

People in the village recall a true, but sad and funny story that illustrates how priests were placed on such a high pedestal. My mother remembers the incident very well; it probably happened during the early 1950s because she said that I had already been born. A wise guy impersonated a priest and was able to fool everybody in the villages into thinking he was a saint. He made people believe that he had no need to eat because the word of God sustained him. He had no need to walk either because people volunteered to carry him on a palanquin from one house to the next or from one village to another. He was worshipped in a different house every night; then as he was carried on a palanquin during processions, some of the men played musical instruments while the women sang hymns of praise.

Even though this wise guy had everyone fooled that he did not eat at all, people would give him turkeys, chickens, pigs, coffee, fruits etc. because they wanted to give something to whom they considered to be a holy man and those were the only things they had available. This charade went on for a while until someone was able to expose the imposter when he was found eating up his gifts in the middle of the night. When people in the village found out about the deception, they were rightfully infuriated. The con artist had to run for his life, along with his accomplice, and he had to leave his animals behind. Hopefully, some people were able to recover some of their gifts.

By the time Father Andrew came to Las Limas, people were no longer that naïve. However, they still believed that priests were above the human condition. More importantly, if a priest broke his vow of celibacy, they still blamed the woman instead of the priest.

Second to seducing a priest, another taboo during my younger years was for a woman to lose her virginity before marriage. While I was growing up, I remember that a few brides had been brought back to their parents the day after their wedding because their husbands had claimed these brides were not the virgins they had expected. Whether that was true or not, no one questioned their judgment, and these men had been able to get away with returning their wives like unwanted merchandise. One can just imagine how humiliating that experience must have been for these women! Besides being severely and consistently punished by their parents, these poor women were completely and forever disgraced in the eyes of society.

For men things were very different of course; the taboos did not apply to them. However, I have to admit that in some way, women have been somewhat responsible for promoting that macho culture. I have heard of cases of very good men that women did not find appealing because they were not like Casanova. Furthermore, for men to be unfaithful they had to find women with whom to be unfaithful with. I believe that as women, we have more power than we realize to turn things around in our favor by not getting involved with a married man. Although, most of the time in this culture men will still lie about their marital status.

Father Andrew and I had been corresponding for several years when I became aware of my romantic feelings towards him. I tried to read between the lines in each letter he sent. I was looking for some indication that he had begun to see me as more than just a candidate for the sisterhood, but I found none. His letters continued to be very spiritual; therefore, I answered them in the same way, trying very hard not to reflect my true feelings for him.

Then, suddenly, something changed! I do not remember when but Father Andrew's gifts to me became more personal. For several years he had been sending me religious books and coconut-filled chocolates because he knew I liked them. He would also send toys for my brother and my baby sister. Not surprisingly, I felt awestruck when on one occasion, he handed me a small jewelry box that contained a lovely necklace with matching earrings. I had never seen anything so beautiful and I will never forget the thrill I felt to receive such gifts! But since Father Andrew was so generous and thoughtful with my brother and sister, it never occurred to me that showering me with gifts, even with the last two special ones, had a romantic connotation.

During one of his trips to the United States, Father Andrew brought me back a heavy coat. I had never seen a coat before, and there was no need to wear one in Honduras because of its tropical climate. Still, I was dying to show off my coat; so I decided to wear it for one of the religious celebrations. I sweated profusely, of course! In addition to feeling very hot, I was the joke of the whole village. I could hear people murmur, "¡Ay! ¡Pero que tonta! Se va a derretir con esa cosa tan caliente." (Oh! What a stupid girl! She is going to melt with that heavy thing on.) No one in Las Limas had ever seen a coat before, and no one had a hard time guessing who had given me that strange gift.

Another gift from Father Andrew that stirred the tongues of the people in the village was a record player. It was battery-operated since we did not have any electricity in Las Limas. Along with the record player, Father Andrew gave me an extensive collection of Mexican music with the most beautiful *rancheras* (Mexican country songs) I had ever heard. I had never seen a record player before, neither had anyone else in Las Limas. People came to my house in groups to either listen to the ranchera songs or to satisfy their curiosity.

I would listen to the love songs over and over again, while daydreaming that the songs expressed how Father Andrew truly felt about me. At times, I even had a dim hope that maybe he had chosen to give me the music of these beautiful love songs because indirectly he was trying to express his feelings for me. But soon reality would set in, and I would give up all hope that Father Andrew loved me in return. Because I worshipped the ground he walked on, I saw him as an unreachable star.

I had tried very hard to conceal from the people in Las Limas who the actual donor of these gifts was. Nevertheless, in a small village everyone knows everybody's business. When people found out about the record player, they began saying, "Ese Padre está enamorado de la hija de María y Don José. No le está dando tantos regalos por gusto." (That priest is in love with María and Don José's daughter. He has not given her all those gifts for nothing.)

I honestly did believe that these gifts were expressions of Father Andrew's loving kindness that had nothing to do with romantic love. Initially, I wanted to stop the gossip mainly because fear of my father's reaction, but I had no idea how to stop people from talking. After a while, I was hoping the gossip was true, and I no longer cared to stop it. However, if my father had been home, things would have been very different. He would have immediately put a stop to the rumors and to the gifts as well.

My father was not aware of what was going on in the village because he was working in Catacamas, a small city in Olancho about sixty-five miles away from Las Limas. He would only come home once a month, and people respected him too much to tell him of any gossip about his daughter. My mother knew about the rumors, but she chose to ignore them. And I am not sure what Father Andrew told her exactly, but he convinced her to allow me to keep the gifts.

After the record player scandal was old news, some of the people in the village made another observation. Now the hot topic of conversation was, "That priest broke his back constructing a road through the mountains; so he can come to Las Limas in his jeep to see his girlfriend." Father Andrew was indeed the first person to bring an automobile from the town of Gualaco to Las Limas. He had been able to accomplish the enormous task of constructing a road through the mountains between Gualaco and Las Limas with the help of a crew of volunteers. In those days, there were no electric tools and all the construction had to be done by manpower. After the road had been completed, a trip that used to take two days on horseback, now it took only about two hours by jeep. Everyone in the province was amazed that Father Andrew had successfully completed such a huge task.

I will never forget the first time Father Andrew came to Las Limas in a jeep. I had never seen a jeep before or any type of automobile for that matter. When I saw from a great distance the red four-wheeled machine coming toward my house, I could not contain my amazement and joy! If my body had wings, I would have flown to meet it halfway. But I was not as curious to see the jeep, as much as I was happy to see Father Andrew.

I was astounded to see a jeep for the first time; but I was more pleasantly surprised that Father Andrew came wearing regular clothes. Instead of his Franciscan habit, he was wearing blue jeans and a white T-shirt. For a brief moment, I separated the priest from the man in my mind. I wanted to embrace him tightly and cover his face with kisses when I greeted him. I also wanted to tell him, "Congratulations on constructing the road! You did it, my love, my hero!" But in this case, my shyness served me well.

I greeted Father Andrew, respectfully as I always did until I noticed that his face was covered with sweat. I went to my bedroom to get a linen handkerchief I had made. The handkerchief had an embroidered pale pink trim and a heart in one of the corners. Inside the heart was the inscription *"Tú y Yo"* (You and I). I gave the handkerchief to Father Andrew to dry the sweat from his face, and he gratefully accepted my kind gesture. After drying his sweaty face, Father Andrew looked at me gratefully and handed me the handkerchief. I did not take it; instead I told him, "I made the handkerchief and I would like you to keep it." He gave me a big smile, and said, "Thank you very much, Chita," and put the handkerchief in his pocket. Chita was an endearing nickname he had given me which means little one.

When I realized what I had done impulsively, I felt so foolish that I could have easily died from embarrassment. Even though I did not reveal to Father Andrew that I had made the handkerchief especially for him, it was probably not too hard for him to figure it out. I made that handkerchief in secret -- even my mother was not aware of it. I had received so many gifts from Father Andrew, that I wanted to make something for him. I made the handkerchief with all of my love, but I could not imagined that I would ever find the courage to give it to him.

After the road had been completed, the rumors about Father Andrew being in love with a girl from Las Limas spread out beyond the province like wildfire. But I honestly believed that the only purpose Father Andrew had for having constructed the road was to make it easier for him to travel from one parish to the next, since he was the only priest and his dioceses included several towns and a few dozen villages. Before constructing the road, he either had to walk or travel by mule. He had a mule called *Relámpago*, which means flash of lightning. It was a very appropriate name because the mule was very fast. Unfortunately, Father Andrew was a poor rider and had been thrown by *Relámpago* more than a few times. It made sense to me that with the experience he already had had with his mule, Father Andrew would certainly try to find a better means of transportation.

Although I was convinced that neither the gifts nor the construction of the road were indications that Father Andrew had fallen in love with me, I was secretly praying and hoping that the rumors were true. It was customary for the women in the village to have some form of worship every night, either praying the rosary or doing a novena. We would have the prayer service at a different house every time, and I had the privilege of being the leader of the prayer group. I would pray aloud for various needs of the community, but in the silence of my heart and with all the fervor of my being, my supplication was always the same, "Please, dear God, let it be true what people are saying that Father Andrew is in love with me."

It was probably my own insecurity and my feelings of being unworthy to be loved by someone as special as Father Andrew that prevented me from believing that the rumors had an element of truth. However, at this point in time, I had to deal with the consequence of the rumors, the hostility of some people in Father Andrew's congregation, especially the pious older ladies who would say things such as, "Leave that priest alone. If you have anything to do with him, you are going straight to hell." Besides not wanting to lose the best priest they ever had, I believe that these pious ladies were also genuinely concerned about my salvation. They were actually convinced that being a temptation to a priest was a mortal sin, which would certainly lead to condemnation to hell, and it would also bring a curse to the whole family of the sinner.

Father Andrew had been in the same parish for nine years during which he had done more for his parishioners than some missionaries had accomplished in a lifetime. He had converted his rectory not only into an orphanage, but also into a school at the same time. He had provided medical treatment and education for the neediest of children in his dioceses with the support of his family and friends in the United States. He also received support in the form of scholarships from the First Lady of the country, who at that time was Mrs. Alejandrina Bermudez de Villeda Morales. When the First Lady found out about some of Father Andrew's incredible accomplishments, she decided to get involved in his work.

Father Andrew was deeply concerned with every aspect of his parishioners' lives. He had instructed farmers on better agricultural techniques and had introduced new grains of corn and beans to them; he had celebrated his masses with music, and had developed a community spirit with his parishioners by introducing outdoor movies and many other activities. According to Father Andrew, "Before one can teach people about God, their basic needs have to be met first." He would often say, "No one wants to hear about religion, if they are hungry." This philosophy explains why Father Andrew was so concerned with helping his people meet their basic needs, become self-sufficient and consequently bring some joy and spirituality into their lives.

One would think that Father Andrew should have been highly praised by his superiors and fellow friars in the United States for the wonderful work he was doing for the missions in Honduras, but instead he had been severely criticized by some of them. "Who do you think you are?" One of his superiors asked him angrily. "We sent you to Honduras to be a missionary, to preach the word of God. We did not send you there to be some kind of social worker."

But in spite of being rebuked and criticized by his superiors, Father Andrew continued to help his people in every way he could.

He was deeply loved by his parishioners not only because of the help he provided for them, but also because of the way he connected with them. Even with the language and cultural barriers at times, he had been able to connect with all of his people no matter what age they were. People were attracted by his kindness and humility. It was not unusual for Father Andrew to visit his parishioners who lived in the most humble huts and to have coffee with them sitting on a bench made of dry mud.

The depth of Father Andrew's charity and humility can be illustrated by the following incident. He had paid a visit to one of the poorest families in his dioceses as he had done many times. The young couple felt honored that the priest was visiting them. After graciously greeting him, they invited Father Andrew into their little hut and to sit on a bench made of mud. When Father Andrew went inside the one-room hut, he saw a baby, about ten months old, sitting on the dirt floor and wearing only a t-shirt. "What a beautiful baby!" Father Andrew exclaimed. Then he asked the proud parents, "What is the baby's name?"

They replied "Gabriel."

"Hola, Gabrielito! (Hi, little Gabriel!) Do you know that you are named after a famous angel?" Father Andrew lovingly said to the baby.

The nice hospitable young lady asked Father Andrew, "Would you like a cup of coffee?"

"Yes, please," he responded. She then proceeded to make the coffee by putting ground coffee beans in a bag made out of cloth and pouring hot water over the bag. Just as she was about to sweeten the coffee with homemade brown sugar, she noticed that her baby had a bad case of diarrhea. The poor woman was probably very embarrassed to have that occur in front of a priest. To make things worse, she could not find anything to clean the baby with. So, she used her index finger to wipe the baby's butt. Then without washing her hands, she stirred the sugar in Father Andrew's coffee with the same finger. In spite of that, Father Andrew still drank the coffee.

Another parishioner who had witnessed the incident later asked Father Andrew, "Why did you drink that dirty coffee?"

"I had no choice," Father Andrew explained, "to hurt the nice lady's feelings would have been completely against Christian charity. I couldn't do that."

Father Andrew's main value was definitely Christian charity. When someone was unkind or rude, Father Andrew would always find a reason to excuse and forgive that person's behavior. When I had lost my shyness around him, I remember telling him: "I swear that if Satan presented himself in front of you, you would find some redeeming quality in him. I hope that when I die and I am judged by God, He will be as merciful to me as you are to everyone else."

Looking at my adoringly and smiling Father Andrew reassured me, "You have nothing to worry about, Chita; you have a beautiful soul. If anyone needs to worry about not going to heaven, that would be me."

As a Franciscan friar, Father Andrew took three vows: poverty, obedience, and chastity. He was a true follower of Saint Francis of Assisi, the founder of his order, and lived by its rules. His brown Franciscan habit was old and worn out. His sandals had been repaired several times, and he was always making penance by denying himself some things, including food. In order to fulfill his vow of obedience, he stayed in the missions in a third world country much too long, but he never complained about his hard life. And as far as his vow of chastity, he never had a girlfriend even before he became a priest. He had never known the delight of being caressed by a woman, or the indescribable joy of holding one's own child for the first time.

After nine years of giving of himself body and soul to the missions, Father Andrew was becoming burned out. However, no one knew about that because he never complained. His fellow friars gave him the nickname, "the Contented Cow," because they assumed that nothing bothered him. Unbeknownst to them, he was becoming very tired, disillusioned and discouraged.

Father Andrew confided to his best friend, my father, "I do not mind the hard work or even the poverty. But I can never get used to the bloodshed during every one of the religious celebrations. Besides, I feel that I am solo in the battleground. My fellow friars and superiors have very different ideas than I do on how to best serve God's people."

The bloodshed Father Andrew was referring to, was that every time during the feast celebrations some of the men would get drunk and would end up fighting with each other. Each man would be carrying a machete, and many times some of them would end up dead or seriously wounded.

Father Andrew and the women in the parish would spend a lot of time and effort getting the churches prepared for the feasts. Everyone in the parish would be having a great time, when suddenly the peaceful crowd would turn into a violent chaos. There would be people screaming and running everywhere trying to get away from the drunken men who were out of control.

Many times, Father Andrew risked his life while trying to bring some order to the crowd, and it was up to him to take care of the dead or the wounded. At that time, there were no doctors in the town or in the villages. Sometimes, Father Andrew had to send a telegram to Juticalpa to request a helicopter to take the wounded to the hospital there. At other times, the wounded people had to be stitched up by *curanderos* (someone who practices medicine without ever going to medical school). The curanderos had no anesthesia available to them. Consequently, the only pain killer the wounded men would receive was the liquor they had already consumed.

Father Andrew's parishioners were completely unaware that he was getting burned out and, more importantly, that he was having a serious vocation crisis. Their biggest fear was that Father Andrew would leave the missions because of me. "Dios quiera que el padre pueda resistir esa tentación," (God willing, the priest will be able to resist that temptation) the pious older ladies whispered to each other whenever they were together in church or at the river washing clothes. Then they would proceed to bombard heaven with prayers to save Father Andrew from me.

Surprisingly, something unexpected happened! A twist of fate took place in my life, which gave hope to the pious ladies that their prayers were going to be answered in their favor. Up until this point, I was sure that Father Andrew was the only man I could ever love, but I would soon find out otherwise.

CHAPTER 5

*B*eing in love for the first time, especially with someone I felt was out of my reach, was a bittersweet experience. Besides feeling terribly guilty for being in love with a priest and worried that my dark secret could have been discovered at any time, I was deeply saddened because I had no hope Father Andrew would ever love me back. I was also very aware that priests are not supposed to get married and that knowledge destroyed any hope I had of having a life with Father Andrew, even if by some miracle he would love me back.

I was also worried about dying and going straight to hell for the unpardonable sin of falling in love with a priest. I prayed very hard to be delivered from this horrible dilemma. When I met Sebastian Alvarado, I thought he was the answer to my prayers. He was the only man I had ever felt attracted to, in addition to Father Andrew. Our eyes locked when we met, and I could not conceal from him the fact that he took my breath away and raised my heartbeat.

Sebastian was a tall, well-educated and strikingly handsome young man from Juticalpa. He had light complexion, black hair and vivacious black eyes. His great looks were certainly enhanced by his gentle manner and irresistible charm.

Sebastian had recently graduated from college and had been sent to Las Limas by the Department of Education in Juticalpa to do some work with my father. They had been assigned the task of assessing the academic level of students in all of the villages pertaining to San Esteban. It was up to them to make the decision of whether the students were to be promoted to the next grade level or not.

The teachers had no say in that particular decision because it would have been considered a conflict of interest. There was a policy at that time that if too many students were not promoted to the next grade in a particular school, the teacher of those students would lose her or his job. The students' academic success or failure in those days was mostly attributed to their teachers' performance.

As a consequence of that belief, the Department of Education had the policy to have the students' academic progress assessed by two qualified but impartial individuals, called "examinadores" (examiners). This policy ensured that teachers would not promote students out of fear of being fired. Each student was assessed individually in all of the academic subjects using both oral and written exams.

However, there was one major drawback with this method of assessment. During the oral exams, some students were too shy to answer questions, even if they knew the answers. Because of their shyness, some of the students would automatically fail the oral test and, consequently, they would not be promoted to the next grade level.

I had, what I thought of as my good fortune, the opportunity of getting to know Sebastian not only because he was a guest in my house while working with my father for several weeks, but also because I was one of three teachers in a village next to Las Limas, called Los Dos Rios. I was only fourteen years old, but appeared older than my age. Officially, I had only grammar school education, but I was much more advanced academically because my father had home-schooled me from the moment I had begun to talk. I obtained my teaching job by simple coincidence or maybe due to a streak of good luck in this case.

The Mayor of San Esteban came to visit my father and met me. I do not remember exactly why this man had started asking me questions about different academic subjects. I wanted my parents to be proud of me, especially my father. So in spite of my shyness, I started answering the Mayor's questions intelligently and in great detail. I had no idea I was being tested, of course.

The Mayor talked to my father about the possibility of having me work as a teacher in Los Dos Rios. My father readily agreed, and he made sure that I met the Mayor's expectation by helping me to prepare classes and instructing me on how to implement them. I was assigned to teach second and fourth grades that year and I had around twenty-five students in each class. My salary was eighty lempiras (forty dollars) per month. I was ecstatic! I thought that salary was absolutely fabulous! However, my father insisted that rather than spending that money in luxuries, I buy a cow every month. His wish was my command, of course. Even though, I would have preferred to buy pretty dresses rather than more cows.

Some of my fourth-grade students were my age and a few even older than I was. But because I seemed older than my age and somewhat on the serious side, I had no problem with a lack of discipline or disrespect from my students. My biggest problem was the jealousy of my two colleagues; they were jealous of the attention I was receiving as a single girl. One of the teachers, who was also the director, was a lady in her forties; she was divorced and had three children. The other teacher was one of the potential nuns that Father Andrew had sent to Juticalpa, but she had decided the religious life was not for her. This teacher noticed how Father Andrew treated me and resented the fact that he had never treated her that way. Both of these women had a reason to feel somewhat bitter towards life, and they made my life very difficult.

Surprisingly, the parents who were, and still are, very critical of teachers, did not seem to complain about me. This was probably because my father was so involved in my performance, that they had a lot of confidence in his ability to guide me, along with the great respect they felt for him. With his help, I completed my first year of teaching successfully and was appointed with the same assignment for the following school year.

My father was a very wise man; when the time came to assess my students, he delegated the job to Sebastian alone. My father did not want to give anyone the opportunity of thinking he was promoting students simply because their teacher happened to be his daughter.

Sebastian tested all of my students and promoted 99 percent of them to the next grade level. He seemed to be very impressed with both of my classes, and he openly praised me on my teaching ability and dedication. In private, he mostly complimented me for being attractive, which was very surprising to me. I was stunned to realize that someone would find me beautiful, especially someone as handsome as Sebastian was.

In addition to feeling extremely happy with the outcome of my first year of teaching, I was flattered and very happy when Sebastian asked me, "Quieres ser mi novia?" (Do you want to be my girlfriend?) I eagerly agreed to be Sebastian's girlfriend. Besides feeling attracted to him, I thought it had been God's will for me to fall in love with Sebastian so that I could forget Father Andrew.

For the few short weeks that I was supposedly Sebastian's girlfriend, I thought of Father Andrew, but not with the same intensity as before. For the first time, I was beginning to have hope that I could get him out of my mind and out of my heart. Also, for the first time, I had peace of mind because I was not dealing with forbidden love. Being happy and at peace were such unfamiliar emotions in my life that I was afraid my happiness would be short-lived.

My fear turned into reality much sooner than I expected. I heard rumors that Sebastian had met my cousin, Graciela, and had mentioned to some people in the village, "When I first met Cándida, I was definitely interested in her, but her cousin Graciela is so much more beautiful, and now I only have eyes for Graciela."

Beyond the pain of being abruptly dumped by Sebastian, I was suffering from the humiliation of having everyone in the village know about this. I had no choice but to believe the rumors were true because Sebastian had stopped showing any interest in me. He had stopped seeing me without providing me with an explanation, and it was common knowledge that he was pursuing my cousin, Graciela.

I was humiliated and heartbroken for days. I never heard from Sebastian again, and neither did I try to contact him. The way he had played with my feelings was too painful. I was completely devastated because his rejection had destroyed my already weakened self-esteem. I was convinced Sebastian had lost interest in me because I was unattractive.

Another reason why a man would lose interest in a girl within this machista culture is if the girl was too easy and had sexual relations before marriage. But that was definitely not the case with me, which lead me to believe that Sebastian's rejection had more to do with my looks. That was the only way I could explain why this romance had ended so abruptly when it was just starting. Sebastian and I crossed paths again, twenty years later; but our roles had been reversed by then.

A few days after this incident with Sebastian, Father Andrew came to my house, and he noticed that I was very sad. I was very happy to see him, but I could not conceal my sadness over feeling rejected by Sebastian. "Tell me what is making you so sad, Chita?" Father Andrew asked me tenderly and deeply concerned. But I could not bring myself to tell him that I was feeling ugly and rejected.

"Tell me what happened," Father Andrew asked me again pleadingly.

After hesitating for a long time, I finally told him what had happened with Sebastian, and my theory of why he had lost interest in me. Father Andrew listened sympathetically to my sad story, and once more, as he did when we met the first time, he placed his hand under my chin. He gently lifted my face, looked me straight in the eyes and said, "Oh no! You are not ugly at all! As a matter of fact, you are the most beautiful flower that has ever grown in this whole valley, and you have a soul that matches your physical beauty."

I was astonished to hear Father Andrew's words of praise, and I was intrigued by what he had said about my soul. "How could you know that?" I asked. "You have never seen my soul," I added.

He laughed and replied. "I have seen your soul; I even saw your soul this morning."

Now I was laughing too, even though I had thought that nothing would ever make me smile. "When exactly and how did you see my soul?" I asked him smiling.

Father Andrew replied with an explanation, "When a lady came by your house this morning on her way back from the river, she was carrying a huge pail of water on her head and a baby on her hip. The moment you saw her coming, you rushed to meet her, took the baby in your arms and carried the baby home for her. I have also seen you help people on other occasions. You are definitely your father's daughter." He emphasized, "José is one of the kindest and most generous human beings I have ever met."

I was speechless! I had no idea that Father Andrew, or anyone else for that matter, would be impressed with such small things. I did not think that I had done anything worthy of being noticed. But even more than that, the idea of being told that I resembled my father in some way was the highest compliment anyone could have given to me, second only to being compared to the most beautiful flower that had grown in the valley.

After my conversation with Father Andrew that day, I felt I had been given a burst of self-esteem, and my sadness was lifted. However, there was a downside to the emotional healing that I was experiencing. My feelings for Father Andrew returned stronger than before. I had not only seen the somewhat poetic and funny side of him, but I was becoming even more addicted to the way he made me feel. No one in my whole life had ever made me feel that way before: beautiful and special.

When I went to bed that night, I probably played a hundred times in my mind the conversation with Father Andrew. I experienced a mixture of feelings more than ever before. On the one hand, I felt so special and even lovable. I even had a glimpse of hope that Father Andrew could reciprocate my feelings someday. On the other hand, as soon as those happy thoughts would come to my mind, I would replace them with negative ones, such as, "Stop fooling yourself! Father Andrew probably thinks that you are so nice because he really doesn't know you, or maybe he only said all those nice things because he felt sorry for you."

The harder I tried to clarify my feelings, the more confused I became. My undying love for Father Andrew, the deep respect and admiration I felt for him, and my eternal gratitude to him were the only things I was sure about, in addition to my feelings of guilt and fear of condemnation for the way I felt about him.

While I was going through this period of conflicting emotions, soul-searching, and confusion, I was distracted somewhat by getting a taste of freedom. My father had gone back to work in Catacamas after completing the end of the year assessment for the students. Without my father at home, now I had the opportunity of going to some parties with my mother because she loved accordion music. We even attended wedding receptions on her side of the family. I did not know how to dance, but in spite of my clumsiness, I would dance the night away and would have a fabulous time.

It was during these parties, while we were dancing, that several local cowboys confessed their undying love for me. However, I was not even flattered by their declaration of love because I was not at all interested in them, and I had strong doubts about their sincerity.

One young cowboy, named Santiago, was silly enough to tell me his true feelings. "I love you so much because you are Don José Méndez's daughter. I would give anything to marry a daughter of his." Obviously, this ignorant cowboy was only interested in the prestige he would gain by being married to someone from my father's family. It had nothing to do with me. My answer was to step on his toes as hard as I could, and I stopped dancing with him.

I distinctly remember another one of my admirers because he made a funny proposal that even now, I am still laughing about it. His name was Hernán, a man from Nicaragua, who had come to Las Limas for business purposes. He was involved with the exportation of meat and also of precious wood called *guayacán*. Hernán seemed to be interested in me since we met at my parents' house, but I was not attracted to him. Then one day, he surprised me by proposing, "Preciosa, por favor cásate conmigo. Podemos ser muy felices en Nicaragua estableciendo un negocio de engordar cerdos." (Please marry me, precious one. We can be very happy in Nicaragua establishing a pig fattening business.)

Fattening pigs was a flourishing business then because people preferred lard to oil. But my idea of happiness was not to fatten up pigs. So I graciously declined Hernán's proposal, trying very hard to keep from laughing. This man was old enough to be my father! But at that time and even now, it was not unusual in my culture for older men to marry young girls.

In those days, many girls preferred to marry a man twenty years their senior or even older. The reason being that since unfaithfulness was prevalent and even accepted within the culture, young women reasoned that if they married someone older and mature, unfaithfulness would be less likely to happen.

Because of the macho culture, some of the men responded to rejection with violence. I remember that during dances, it was not unusual for a woman to get hit on the head with a flashlight if she refused to dance with a particular man. In other cases, a man would resort to a more serious violence, including rape, because he could not deal with being rebuffed by a young lady. To make the assault even worse for the victim, in certain instances her parents would force her to marry her rapist because they reasoned that he had already disgraced her in the eyes of the society.

Luckily, it had not been dangerous for me to get rid of the cowboy and the businessman but, as I was soon to learn, dealing with a self-entitled gunslinger was another story entirely.

CHAPTER 6

Once again, six years later, I found myself in the luxurious house of Don Maximiliano Luna, the place where I had met Father Andrew for the first time. I was no longer a shy little girl, and the occasion was not a religious ceremony. It was a political campaign for a friend of my father who was running for president. His name was Roberto Rodas Alvarado. I had never seen such a big crowd. The meeting took place on the well-landscaped grounds of the enormous hacienda. People from nearby villages were there to support this very popular candidate. Mr. Rodas Alvarado arrived accompanied by eight other politicians.

The political speeches were very long; most of the politicians took turns speaking. The crowd was clapping enthusiastically. I clapped too, but I was not listening to what they were saying. I was daydreaming almost the entire time. I was remembering my first meeting with Father Andrew. I could still hear him asking me, "Muchachita, te comieron la lengua los ratones?" (Little girl, did mice eat your tongue?)

"How did it happen?" I asked myself. "How could total indifference have bloomed into an all-consuming and forbidden love?" Thoughts about Father Andrew occupied my mind during all of my waking hours, and he was also in my subconscious mind when I was sleeping. But thinking of him only made me sad. Even in my wildest fantasies, I could never imagine or even dream that my love would ever have a happy ending. Because of his commitment to the priesthood, I considered Father Andrew as inaccessible as a star, and I hated myself for aiming so high.

The claps and cheers of the lively crowd brought me back to reality. In order to pretend I was paying attention to the speeches, I looked across the crowd, and I noticed that someone was looking at me. I glanced again and our eyes met. From then on, I felt his gaze on me the remaining time the speeches were going on. He was about twenty-one years old, of medium height, very light complexion and brown hair. His abundant hair was neatly combed, and in his tailored brown suit, he resembled a model in a magazine.

I had not seen this young man for many years, but I recognized him. He had distinct Spanish features, which gave him an air of distinction and sophistication. His name was Alejandro de la Vega, the favorite grandson of Don Maximiliano, the wealthiest man in the area.

Alejandro was born in Las Limas, but he had been in Catacamas for several years studying to be a veterinarian. No one in the village was surprised that Alejandro had chosen that particular profession. It was common knowledge that even though Don Maximiliano had at least a half dozen children and many grandchildren, he had designated Alejandro as his only heir. Some people claimed that Don Maximiliano favored Alejandro because of his great looks and background. He was the son of Don Maximiliano's oldest daughter and a gentleman from Spain. Alejandro grew up with his mother and grandfather because his father had gone back to Spain and never returned to Honduras.

Since Alejandro was the grandson of someone as prestigious and wealthy as Don Maximiliano, he was as much the center of attention during the gathering as the candidate for the presidency. There was a line of people waiting to talk to him, but he gracefully excused himself and made a point to very respectfully greet my mother and make her feel welcomed. This was probably the first time my mother had been to his fancy house, and he could probably sense that she was feeling very uncomfortable. My mother knew very well that Alejandro's family considered her beneath their social class. Whenever they had a function, they would only invite my father. But this time, everyone had been invited since the candidate for the presidency needed all the votes he could get.

After putting my mother at ease, Alejandro directed his attention to my sister and me. He greeted us briefly, and then he commented, "Cándida, I hardly recognized you! You are so tall, so beautiful, and all grown up. The last time I saw you, you were nine or ten years old."

I was less shy now, but still compliments made me cringe. My face probably looked like a red tomato from embarrassment, but I was able to utter a soft, "Thank you very much."

Then Alejandro went on to ask my mother how she was managing the hacienda since my father was in Catacamas. My mother replied, "It's not easy. It's a lot of work. And one of the cows is sick." Alejandro readily said, "A sus órdenes. (At your service.) I'll be more than happy to check your sick cow." And he did.

Alejandro made his very first house call to see the cow the next afternoon. He also continued to come over to my parents' house on a daily basis for the following two weeks, supposedly to check on the sick cow. His daily visits were always at the same time, late in the afternoon after school was out. I believe that no cow ever received as much attention from a veterinarian as ours did. His daily visits continued even after the cow got better.

I was so naïve that I honestly believed Alejandro was coming over to my house only to check on the cow. I figured that since he was a new veterinarian, he was looking for every opportunity to put into practice the professional skills he had acquired. My mother didn't mind his daily visits. He was very pleasant, and she liked him. "Alejandro is so different from his family, "He is such a nice and polite young man." She mentioned a few times. At this point, neither my mother nor I knew he was interested in me.

I found out otherwise when one of my students, who happened to be Alejandro's cousin, brought me a letter to school. I should have known not to accept the letter because by doing so, in my culture, I was sending the message that I was interested in the sender. I was flattered to receive a letter from someone as distinguished, charming and educated as Alejandro. But I did not feel attracted to him initially. I accepted the letter more out of curiosity of its content than anything

---

else. This was the first real love letter that I had ever received. I still remember some parts of the letter because I read it over and over again.

Candida, my love,

I hope you agree to accept this letter. I have to confess to you that since I met you all grown up, I have been bewitched by your beauty and now I am a slave of your love. There is not a moment of the day or night that I do not think about you. I assure you that my intentions for you are serious and respectable.

I beg of you to allow me the opportunity of showing you how profoundly I love you. My most fervent wish is to make you the happiest woman in the world.

With all my heart I hope you reciprocate my love. I need you like a baby needs its mother. I need you as much as a flower needs the rain and the sun in order to bloom.

Please answer me today. I will be anxiously awaiting your reply.

With all my love, which is yours forever,
Alejandro de la Vega

I was deeply touched by Alejandro's letter, and I wanted to believe everything he said, but I knew better. I knew that in my culture, men would say anything, whether they meant it or not, when they wanted to conquer a woman. The more difficult the conquest, the more exciting the chase became for them. They seemed to enjoy the challenge of conquering a woman, more than the conquest itself. But as soon as they had what they wanted; they were no longer interested in the woman. It was very hard for a woman to be sure whether a man was sincere or not.

I replied to Alejandro's letter, but my answer was probably not what he wanted to hear. I explained to him my inability to reciprocate his love because my heart already belonged to someone else. I expected another letter from him the following day, but he did not write. Instead, he came to the school in Los Dos Rios where I was working. He arrived during my lunch time. He knew that most of the students had gone home for lunch or had gone swimming in the river.

Alejandro demanded to know who had stolen my heart from him. "My heart was never yours," I replied, "and I don't owe you an explanation."

"Well," he said, "you are not at the altar yet; and until you say I do, I will never give up on you."

I reassured him he was wasting his time because I was not going to change my mind. I also asked him politely to leave the school. "The students are about to return from lunch for the afternoon session," I explained.

"Okay," Alejandro answered, seemingly disappointed, "but I will see you later. Alejandro de la Vega no se rinde." (Alejandro de la Vega doesn't give up.)

I had never met anyone as persistent as Alejandro. He would not listen to my reasons nor accepted "no" for an answer. He continued his daily visits to the school during my lunch time and to my house late in the afternoon. This young man did everything he could to convince me to fall in love with him, and he was coming across as someone desperate, begging to be loved. I had been completely honest with him about my feelings, but he flatly refused to give up the chase.

During the whole time that Alejandro was aggressively pursuing me, Father Andrew and I kept on corresponding by letter. He came to Las Limas once in a while as usual, but I did not tell him about Alejandro. I did not want him to think that I was encouraging Alejandro and that now I had a boyfriend.

However, both men happened to meet one evening at my house. It was already dark when Father Andrew was leaving my home. Alejandro volunteered to take Father Andrew to my uncle's house where he was staying. I became suspicious of Alejandro's motive for being so nice to Father Andrew. I was sure he was aware of the rumors about Father Andrew and me. I became very worried and with good reason.

By now I knew that Alejandro was crazy, obsessed, and dangerous. He was always armed with two guns around his waist in a twin holster and a belt loaded with bullets. He loved to show off, and without warning anyone, he would pull both pistols out and would fire them into the air. After one of Alejandro's shooting rampages, my brother, who was about ten years old then, exclaimed, "I wish I was old enough to put a stop to this madness."

My mother and I were scared of Alejandro when he went into a shooting rampage as most people in the village were, but there was nothing anyone could do. There were no laws in place to protect people, and no one would dare complain about the grandson of the most wealthy and powerful man in the village.

On that night when Father Andrew and Alejandro met at my house, I tried to convince Alejandro that there was no need to take Father Andrew to my uncle's house because he knew the way. I guess Alejandro sensed my fear or read my mind because he assured me, "Do not worry about your priest; he is perfectly safe with me. My grandfather told me, 'If you ever harm a priest, you will go straight to hell.' I certainly don't want to go to hell or upset my grandfather."

That comment put my mind at ease because I knew that Alejandro would never do anything to displease his grandfather. I was sure that his fear of losing his grandfather's inheritance was greater than his fear of going to hell. Alejandro kept his word and took Father Andrew safely to my uncle's house.

Shortly after this incident, Father Andrew returned to Las Limas, but for a very different reason. He had been notified that his father had died suddenly from a heart attack, and he was on his way to the United States. He came to Las Limas to take a small plane to Tegucigalpa.

I watched the plane take off, as I had done in wonder so many times throughout my childhood. But this time watching the plane take off, gave me a very different sensation. The noise of the engines seemed to penetrate through the very core of my being, and I felt my heart break into a million pieces. As the small plane took off, I felt that a piece of my heart was leaving my body, along with my hopes and dreams.

But in addition to feeling badly for Father Andrew's loss, an overwhelming fear came over me. I was afraid that I would never see Father Andrew again. I was sure that this time he was not going to return from the United States. I knew he was an only child and that his mother was very sick. "I lost him forever," I told myself. And that thought cut through my heart like a knife.

Father Andrew remained in the United States for five long weeks, but during that whole time, he kept in touch with me through letters and postal cards. He even sent me a postal card of President Kennedy with a message explaining that he knew President Kennedy personally. "We met as teenagers in the Boston area, and later I saw him again when I officiated my cousin Vito's wedding. Young John Kennedy happened to be the best man," Father Andrew wrote on the post card.

I felt an indescribable relief and excitement every time I received a letter or a postal card from Father Andrew. His consistent correspondence was my assurance that he had not forgotten me. But although he was showering me with attention from over two thousand miles away, I did not get the hint that Father Andrew had fallen in love with me.

Besides being naive about matters of the heart, my lack of perception that Father Andrew had developed romantic feelings toward me was probably due to the way I felt about myself. I considered myself so unworthy of his love. As a matter of fact, the fear that Father Andrew was not coming back encouraged me to put up with Alejandro's madness. By this time, he had developed a new tactic to win me over, if not my heart, my pity.

In light of the fact that all of the previous strategies that Alejandro had used to make me fall in love with him had failed, he came up with a brand new one. He wrote a letter of suicide to me. The gist of the letter was as follows:

Since you are not willing to open your heart and love me in return, I feel that my life is not worth living. Because I cannot live without you, I am going to commit suicide in two weeks. My death will be on your conscience. Can you live with that?

In order to make the threat more believable, Alejandro even stated in the letter the date and time when he was going to commit suicide. He also explained, "I decided to take my own life in two weeks from now because I need time to put my affairs in order."

I was astonished and deeply concerned when I learned about Alejandro's suicide threat. I considered him capable of doing such a crazy thing. "On the other hand," I said to myself, "he could be lying. He has lied before about so many other things." Since I was not sure what to do, I decided to seek my mother's advice. I read Alejandro's letter to her and her reaction was, "Oh my God! If that crazy fool kills himself, his family is going to blame you." My mother's reaction led me to believe that she took Alejandro's threat seriously and so did I.

I had no idea how to stop Alejandro from doing something so terrible and foolish. The only thing I could think of was to buy some time by pretending that I really cared about him, until I could find a better solution. I begged him to forget such a crazy idea. "I can only do that with one condition, if you accept to be my girlfriend," Alejandro bargained.

"Okay, okay," I reluctantly replied. I felt I had no choice because I had taken his threat seriously.

While I was playing this game, supposedly to buy time until I could find a better solution, Alejandro proposed marriage several times. Every time he mentioned marriage, my answer was always the same. "If you really love me, please give me some time to sort out my feelings and make up my mind." I made sure to never accept his marriage proposal even while pretending. I was sure that if I did that, he would oblige me to keep my word at gunpoint. No kidding!

At that time in my culture, if a girl accepted a marriage proposal, she was forced by the man to keep her word. If she changed her mind about getting married for whatever reason, she would be risking her life.

Buying time until Alejandro came to his senses and give up the suicide idea did not seem to be a very dangerous game at first, but I was wrong. Alejandro got tired of just talking. He wanted to hold and kiss me passionately. I kept him at arms' length as long as I could. But at some point, he was becoming suspicious that I was playing a game. First, I allowed him to kiss me because I was afraid of what he would do if he found out that his hunch had been right. But I never expected to react the way I did! I loved his passionate embrace. I was delighted by his kisses. I experienced feelings I never had before. "Could this be love?" I asked myself.

I had never been kissed, and the sweet sensation was so new to me that I wanted to experience it over and over again. After the first of many kisses, I started having romantic feelings towards Alejandro. I did not discourage these feelings from developing because again, like in Sebastian's case, I thought it was the will of God so I could get Father Andrew out of my heart and out of my mind.

I thought that God was giving me the opportunity of falling in love with someone available, whose love would not risk the condemnation to hell of my immortal soul. I was actually thinking of two different hells. The hell I was going through by loving someone out of my reach, and the hell that would come after I died if I stood between a priest and his vocation.

The pious little old ladies had convinced me, "Te vas a ir derecho al infierno si haces caer a ese padre." (You are going to go straight to hell if you make that priest fall.) After hearing that warning so many times, I came to believe it. I was definitely afraid of going to hell and I tried very hard to do the right thing. But to rip out Father Andrew from my heart, was as impossible as asking the sun not to shine.

However, these new feelings for Alejandro gave me a dim hope that my redemption from hell could be possible. However, loving Alejandro did not replace what I was feeling towards Father Andrew. This new awareness of conflicting emotions took me by surprise. Now my heart was divided between Father Andrew and Alejandro.

I had no idea that it was possible to love two men at the same time. My strongest feelings were always toward Father Andrew, but I loved Alejandro too. I was completely confused! I had to talk to someone to try to make some sense of my confusion. I was losing sleep over it and I could not focus on anything else. It was bad enough to be in love with the wrong person, but to have one's heart divided was even worse.

I decided to seek the advice of a mature lady, a friend of mine named Sofía, who lived near the school where I was working. She already knew about Alejandro because I used to meet him at her house, with her permission of course. Whenever he went to the school during my lunch time, I would tell him to wait for me at Sofia's house.

When I told Sofía about my feelings for Father Andrew, she responded, "Having feelings for a priest is wrong and sinful." She then asked, "Are you sure you aren't infatuated with him because he's from the United States? Do you think all you want is a trip to the States?"

I was very surprised that I had not received any sympathy from my friend Sofia, and I found her questions quite insulting. After pausing for a while, thinking about what Sofia had asked, I responded, "I do admit that going to the United States is very appealing. But I don't love Father Andrew because he was born there." Then I continued explaining, "I adore him because of the person he is. If by some miracle, he did marry me, I would happily spend my life with him in any corner of the world."

Before I could go on, the mature woman that I had considered a good friend, interrupted me by asking a series of questions and giving me advice at the same time: "Don't you know that priests cannot get married? Why don't you stop kidding yourself? Why don't you focus your attention on Alejandro? He is crazy about you! He is a great catch! Any girl's dream! So you see, you can't go wrong with him."

I thanked Sofia for her advice and reassured her that I would think about it. I was not surprised that she would consider my feelings for Father Andrew a sin, and that she was so eager to endorse Alejandro because she was somewhat related to him on his mother's side of the family. Furthermore, she certainly considered him a great catch because he was wealthy, sophisticated and good-looking. But most importantly, she firmly believed that being in love with a priest was a mortal sin and she was trying to prevent me from going to hell.

Sofía was not the only one who thought of Alejandro as quite a catch; almost everyone in the village did as well. Plenty of girls, not only in the villages but in the nearby towns were interested in him. I could not understand why he was pursuing me so relentlessly. I questioned Alejandro's sincerity, but he did not seem to be interested in any other girl. According to him, he only had eyes for me. To prove his sincerity to me, he ripped up a bunch of pictures of other girls in my presence. These pictures were of former girlfriends or present admirers of his. I felt badly to see those beautiful pictures being destroyed. But he did it before I could stop him.

When I went home that day after talking to my friend, Sofia, I reflected on our conversation time and time again. I pondered if my love for Father Andrew had anything to do with wanting a trip to the United States. I asked myself. "Would I be happy with him if we had to live in Honduras?" The answer was the same as I told Sofia, that I could be happy living with Father Andrew in any corner of the world as long as we were together – as long as I was with him, the place would not be important.

Then I questioned myself, "Can you say the same thing about Alejandro?" My answer was definitely "no." It was then that I became aware that I had confused passion with love. I also realized that I had played a very dangerous game with Alejandro, and now I needed to tell him the truth. I certainly felt more afraid for my life than for his when he had threatened to commit suicide.

CHAPTER 7

$\mathscr{I}$ agonized for a couple days trying to find the courage to tell Alejandro the truth about my feelings, but I could not bring myself to do it. By now, I was more afraid than ever because he had already perceived that something was wrong, and he had started following me to the river and everywhere I went. I used to go with some of my female students to swim in the river during our lunchtime. But now, I could not even enjoy a swim on a hot day. I was certain that Alejandro would be hiding behind the bushes or trees watching me.

For the first time, I wished that my father had never left for Catacamas. If my father had been at home, none of this nonsense would have happened. Alejandro would not be following me like a shadow or emptying his two guns in the air every time he felt like shooting. He would not do any of those things out of respect for my father.

I did not dare tell my mother that Alejandro was following me and that I was becoming increasingly afraid of him. I was sure that she would blame me, and I was afraid of her wrath. I could anticipate her screaming, "How could you have been so foolish as to lead on a crazy, armed and dangerous man? Don't you know what could happen to you?" My mother had stopped beating me by this time, but if she knew about the dilemma, I had gotten myself into, I was sure she would soon start mistreating me all over again.

Before I could settle things with Alejandro, I received a telegram from Father Andrew with the following message, "I am back in Gualaco. I have something important to tell you. I will see you tomorrow." I was absolutely ecstatic to learn of the fabulous news! During the entire time

Father Andrew had been in the United States, I was afraid he would never return to Honduras.

I remember jumping for joy and kissing the telegram upon receiving it. But the next day seemed like an eternity to me. I had been awake the whole night wondering what was so important that Father Andrew wanted to tell me. I would go back and forth from being somewhat hopeful to complete despair by telling myself, "Father Andrew is either going to tell me he has fallen in love with me or that he is going back to the United States for good, and I will never see him again."

The long-waited day finally came; it was Friday, September 13, 1963. When Father Andrew came to my house, I greeted him with such a long and tight embrace as if I wanted to hold on to him forever. When we parted from each other's arms, he said, "Chita, I need to talk to your mother." Then he and my mother went into the kitchen to talk in private. I had no idea what the talk was about.

After what seemed like a very long time to me, even if it had been probably only a few minutes, I was anxiously waiting for Father Andrew in the garden. Whenever I was nervous or wanting to distract myself, looking at the beautiful flowers always had a calming effect on me. When Father Andrew found me, he reached out for my hand, and said somewhat seriously and as if in a hurry, "I need to talk to you, Chita, about something very important. Please come with me. I have your mother's permission for us to talk alone under the Guanacaste tree (a tall tropical tree with an enormous round crown that exceeds its overall height)."

My mother chose the Guanacaste tree as a place for us to talk because it was situated in front of the house and in plain view not only of her, but of the nearby neighbors. This was her attempt at preventing any more gossip about Father Andrew and me.

Father Andrew and I sat under the Guanacaste tree. It was a glorious warm day. The sun had already set, and the cool breeze caressed our faces. I was wearing my prettiest dress; a princess-cut light blue dress that one of my aunts had made for me. I was also wearing the only jewelry I had, the precious necklace and matching earrings that Father Andrew had given to me. And as usual, after styling my shoulder-length black hair, I had placed a gardenia on the left side of my head.

Being that close to Father Andrew and alone for the very first time made me very nervous. I thought that my heart was going to come out of my chest; however, I tried very hard to keep my composure. After making some small talk to put me at ease, Father Andrew took both my hands into his; he looked adoringly into my eyes and said, "Chita, you know that my father died."

I could not even bring myself to say, "I am sorry." The touch of his hand and the look of love in his hazel eyes were so captivating that I froze and remained speechless. Still immersed in my eyes, Father Andrew continued, "My mother is sick and alone; I am her only child. I have decided to go back to the States to take care of her. I could go home alone and grow to be a lonely and bitter old man (he was thirty-six years old at that time), or I could go home feeling like the luckiest man in the whole world being married to you. Will you marry me, Chita?"

I was astonished, deliriously happy and terribly embarrassed at the same time! Now I knew that Father Andrew was definitely aware, and had probably been aware right along, that I was in love with him, and I was terribly embarrassed. My dream was coming true, but my secret was also exposed. I felt as if my soul was completely naked in front of Father Andrew for the first time. I wanted to shout, "Yes, yes, I would love to marry you!" But instead, I pulled my hands away from his and verbalized a firm and convincing "No! How did you get the idea that I am interested in marrying you?"

Father Andrew was very surprised, deeply hurt and utterly disappointed. He did not ask me for an explanation, and I did not volunteer one. He was silent for a while; then he sadly said, "I am so sorry, Chita! I thought you loved me as much as I love you. I guess I was wrong. Let's go back to the house."

When we went back to the house, Father Andrew talked to my mother for a little while. Then he quickly left on his jeep without saying goodbye to me.

I sadly watched Father Andrew disappear in the distance, taking with him all my joy, hopes, and dreams. I ran to the living room; stood over the record player he had given me, and I cried profusely. After a while, my mother came into the room. When she saw that I was crying and sobbing, she did something completely unexpected. For the first time in my whole life, my mother comforted me. Showing much love and compassion, she tenderly stroked my hair and said, "Don't cry anymore, foolish girl. He will be back." I lifted my head, made eye contact with her between the tears, and asked my mother, "How can you be so sure he's coming back?"

She replied, "Because I know how much he loves you." My mother spoke with such conviction that I started thinking, "Maybe she knows something that I don't." Her reassurance that Father Andrew would return, brought life back into my body and joy to my heart.

After processing in my mind, the events of that afternoon, I could not believe what was happening! Not only did I find out that Father Andrew was in love with me, but that he also wanted me to marry him. The happiness I felt at that moment was indescribable! I will never have to wonder how it might feel to win a Miss Universe beauty pageant or winning the lottery! Nothing can surpass the happiness I felt when I found out that the man I had adored in silence for years, someone I had considered unattainable, was in love with me.

Father Andrew's revelation of his love for me and marriage proposal came so unexpectedly that I did not know how to respond. Even now I am not sure why I reacted the way I did. How could I have done such a foolish thing as to say "no" to a marriage proposal that I had dreamed about, wished and hoped for with all my heart, and had fervently prayed for?

I remember that my mother had always told me, "It's a good idea for a woman to play hard to get. That will make a man respect her more and become more interested in her." Alejandro's behavior was proof that my mother's theory was right at least in my culture. Maybe I was taking my mother's advice and I had been brainwashed to react that way. It could also have been the embarrassment of knowing that the feelings I had tried so hard to hide from Father Andrew, had not been hidden at all – he would not have proposed marriage, unless he had been sure I was in love with him.

After finding out Father Andrew's feelings for me, I felt the urgency to resolve my situation with Alejandro more than ever. The possibility of marrying Father Andrew gave me the courage and determination I needed to be honest with Alejandro, no matter how dangerous it could be.

It was Alejandro's routine to visit me at school every day. When he arrived the following day, I told him to wait for me at my friend Sofia's house because we needed to talk. He seemed cheerful to hear that. I imagine he thought that I had come to my senses and had decided to accept the marriage proposal he was pressing so hard for. I was still very much afraid of his reaction when he learned that I did not want to see him anymore. Fortunately, Sofia's husband and two of her sons were at home that day, and I felt somewhat protected by them.

When I arrived at Sofia's house, Alejandro was anxiously waiting for me in the veranda. He motioned for me to sit beside him, but I remained standing. I made eye contact with him and trying very hard to conceal my fear and apprehension, I said, "Alejandro, I like you as a friend. I have tried very hard to love you as a boyfriend, but I can't do it. Please believe me. I am so sorry! I really think it's best if we no longer see each other."

As if trying to process what I was saying, Alejandro was puzzled and silent for a while. He avoided eye contact with me and remained looking down for what seemed like a long time. Then he looked at me angrily and shouted, "What do you mean by that? You have no feelings for me? I know you felt something when we kissed."

Before I could respond, he warned me, "If you were faking it, you have taken me for a fool. You played with my feelings. Nobody takes Alejandro de la Vega for a fool and gets away with it!"

I was thinking how to reply to his threat, but before I could squeeze in a word, Alejandro asked, "Does this decision of yours have anything to do with that damned priest coming back?" I firmly answered, "Of course not! You are too smart to believe those stupid rumors."

Then Alejandro grabbed me by my shoulders, shook me a couple of times and with fire in his eyes, warned me, "I am not sure if the rumors are true or false, but I am damned sure of one thing. If you ever marry that priest or anyone else for that matter, I swear to God I will kill you."

Trying to pull away from his strong grip I said loudly, "Let me go before I scream!" Then reluctantly he took his hands off of me.

After a short while, Alejandro seemed to somewhat compose himself. Touching his forehead and with a puzzled look in his eyes, he said softly, "I don't understand. Any woman in this damned country would cut off her right arm to marry me. I am offering you the privilege of being my wife, and you refuse? What is wrong with you?"

Playing into his ego and making eye contact with him to conceal my fear, I answered him firmly, "Maybe you are right. Maybe there is something wrong with me. So please go away. Please do me the favor of giving that privilege to another woman."

Sofia heard my voice from the kitchen and came running to the corridor. "What's going on here?" she asked very concerned.

"Everything is okay, Sofia," I replied. "Alejandro was just leaving."

Then he slowly walked toward his horse and rode away. As he was leaving, he looked back and shouted one last warning, "Remember what I said! I wasn't kidding! I promised my grandfather to keep my hands off that damned priest. But I never promised him not to get even with anyone who takes me for a fool!"

I took Alejandro's threat seriously, and I was really afraid for my life. I had a very long and sleepless night. I had nightmares while awake. I was remembering horrible incidents I had been told about which had happened in nearby villages. In one particular instance, a jealous ex-boyfriend had killed a young woman while she had been holding her newborn baby in her arms.

The next day I made sure I was always accompanied by several women when I went to the river and by several students when I walked to school. I considered not going to work that day, but I changed my mind. I feared my mother's wrath as much as I feared Alejandro's threats. If I stayed at home from work, I would have needed to give my mother a good explanation, and I did not want her to know the truth.

As lunchtime approached that day, my panic increased. But to my relief and surprise, Alejandro did not show up at school. Neither did he come to my parents' house in the afternoon. I was very relieved, but I could not help wondering what had happened. The suspense did not last long. News spreads out in a small village like a wildfire.

It was public knowledge in Las Limas that after Alejandro left Sofia's house the day before, he had gone to a cantina in San Esteban. Witnesses claimed that while he had been very drunk in the cantina, he had started bragging, "Yo soy un verdadero hombre, y tengo mucho dinero. Siempre tengo miles de lempiras en mi bolsillo, y puedo tener a cualquier mujer que me dé la gana." (I am a real man, and I have a lot of money. I always carry thousands of lempiras in my pocket, and I can have any woman I want.)

Reliable sources had confirmed that Alejandro was telling the truth as far as the money. He used to carry large amounts of money at any given time because he had been addicted to gambling. He took pride in bragging, even when he wasn't drunk, about the large amount of money he usually carried. But this time, his bragging had been heard by the wrong people.

Supposedly, Alejandro had left the cantina very late that evening. It had already been dark, and he still had several hours to travel by horse. At some point on his way home from town, he had been severely beaten and robbed. Someone found him on the road the following morning and took him home. Immediately Alejandro's family sent him to Tegucigalpa for medical treatment, and also to get him away from the men who had mugged him.

When I heard the story about what had happened to Alejandro, I felt saddened and relieved at the same time. Knowing how protective his family was of him, I knew that Alejandro would be away for a very long time. "Thank God I am safe." I said to myself. "Thank God this nightmare is over."

It appeared that my luck was finally turning in my favor. The same day Alejandro left, Father Andrew returned. However, things did not work out as I had hoped they would. I had rehearsed hundreds of times in my mind what I was going to say to Father Andrew if he returned. But before I could speak a word when I saw him, he confronted me about my relationship with Alejandro. I had a lot of explaining to do, and I had no idea how he had found out about Alejandro.

My mother later explained that when Father Andrew had arrived at my house that day, I had not been at home. Usually in that case, he would wait for me resting in a hammock on the veranda. But because it was raining that particular afternoon, she asked Father Andrew to wait for me in the living room. I had left a bunch of letters and pictures that I meant to return to Alejandro, on top of the record player located in the living room. When Father Andrew went to play a record, he could not help but discover the pile of letters.

It was a custom in those days that if a girl broke up with her boyfriend, she would return the letters, pictures and any gifts he had given her. In Alejandro's case, all I had to return were letters and pictures because I had not accepted any gifts from him.

Not knowing that Father Andrew had discovered the letters, when I was returning home that afternoon and saw from afar Father Andrew's jeep parked in front of my house, I ran the rest of the way. I could not contain my excitement! But just before approaching the house, my mother rushed to meet me, which was unusual. I knew then that something was very wrong. "Cándida," she whispered, "He found Alejandro's letters! How could you be so foolish as to leave those letters around? Why didn't you burn or hide those stupid letters?" My mother asked me, very annoyed.

With an expression of dismay, I replied, "Oh my God! What am I going to do now?"

"The only thing you can do," my mother advised, "is to tell Father Andrew the truth and pray he believes you."

When I entered the living room, I noticed that Father Andrew was very subdued, but I could understand why. Even though he might not have been aware of the content of the letters, he probably knew what accepting those types of letters meant in my culture. In those days, a girl would only accept letters from a man if she was interested in having a relationship with him. I had several letters tied with a colorful ribbon along with some pictures of Alejandro.

Before I could greet Father Andrew, he got up from where he was sitting, picked up the bunch of letters and placed them close to my face. "Now I know why you didn't want to marry me," he said in a soft and sad tone with a hint of anger. "Why didn't you tell me Alejandro de la Vega is your boyfriend?" he asked.

"Alejandro is not my boyfriend," I replied, trying to sound as convincing as I could. "If you would please listen and give me a chance, I can explain the letters."

At that moment, Father Andrew, the priest and not the man, listened attentively to my long story about Alejandro. Not only did he believe me, but he also acted sympathetically toward Alejandro. At some point and with sadness in his voice, Father Andrew commented, "That poor young man! I can perfectly understand why he has lost his head over you."

I told Father Andrew the whole story about Alejandro, but I could not bring myself to tell him a couple of details. I had omitted telling him that Alejandro and I had kissed. I had also left out that at some point I had thought I had romantic feelings toward Alejandro.

Fortunately for me, Father Andrew never became aware of the contents of the letters. If he had read the letters, I would have had a lot more explaining to do because Alejandro had made some reference about our passionate kisses. "I have kissed many lips before," he wrote, "but I have never experienced such ecstasy as when I kiss yours. Your kisses have a way of transporting me from earth to paradise."

I concluded the story about Alejandro by telling Father Andrew, "I am so sorry! I know what I did wasn't right. But I was very afraid of Alejandro." For a moment, I overcame my shyness and brought myself to add, "Besides living in fear, I was enduring the pain of missing you terribly while you were in the States."

Father Andrew was obviously very pleased to hear that I had missed him. He embraced me tightly, looked deeply into my eyes, and asked me smiling, "Did you really miss me that much?"

"Of course," I replied, smiling back, "Between missing you and worrying you wouldn't come back, the pain was unbearable."

"Then I was right," he said, and asked for reassurance, "Do you love me?"

"Oh, no!" I responded jokingly, "I do not love you. I adore you totally, completely, absolutely and forever."

"This gringo adores you more, but right now this dumb gringo is very confused," Father Andrew said perplexed, still smiling.

I thought the expression this "dumb gringo" was very funny, and I started laughing. I was about to ask, "What are you confused about?" when Father Andrew questioned, "Why didn't you agree to marry me?"

I tried to explain to him about my embarrassment of knowing that my secret feelings for him had not been secret at all. "You were not the only one who was trying to keep your feelings a secret," he said, no longer smiling.

Now I became very curious and asked Father Andrew, "Does that mean that you have been keeping a secret too?"

Motioning with his head, he responded, "Oh yes, I even kept the secret from myself for a long time."

Tell me, I asked pleadingly, "When did you let yourself know the secret?"

"It's a long story, my love," Father Andrew said, "but if you want to know the details, I will write a letter to you."

"Oh, please do!" I begged him. "I want to know every single, small detail about your secrets."

"I will write you the letter," he promised. "But now I have something important to ask you again."

Holding my hands again, but this time kneeling on one knee, Father Andrew asked me, "Chita, do you agree to make this gringo the happiest man in the world by becoming my wife?"

I quickly replied, expressing in my voice the excitement I was feeling at that magical moment, "Yes, yes! With all my heart I want to marry you."

Our faces mirrored each other's ecstasy. Father Andrew then took me in his arms and kissed me for the first time. The feeling of being kissed by his chaste lips brought to surface feelings I had never experienced before. First, we started kissing gently, maybe due to shyness or lack of experience. Then a wave of passion took over our bodies, and we surrendered to our feelings. For that brief moment, we could feel each other's heartbeat as if our bodies had become one. Neither of us had experienced such bliss and tenderness.

We were still kissing when my mother came into the living room. When we saw her, we felt very embarrassed and pulled away. I was sure she was going to be furious at us for crossing the line that we had so carefully guarded up until that point. But jokingly, she said, "I see that the two of you have worked things out."

Smiling, Father Andrew replied, "We did better than that 'suegra' (mother-in-law); your daughter has agreed to be my wife."

Then he asked her, "Will you give us your blessing and your consent?"

My mother responded, "I gladly give you my blessing, but for the consent, you will have to ask Cándida's father."

Father Andrew sent a friend of his, someone very respectable, to ask my father for my hand in marriage. Since my father was in Catacamas and was not aware that his best friend and daughter were even in love, he reacted not only surprised, but upset as well. Trying to mask his anger, he politely declined, "It's up to Cándida's mother to make such a decision. I leave it up to her."

I felt that my father, whom I had adored and respected so much throughout my life, had disowned me by washing his hands about such an important decision, as my marriage. I was deeply hurt of course. But many years later, my father explained to me the reason, "During my lifetime I heard a couple of stories about priests, who had taken young girls away supposedly to marry them. But after taken advantage of those young girls, they had gone back to the priesthood. Knowing Father Andrew as well as I did," my father continued, "I hardly had any doubts about his honorable intentions. However, I did not want to take the chance of being responsible for your disgrace in case my judgment was wrong."

Father Andrew asked my mother again to give her consent for us to get married. After a long pause, carefully weighing all the advantages and risks of such a difficult decision, my mother finally agreed. We were overjoyed that my mother was supportive of our marriage plans.

I was surprised that my mother took the chance of giving us her consent for us to get married. I knew that she had had to deal with my father's wrath when he came home. It even crossed my mind that her main motivation for being supportive of our marriage was to get rid of me. But I did not care. All I wanted was to spend the rest of my life with the man I loved.

I asked my mother many years later, "Why did you agree for me to marry my husband?" She replied with conviction and without any hesitation, "I reasoned that I would rather take a chance, and have you marry a priest than allow you to marry Alejandro de la Vega and end up as a servant or maybe even a slave in his huge hacienda."

Father Andrew started the process of obtaining a visa for me to travel to the United States. He also mentioned that he was working on arranging our marriage, but he did not describe the specific details. He wrote to his mother asking her to lend him the money for the plane fare for both of us to the United States, because he did not want to touch even a penny that belonged to the church.

I knew that Father Andrew was working on securing our future together. But I had no idea how fast until I was put on the spot.

Only a few days after my mother gave her consent for us to get married, without any warning at all, Father Andrew came to my house with one of my uncles and the justice of the peace from San Esteban. My mother and I thought that the three men had come to pay us a visit, when Father Andrew informed me, "Your uncle and the justice of the peace are here to marry us."

I was astonished to hear that! Without even trying to hide my disappointment, I asked him "What did you say? Getting married just like that, with no white dress, no cake and no preparation? No way!" This time, when I said "no," I meant it.

Poor Father Andrew! He was so shocked at my reaction, that he did not say anything else. My uncle, who is also my godfather, asked to talk to me in private and gave me a piece of his mind. He angrily asked me, "How can you waste the best opportunity of your life because of a stupid wedding dress and a cake?"

Then my uncle went on and on with a long lecture: "Be smart! Go ahead and marry Father Andrew now, while you have the chance. If you miss this opportunity, you may never get it again. Sometimes, luck only knocks once at our door." Then he gave me one last warning. "If that were to happen, you're going to end up messing up your life for sure."

But even after that strong and convincing speech from my uncle and godfather, my answer remained the same: "I do not want to get married without any preparation. I want a white dress, a cake and flowers."

"That's ridiculous!" my uncle replied, rolling his eyes with exasperation.

Looking back, I cannot believe that the fantasy of getting married in a white dress with all of the trimmings was greater than securing my marriage to the man of my dreams. Poor Father Andrew! I had disappointed him again, and I had no idea that I was heading for a huge disappointment myself. I had made a big mistake by refusing to marry the love of my life while I had a chance.

I found out later that Father Andrew had a good reason to come up with that impulsive marriage plan. He had become aware that the bishop knew by now that the rumors about us were factual. Father Andrew was sure he would be confronted by the bishop very soon, and he wanted to marry me before that happened. He reasoned that once we were married, the pressure of staying in the priesthood from the bishop would lessen.

Father Andrew's hunch about having to face the bishop in the very near future was correct. Soon after his unsuccessful attempt to marry me, he received a telegram from his bishop in Juticalpa, demanding to see him immediately. Father Andrew had not choice, but to obey the orders of his superior.

CHAPTER 8

Soon after receiving the telegram from the bishop, Father Andrew went to meet with him at his residence in Juticalpa. The bishop politely asked Father Andrew, "Are the rumors true about your impending departure with a young girl from Las Limas?"

When Father Andrew confirmed the rumors, the bishop rose from his desk and reached for a book in his bookcase. He handed Father Andrew the book. It was the Rite of Priestly Ordination. Speaking with authority, the bishop then reminded Father Andrew, "Nine years ago, you made a solemn promise to be the "Persona Christi" (person of Christ) for his people. I suspected that you might have encountered problems with your vocation because you have acted more like a social worker than a priest. Have you considered the impact this decision will have on the church and our people?"

Father Andrew remained silent, and the bishop continued, "If you should reconsider your decision, I will reward your fidelity to the church by consecrating you as a bishop. You can have a new start in another province of Honduras or in the States, if you wish."

Father Andrew became incensed with the offer and whispered under his breath: "Sit transit gloria mundie" (So passes the glory of the world). When the bishop asked him to explain his reaction, Father Andrew replied, "I have never been interested in the power or politics of the church; neither was our founder, Saint Francis. Your offer is a simple bribe, and I flatly refuse it."

A wave of fury gushed from the bishop, as he yelled at Father Andrew, "I have tried to exercise patience and discretion, and you accuse me of wrongdoing? Saint Francis loved the Church, and a true son of Saint Francis would not abandon the Church. Don't you dare lecture me about Saint Francis."

Their discussion continued without an agreement. Father Andrew was about to depart the bishop's office, and in exasperation the bishop exclaimed, "You were the last person anyone would have expected to betray the church. I can only hope and pray you come to your senses before it's too late."

Father Andrew left without saying another word.

After the heated discussion with the bishop, Father Andrew was more convinced than ever that he wanted to leave the priesthood. He had come face to face with the politics of the church as never before, and he was deeply disappointed.

Since Father Andrew was already in the city, he decided to buy my wedding dress and the whole works: veil, bouquet, cake, and even some wine.

Two days later, he came to my house again unannounced. He proudly presented me with all the wedding paraphernalia and said with a huge smile, "Now you have no reason for not marrying me today because I brought everything you wanted." My eyes could not believe what they saw when I anxiously opened the boxes! Father Andrew had brought everything that I had considered necessary to have the wedding of my dreams.

I had never seen such a beautiful wedding dress! It was a classical princess-cut white gown with intricately detailed lace overlay and a matching veil. I rushed to my bedroom to try it. And to my amazement, it was the perfect size. I was wondering, "How did Father Andrew know my dress size?" When I asked him, he replied, "I had a little help from your aunt, the dressmaker." He smiled, obviously beaming with pride and satisfaction.

It was at about 9:00 a.m. when Father Andrew came to my house with the wedding paraphernalia, and he proposed for us to get married later on, at 2:00 p.m. He needed time to go to San Esteban to pick up the Justice of the Peace and also my uncle, who had offered to be one of the witnesses. This time, both my mother and I agreed to have the marriage ceremony that day.

I was deliriously happy but frantic as well! I had only five short hours to get ready for the biggest day of my life! And I wanted to be the most beautiful bride Father Andrew had ever seen. During his nine years of officiating weddings, he had seen hundreds of brides. I needed all the help I could get.

My mother sent for some of her sisters and nieces to come to our rescue. Some of the women were in charge of decorating the house with roses, gardenias, and any flowers in the garden that happened to be in bloom. Others were helping my mother in the kitchen preparing a special dinner for the occasion. My youngest aunt and some of my cousins had the most difficult task: to make me as beautiful as possible.

When my aunt and cousins were finished, performing what I was sure would be a miracle, they told me excitedly, "Go see yourself in the mirror." I could not believe that the reflection in the mirror was really me! Not only did the dress look beautiful, but also the reflection of the young lady in the mirror looked stunning. "How can it be?" I asked myself. "My whole life I have considered myself unattractive and now I look so beautiful." I felt beautiful too.

Everything was working out as I had hoped. The veranda in front of the house where the ceremony was going to take place looked splendid! Besides being beautifully decorated with all kinds of flowers, the floor was completely covered with pine needles. It was a custom that during festive occasions, people used pine needles to give the house a pine smell. Between the dozens of gardenias and pine needles, the veranda smelled absolutely heavenly. Now I could not wait for the return of my groom-to-be! I could imagine how happy he was going to feel that everything had been beautifully prepared for our marriage. I could not wait to surprise him!

I had no way of knowing then that the big surprise was going to be mine. Father Andrew returned from town with no Justice of the Peace and extremely disappointed. This man, who was so willing to marry us before, now completely refused to get involved. Now the news about our possible marriage had spread. The people had pressured the Justice of the Peace not to perform the ceremony. They warned him over and over again, "If you have anything to do with marrying that priest, you and your family will be cursed. The curse that will come upon the priest for leaving his church will surely fall on you and your family too." No amount of convincing from Father Andrew was able to change this man's mind.

My uncle, our witness, was still willing to come to Las Limas with Father Andrew. He was aware there would be no wedding that day, but he pretended to offer us unconditional support. However, I knew better. My uncle wanted to come to Las Limas for one reason only. He could not resist the opportunity of telling me to my face, "I told you so, stupid girl!"

My heart sank with disappointment when I saw Father Andrew and my uncle return from San Esteban with no Justice of the Peace. I quickly ran to the living room and closed the door. I wanted to conceal my tears and take off my wedding dress. But someone knocked on the door. I quickly opened it, assuming it was my mother or one of my aunts.

When Father Andrew saw me dressed as a bride, his expression of disappointment rapidly changed into awe! Staring at me adoringly he exclaimed, "Oh my God! You look so beautiful!" Gently placing his right hand under my chin and lifting my face as he had done the first time, gazing into my eyes, he continued, "You have the face of an angel. I fell in love with you for the beauty of your soul and the nobility of your character. But you are just as beautiful on the outside." He embraced me tightly and kissed me for a long time with the same passion of our first kiss. It was such an unfamiliar sensation for me to feel beautiful and adored. I was also experiencing the disappointment of my cancelled wedding after everything had been ready. The mixture of these conflicting emotions brought tears to my eyes of joy and sadness at the same time.

When Father Andrew saw the tears running down my face, he took out from his pocket the linen handkerchief I had made for him. After drying my tears tenderly, Father Andrew reassured me, "Don't worry, Chita. Everything is going to be all right. I will find someone to marry us; even if I have to go to Tegus (short for Tegucigalpa)." While reaching into his pocket for the handkerchief, he remembered something, and said excitedly, "The letter, Chita! I forgot to give you the letter." He quickly took out the letter from another pocket and gave it to me.

Even more than Father Andrew's soothing words of reassurance, receiving my first love letter from him definitely cheered me up. I could not wait to read it, but I waited until he left that day to read it because I wanted to relish every single word.

In the course of the several years that Father Andrew and I had corresponded, we had written to each other more than two hundred letters and I treasured them all. But his first love letter was as meaningful to me as our first kiss. I had no idea that Father Andrew and I had so much in common until I read his letter.

October 25, 1963

My dearest Cándida

This is my awkward attempt to write you a love letter. I have composed this letter a hundred times, but each draft found its way to the trash.

A part of me thought that if I put my feelings for you on paper that would be enough to get rid of them. It wasn't. My love didn't disappear. Another part of me thought that if I destroyed the letters, I could destroy any evidence that I am in love with you. I failed again. Somewhere, somehow, I found a little courage along the way to make sure that this letter would make its way to you.

For months I've kept my feelings for you a secret, even from myself. I don't know exactly when my feelings changed from loving you as a child of God to loving the beautiful woman that you have become. Neither do I know when I changed from wanting you for the bride of Christ to be a bride for myself.

God knows I've tried to purge you from my physical body. I even wore a heavy metal bracelet on my left arm as a penance for loving you. The bracelet tore my skin, but no amount of penance was able to get you out my thoughts or to exorcise you from my heart.

Remember the day you were so sad because Sebastian left you? The priest in me felt your pain and I wanted to console you. But inside the priest was a very jealous man, who was glad that Sebastian was out of your life. That was the day I could no longer deny to myself that I was in love with you.

I went to the States for five long weeks after my father died. I was hoping that time and distance would put my feelings in their proper perspective, but the opposite happened. Time and distance only made me realize that I couldn't live without you. My world has become so meaningless without you. That's when I realized that I had lost the battle and my only choice was to surrender. It was not an easy decision because I had made sacred vows to be a priest for life.

I was already a tortured soul because I knew I could no longer be faithful to my priestly vows, but the uncertainty of your love for me added more pain to my torment. I considered it impossible for a beautiful woman like you to fall in love with an overweight gringo like me. But when you gave me the handkerchief, it gave me a dim hope that you could love me back.

Cándida, you have no idea how my world came crashing down when you rejected my marriage proposal. But thanks to your mother, I didn't give in to despair. Before I left your house that day, Maria told me, "I know my daughter, and I know she's in love with you."

And now my love, I feel the luckiest gringo in the world because I have a renewed sense of hope that you love me. Can you do me a favor? Just save me. Please be my wife. I cannot imagine greater happiness than spending the rest of my life with you.

Love always,
Frank

(Frank was Father Andrew's legal name before he entered the seminary.)

I cannot put into words how happy and surprised I felt when I read Father Andrew's letter. I was deliriously happy to find out that he loved me with the same depth and intensity that I loved him. I was very surprised that we both had tried so hard to keep our feelings for each other a secret. But it was even more surprising that he felt unworthy of being loved by me. I have read this letter hundreds and hundreds of times, and every time I am amazed that Father Andrew and I had in common not only our secret love for each other, but also our insecurities.

When Father Andrew reassured me that he would find a Justice of the Peace who would be willing to marry us, he had no idea how difficult it would be to keep that promise. Mayors and lawyers were also authorized to officiate civil unions, but none of them in the surrounding towns near Las Limas were willing to marry us for fear of repercussions from the people. Within a few days, the news of a priest trying to marry a young lady but everyone refusing to marry them, was public knowledge. The news had spread out not only from mouth to mouth, but also by radio throughout the whole country.

I hated to admit, especially to myself, that my uncle had been absolutely right. I should have married the man of my dreams when I had the chance. Now the fantasy of getting married in a bridal dress seemed unimportant. "Will we ever find anyone brave enough to marry us?" I asked myself in dismay. I was hoping we would, but I had serious doubts.

It was now the beginning of November 1963. Seven weeks had gone by since Alejandro had left Las Limas. I was almost beginning to forget the nightmare I had lived with him. But suddenly after all this time, it was right back in my face. A telegram from him had arrived with the following message:

From here I am thinking of you with all of my heart and soul. Soon I will be back for you.

Eternally yours,
Alejandro

A chill ran through my bones, as I read Alejandro's telegram. "Why now?" I asked myself in exasperation. "Why has Alejandro decided to rise from the dead after all this time?" I do not need any more fear and confusion in my life.

This time I did not keep Alejandro's threat a secret. I told my mother about the telegram and showed it to Father Andrew. His reaction was one of urgency, "Oh my God! We need to act quickly for more reasons than one."

Two days later, Father Andrew, my mother, and I boarded a small plane in Las Limas and went to Tegucigalpa. Since the trip was so rushed, I had no time for sentimentality or even to say goodbye to anyone. I was about to finish my second year of teaching. There were only two weeks left for the school year to end. The school year in Honduras begins in February and ends in November. I felt terrible about leaving untied loose ends. I especially regretted not being there when my students had to take their final exams.

Another part of me was somewhat relieved that I did not have time to say goodbye to anyone. I didn't tell a soul about my trip to Tegucigalpa or my impending marriage to Father Andrew. "I do not want to be the laughingstock of the village on my return," I told myself, fearing we would not find anyone willing to marry us in the capital city either.

When we arrived at the airport in Tegucigalpa, a taxi driver named Rubén, a friend of Father Andrew, was waiting for us. He kindly offered to put us up in his humble home in the outskirts of the city. When Ruben and his wife found out the purpose of our trip, they were not happy at all. However, they remained hospitable to us out of gratitude to Father Andrew. Ruben confided in me, "I was working for someone who owns a taxi. But I could hardly support my six children, because I had to share my daily profits with the taxi owner. When Father Andrew became aware of my predicament, he found a way of helping me to buy my own taxi."

We had been in the capital city for a couple days, had knocked on many doors, but instead of finding someone to marry us, we found an additional problem. I had two original birth certificates with the same day of birth, but with a different year. According to one I was born in 1946 and the other one in 1949. "How did that happen, Chita?" Father Andrew asked me. I had no choice, but to confess that I knew about the discrepancy on the birth certificates.

It had happened during the presidential elections of 1963, when a politician in San Esteban was trying to get as many votes as he could for his party. So that I would qualify to vote, the politician had provided me with another original birth certificate, altering the year of birth. I had no saying in the matter; I did not even know that altering a legal document was committing fraud. However, I was guilty of using the fraudulent birth certificate in my favor to make Father Andrew believe that I was older than I really was.

Father Andrew's reaction was one of shock and disbelief! "Why did you lie to me, Chita?" Trying to save face, I responded, "I didn't lie to you, honey. I just didn't tell you that the birth certificate had a false year when I showed it to you." Forcing a quick smile, he concluded "Oh well! You are more mature than any almost fifteen-year-old girl in the States and now it's too late to turn the clock back. So let's continue with our plans."

We had almost lost all hope of ever finding someone to marry us when a miracle happened! Father Andrew finally found a lawyer, who was not only willing to marry us, but who would also speed up the legal process for us to travel to the United States. He used my true birth certificate, and since my father had not given me his last name, I only needed my mother's authorization to get married. On this particular situation, the saying "Every cloud has a silver lining," turned out to be true.

We were married in the lawyer's office on November 10, 1963, at 8:00 p.m. As soon as the lawyer agreed to officiate our marriage, we asked him to do it immediately. We did not want to take any chances about him changing his mind.

I have no recollection what I was wearing for my marriage ceremony. I do not remember the ceremony either because it was just a rushed legal formality. How ironic! I had brought my wedding dress to the city, but I had not been able to wear it. My marriage ceremony turned out to be exactly as the first one Father Andrew had proposed: no wedding dress, no veil, no cake, no flowers, and no preparations at all.

Nevertheless, we finally became husband and wife. When we left the lawyer's office, we went directly to Ruben's house. But there were no congratulations, no champagne, and no wedding cake waiting for us. All we received were stern looks of disdain and disapproval from Ruben's wife and some of her neighbors. Ruben was the only one, who had remained civil toward us. He cared and respected Father Andrew too much to act otherwise.

Even my mother, who had been very supportive of our marriage, now was having second thoughts about her decision. "Maybe I made a huge mistake going along with this marriage," she told me, questioning herself. "If looks could kill, you would be dead already." She was referring to the reaction of Ruben's wife and her neighbors.

My new husband and I decided to get away from such a somber and depressing atmosphere. We held hands and stepped out to the garden. With the stars as our only witnesses, we professed our eternal love and commitment to each other. For a few hours, we experienced the delight of being in each other's arms. We embraced each other tightly and kissed with an explosion of passion. For a while, we forgot everything we had gone through to get to this point.

Still holding me tight and gazing into my eyes with the look of love, my new husband whispered, "I love you so much. I wish with every fiber of my being that this moment could last forever." I was wishing the same thing when I heard my mother's footsteps looking for me. I reluctantly pulled away from the loving embrace of my new husband and sweetly whispered in his ear, "I am so sorry, darling. I have to go now. I love you so very much."

He smiled and whispered back, "I understand my love. I love you more, Mrs. DeVito."

That was the first time I was called by his last name. It then dawned on me that both of us had to change our names. I had to take my husband's last name and he had to give up his religious name. Now he was Frank DeVito, his legal name. It took me a long time to get used to this change. I think that in my heart I never did. My husband would always be Father Andrew to me because it was Father Andrew who I fell madly in love with. However, that was not a bad thing – it kept my deep love and great respect for him very much alive throughout the years of our marriage.

Several people have asked me, "When did you make the transition from Father Andrew to Frank?" Honestly, it took several years after we were married for me to get used to calling my husband Frank. I used to call him endearing names; such as honey, darling and sweetheart to avoid calling him Frank. However, in my heart of hearts and somewhat on my mind, I never made a complete transition from the priest to the man.

We had to wait three long days after our marriage before we could travel to the United States. The attorney was working as fast as he could, but it was not an easy task to get all documents in order. It helped that on my birth certificate I appeared with my mother's last name only since I did not need my father's permission to get married or to travel to another country. But the attorney needed to confirm with the birth registration office of San Esteban which one of my birth certificates was the legal one.

While we waited to leave for the United States, we had to keep our marriage a secret as much as we could. Not only did we fear the reaction of people, but we also did not want the news of our secret marriage to get back to the bishop until after we had left the country. Father Andrew, now Frank, was very busy during these three days putting the affairs of his former parish in order and making sure the attorney was on task getting our documents ready to travel to the United States.

My mother and I had not much to do during these three days, and we no longer felt comfortable in Rubén's house. Now his wife acted very cold and distant toward us. Just to get away from the uncomfortable atmosphere, we would spend most of the day roaming around stores and sightseeing. I went directly from a small village to a big city. Everything was so new and such a wonder to me!

During the third day of exploring the city, my mother and I were finally exhausted. We decided to rest in Parque Morazán (the central park) and had a picnic lunch there. It was a glorious sunny day and with nothing else better to do, we remained most of the afternoon in the park. Just as we were about to leave, someone said hello to us and called us by name. We recognized him at once. He was Don Julio Padilla, a businessman from San Esteban.

Don Julio was surprised to see us, and asked, "What are the two of you doing in the big city?"

Without thinking my mother responded, "Cándida came here to marry Father Andrew."

The man acted surprised and burst out laughing. I had no idea what was so funny and before I could ask, Don Julio said. "I guess that Alejandro de la Vega has lost on the bet big time."

"What bet?" I asked curiously.

He hesitated to respond, but finally said, "I am so sorry; I thought you knew."

"Knew what?" I insisted.

Then Don Julio explained to us, "Alejandro made a bet with some people in San Esteban that he could take the priest's girlfriend away from him. A lot of money was involved in that bet!" Then he added, "Alejandro is not going to be happy at all! He has lost big time!"

I could not believe it! The news fell on me like a ton of bricks and it infuriated me! Soon I started wondering, "Did Alejandro ever love me at all? Was all that relentless pursuing just to win a bet?" Now I felt more foolish than ever for having believed his lies, for allowing him to kiss me and for thinking at some point that I had feelings for him. "How could I have been so stupid?" I asked myself.

I could not stand the idea that I had been completely fooled and I had been unable to see through Alejandro's dirty scheme. So, I asked my mother, "Do you think it's true that Alejandro was trying to convince me to marry him only to win a bet?"

I was hoping for reassurance that Alejandro really loved me, but my mother responded, "Well, I don't know for sure, but he has a serious gambling history."

That was not the answer I wanted to hear from my mother. But I could not deny that she was right. I knew for a fact that Alejandro had a gambling problem and had lost a lot of money due to this addiction. "How could I have believed the lies of a con artist?" I asked myself over and over again. After I had tortured myself enough, I finally concluded. "I was very lucky not to have fallen into his trap any further than I had." For me that was the end of Alejandro, but my mother was not as lucky. She had to deal with him upon returning home.

Frank and I left for the United States the morning of November 13, 1963. Rubén kindly drove us to the airport. While my husband had been checking the luggage, Rubén had given me some important advice. He told me, acting somewhat sad, worried and very concerned. "You are a very lucky young lady. You are married to the best man I know in the world. But you are too young to know what you have done. No matter what comes ahead, please don't look back. Be brave! Be strong and stand by your husband."

I had no idea then what Ruben was trying to tell me. Neither was I aware of the wisdom of his advice. Very soon I found out that I needed to take Ruben's advice. For my marriage to survive the hell that was to come, I had to be very brave, very strong and hold tightly to my man.

After the ticket agent carefully checked all of our documents at the airport, he gave us the okay to board the plane to Miami. We both let out a long sigh of relief. "We made it, Chita," my husband exclaimed, deliriously happy, "We are on our way home." I kissed his hand and smiled thinking that a life of eternal love and incredible bliss was waiting for us.

Before reaching Boston, our final destination, we had a two-day glorious honeymoon in a hotel located at Miami International Airport. I was very nervous when we entered the hotel room, mostly because I was very bashful, and I did not know what to expect. Talking about sex was taboo in my culture; I only knew what I had heard from other girls in school when I was about ten years old. One girl told me, "The first time is very painful." Another girl added, "And bloody too."

Not knowing if my classmates had the right information or not, when I was about thirteen years old, I mustered the courage to ask one of my youngest aunts, who had just had a baby. "Is it more painful to have sex the first time or to give birth?" I asked her naively.

"They are both about the same," my aunt quickly replied.

That really scared me because many times I had heard the horrible screams of women while giving birth.

Besides being petrified, I was more curious than ever, and I had another question for my aunt. "What about the blood the first time you have sex, how bad is it?"

She paused for a few seconds, then responded, "It's probably like the worst day of your period."

I knew what she was talking about because I had started having my period when I was twelve years old. "Oh my God!" I thought. "My classmates were right. It is a painful and bloody experience."

I had no reason to think that my aunt had given me inaccurate information; so I had believed everything she had told me. Therefore, when my husband and I went into the hotel room, I headed directly for the bathroom. I stayed there a long time, trying to find the courage to take my clothes off and also trying to figure out how to clean the bloody mess. "I am not ready for this!" I told myself in panic. "I will be so embarrassed if I stain those nice white sheets."

I was still thinking how to solve my dilemma, when my husband knocked on the door and asked very concerned, "Are you okay, Chita?"

I opened the door, still dressed and pale as a ghost. I could not bring myself to utter a word. He could see how frightened and embarrassed I was; then he took me in his arms, held me close to his heart and tenderly whispered, "Don't be afraid Chita. I would never do anything to hurt you or make you feel uncomfortable." We kissed for a long time until passion overtook us.

I asked if he could turn off the light and he complied. Then he slowly took my clothes off and finally our honeymoon began. Surprisingly, I was able to separate the man from the priest in my mind. I did not have any feelings of guilt at that moment. I felt that I was making love with Frank and not with Father Andrew.

Both of us were making love for the first time. Besides feeling embarrassed to reveal our naked bodies to the other, we were extremely clumsy and naive. But after a while, we just let our senses and instincts take over. Making love for us was more than the union of two bodies. It was the union of two souls, bonded by the purest of loves, respect and admiration for each other.

My husband was extremely tender and caring. I did not experience the pain I was expecting or the blood that I had been so concerned about cleaning. However, when I did not see any blood, I was very disturbed for another reason. Trying to sound as convincing as I could, I told my husband. "I have no idea what happened. I swear on the bible that I never had sex before."

He smiled, kissed my forehead and explained, "You have been riding horses all your life; that can be a cause for a woman's hymen to break. So, don't worry my love. I know you are as pure as an angel."

My husband's explanation put my mind at ease. It also made me realize why some brides, who were actually virgins, had been humiliated by their husbands and had been returned to their parents in disgrace, like used merchandise. I would have been one of those poor humiliated brides, if I had married a man from my own country.

The same day that Frank and I left for the United States, my mother went back home. I do not remember our goodbye, and I was oblivious to the pain that my departure was causing her. She had told me so many times, "I will be happy the day I get rid of you." And I believed she meant exactly that. Later on, I found out that my mother had said a lot of things she did not mean. But at that time, I took everything she said literally. I was too young to know any better.

Years later, my mother gave me an account of what had happened when she returned home from Tegucigalpa after my marriage to Father Andrew.

The day you left for the United States, I returned home completely heartbroken because I missed you already; and also because I wasn't sure I had done the right thing by letting you go. First, I had to deal with the explosive reaction of the people. They were enraged because Father Andrew had left the church and they blamed you and me. I was even told by some of the people (with different words, but the same message): 'When a priest leaves his church, it awakens the wrath of God. Not only could the whole village be cursed, but the whole country too. And it will be your fault, Maria! You helped your daughter make a man of God fall out of grace. You went along with their marriage. How could you have done such a terrible thing?'

I dealt with people's accusations the best way I knew how. No amount of explaining did any good to change anyone's mind. So I stopped trying to defend myself. I decided to let people talk. I let their comments go in one ear and out of the other.

When your father found out about the scandal your marriage had caused, he came home from Catacamas. The main purpose of his trip had been to give me a piece of his mind and to confirm you were really married. 'How could you have done such a stupid thing?' your father asked me angrily. Then he continued, 'I know that I left the decision in your hands, but I never dreamed that you would be foolish enough to actually take the chance of having your daughter risk being left abandoned in a faraway land and maybe never hear or see her ever again.'

Without giving me a chance to even respond, your father kept on asking me, 'Are you sure they got legally married? Can you swear on the Bible they just didn't take off without being married?'

When I could squeeze in a word, I told José, 'Yes, they got married in the lawyer's office.' But that was not enough for him. He kept on asking the same questions over and over again. I got furious and yelled, 'How many times do I have to tell you the same thing? Why do you keep asking the same questions?'

José responded, 'Well, you are so simple. Maybe they just went through the motions to fool you. Maybe they are not married at all.'

After your father made that very insulting comment, I lost my temper and screamed at him, 'If you were so worried about your daughter, why did you act like Pontius Pilate? Why did you wash your hands off of her? And since you're the smart one, why didn't you go to Tegucigalpa to make sure she got truly married?'

Your father didn't want to hear me anymore. So he said, 'That's enough, woman! There's nothing we can do now. Let's pray and hope for the best.' Your father finally stopped giving me a hard time, but he was very sad for a long time.

After dealing with your father, I also had to deal with Alejandro. He returned to the village before your father went back to Catacamas, but he waited until I was alone again to pay me a visit. I was hoping he would come because I could hardly wait to confront him about the bet.

Alejandro came to the house one afternoon. He said, 'Buenas tardes' (good afternoon) very coldly but polite. I answered him the same way. After some small talk, Alejandro said, 'So you let your daughter marry that damned priest, didn't you?'

I answered him rather angry, 'Yes, and it's none of your business.'

Alejandro got up from the chair and answered with fury in his voice, 'It is my business! I love Cándida, and I was going to marry her.'

Were you going to marry my daughter only to win a bet? I asked Alejandro.

'I have no idea what you are talking about,' he answered.

Now I got up from my chair too, looked at him straight in the eyes and told him. 'Stop lying to me, Alejandro! I know all about the bet. You have told so many lies. How can anyone believe anything that comes out of your mouth?'

At this point, this macho man, who took pleasure in scaring people by firing two guns into the air, sat again on the chair, covered his face with both hands and began to cry like a baby. I don't know if he was crying because he had lost the bet or because he had lost you. Nobody knows for sure, but I saw real tears dripping down his face. He finally admitted that it was true about the bet, and he tried to explain his side of the story.

He began by saying, 'It was more than just a bet! The people wanted Father Andrew to stay here, including my own mother. I thought that if I could get Cándida to marry me, Father Andrew would continue to be a priest here. I admit that at first, I wanted Cándida to be my girlfriend because of the bet, but I ended up falling in love with her. I was going to marry her for love.'

Alejandro was either telling the truth or he was a very good liar. He convinced me that he really loved you. I believed his version of the story, and I felt very sorry for him too.

When my mother concluded telling me about the consequences of her decision, I felt very sorry for her and somewhat for Alejandro too. I also began to realize that she had made the choice, of allowing me to marry Father Andrew, out of love and not to get rid of me as I originally suspected.

Following is an excerpt of a letter I sent to her shortly after learning the details of the ordeal she went through:

I can imagine how difficult it was for you to make the decision of authorizing my marriage to Father Andrew and to have to deal with the consequences of that choice. Not only did you see your young daughter move to a faraway country, but you also had to endure the wrath of people, especially of my father. I now believe you made that difficult decision out of love and because you wanted a better life for me.

I wish to assure you that you made the best decision for my life and what you were hoping for was granted. It's true that I encountered many trials and tribulations along the way because that's the human condition, but I can promise you that I have no regrets. Life has blessed me with more roses than thorns and I feel that I am one of the luckiest women in the world.

Ironically, at the same time that my mother had been facing the repercussions of my marriage to a priest in the early 1960s in Honduras, my husband and I had to deal with the scandal and persecution that were waiting for us in Boston, his birthplace.

CHAPTER 9

My husband and I arrived at Logan Airport in Boston on November 15, 1963, at 11:00 p.m. I was wearing a summer dress because I did not know how the weather in Boston was during wintertime. When we stepped outside the airport to wait for a taxi, I received the shock of my life. It was so cold! I never knew that such a degree of cold temperature existed. Miami was nice and warm, which supported the erroneous and naive belief that the whole world had the same warm climate as Honduras.

I had left the heavy coat Father Andrew had given me (months before) in Las Limas. It never crossed my mind to bring it to the United States. When my husband saw me shivering with cold, he took off his black jacket and insisted that I wear it. He lovingly put his arms around me and held me close to his chest to keep me warm.

The taxi brought us to my mother-in-law's apartment building located in the Beacon Hill section of Boston. It is a beautiful neighborhood with cobblestoned streets and ivy-covered houses with gas streetlights. Beacon Hill is known as one of the most historical and expensive areas in Boston. Just before going into the apartment, I was still asking my husband, "How can it be that a tunnel is built under water?" He had explained to me that the Sumner tunnel had been built under the Boston harbor, and I could not understand how that was possible. The cold temperature and the Sumner tunnel were my first impressions of Boston and I was amazed that these wonders were even possible.

By the time we arrived at my mother-in-law's apartment building, it was already midnight, but she was still up, waiting for us. Doña Alicia, my mother-in-law, was 68 years old then, a short and chubby woman with gray hair and brown eyes. She seemed healthy to me and much younger than her age. But immediately after meeting her, she gave me the impression that she was very sick. My mother-in-law warmly greeted me by kissing me on both cheeks, and then she told me in Italian, "E bello averti qui. Mi aspetto la mano di Dio in qualsiasi momento." (It's so good to have you here. I am expecting the hand of God at any time.)

I understood most of the words she was saying because Italian is very similar to Spanish, but I had no idea what she was talking about.

My husband explained to me, "Expecting the hand of God at any time meant that she was going to die soon." Then he added, "My poor mother has been suffering from high blood pressure for years. She also has an enlarged heart, and she has told me about her premonition that her end is very near." I was engulfed with sorrow for my mother-in-law's fragile condition.

I took my mother-in-law's claim about her health and impending death literally. The very next day, I started taking care of her as if she were approaching death. Within a few days of my arrival, I took over not only of the cooking and cleaning, but also of her personal care. I started bathing her, washing her hair, and giving her back and leg massages because she complained of poor circulation. I asked my husband to instruct me about her medications, and I made sure that she took all of them as prescribed by her doctor. I also brought nice warm meals to her room three times a day and I fulfilled her every whim.

My mother-in-law enjoyed my constant pampering. To my surprise, she even liked my cooking. Her only suggestion was to use less salt because it was not good for her high blood pressure. I made that adjustment of course. I tried to please her in every way I could because I thought she had such a short time of life left. "I am going to give this poor "moribunda" (dying lady) the best care possible; I do not want to deal with any guilt feelings or regrets after she dies," I told myself. I had no idea then that the hand of God would be delayed for twenty long years. I was completely blissful and unaware that my living hell was about to begin.

The warm and peaceful welcome that Doña Alicia had given to us was short-lived. As soon as the news spread that her only son had not only left the priesthood, but he was now married, suddenly all turned to chaos. She had been bombarded with negative feedback from most of her family members and friends. She had been interrogated over and over again by different people, with questions such as: "How could you have allowed this to happen? How can you have sinners living in your home? When are you going to throw them out?" The same week we arrived in Boston, Doña Alicia succumbed to the negative pressure, and she was in a rage every day.

When I came to the United States, I hardly spoke English. I never imagined that not being able to understand the language in one's surroundings could be a blessing. But in my case, it was definitely a blessing. Thank God I did not understand when my mother-in-law used to curse us and called us all kinds of names. She would take turns cursing us in English and at other times in Italian. She would call me, "Porcachona, porca fedente, spacima, etc." I did not have to understand the language to realize that my mother-in-law was calling me terrible names. I am still not sure what the English translation is for those words, but they all felt very insulting.

Doña Alicia was just as mean and unkind to her own son as she was to me. "Bum, lazy, good-for-nothing" were some of the derogatory names she would call him on a regular basis. We had been living with her less than a week, when she demanded that we pay her back immediately every penny she had loaned us for the plane fare to come to the United States; but we had no money to pay her, of course.

My husband started looking for employment two days after we arrived in Boston. But at that time, degrees from religious institutions were not recognized as official degrees. My husband had a Master's degree in both theology and philosophy. But outside of the religious community, his degrees were not worth anything. To make things even worse, lack of work experience and references together with his religious education not being recognized, it was impossible for my husband to find any decent employment right away. The only job available immediately was working in maintenance in one of the big department stores in downtown Boston.

My husband was forced to take this menial position because his mother was relentless in demanding that he pay back at once the money he had borrowed from her. Her unreasonable request was not because she needed the money, but because she was very upset that he had left the priesthood. She became so vicious with her tongue that her son was willing to do anything to satisfy her demands.

Words cannot describe the pain I felt when I found out that the same hands, which were once consecrated to change water and wine into the body of Christ, were now even cleaning toilets. "How did this happen?" I used to ask myself, "Where did our happiness go? Is this only the beginning of the punishment for our sin?"

The silent pain and sadness I was feeling, was soon to be shared by the whole country, but for a very different reason. I had been in Boston less than two weeks when a horrible tragedy struck the whole country. I was walking by the Boston Common on my way to my second English class at the Berlitz School, a famous language school, the afternoon of November 22, 1963, when I saw people running, screaming, and desperately crying everywhere. I knew that something terrible had happened, but I could not understand what was going on. All I could think was, "Oh my God! The third world war has probably just begun!"

I tried to ask my teacher at the Berlitz School what had happened, but she did not understand me. I hardly spoke any English and she did not speak Spanish. I finally gave up asking. She went on with her lesson, pointing to a number of pictures and slowly repeating the name of each picture in English. I went through the motions repeating words like a parrot. But my mind and my heart were not in the lesson. I could not wait for the lesson to end.

On my way home from school, I went by the Boston Common again, and I witnessed the same commotion and desperation. Most of the people were crying. I soon joined them, without even knowing what I was crying for. I had to wait until my husband returned from work that evening to find out that President John Kennedy had been assassinated. That was such terrible and sad news! I had loved President Kennedy even before I left Honduras. My husband had told me so many wonderful things about him. So along with the rest of the country and most parts of the world, I grieved deeply for such a great loss.

Besides our personal problems, our timing for arriving in Boston had not been the best moment. In addition to the assassination of President Kennedy, it was also the peak time of the Boston strangler. It was a very frightening time for the whole city. This serial killer had been responsible for taking the lives of thirteen women in the Boston area. I knew this information, and I lived in constant fear. I was instructed by my husband never to open the door of the apartment when I was alone. Thank God it was not that often. Since my mother-in-law was supposedly very sick, the only time she had gone out was to attend doctor's appointments.

The first time someone knocked on the door when I was alone, I nearly died with fright. I thought for sure it was the Boston strangler! I did not open the door, of course, and I did not move for about two hours until my mother-in-law came home. I spent all that time under the bed. I was even afraid to breathe because I was sure the Boston strangler was just outside the door waiting to make me his next victim.

Later that day, a handsome policeman came to the apartment. By that time, my husband and his mother were both at home. The officer was my husband's cousin, (also named Frank DeVito) who worked for the Newton Police Department. He happened to be working nearby and had decided to visit his relatives. After a quick greeting, the officer told his aunt and cousin, "I was here before, but there was no one at home." I realized then that I had spent a couple of agonizing hours for no reason, even though I still felt that I had done the right thing by not opening the door.

However, my fear of the Boston strangler seemed pale in comparison with the fear of being left by my husband. Only a few days after we had arrived in Boston, priests from my husband's order started coming to see him. Sometimes, they would come individually and, at other times, in groups of two or three. Occasionally they would come a couple times a week and at other times on a daily basis. The purpose of each and all of their visits was the same. They had one mission only, to convince Father Andrew to return to the priesthood. And the more he was pressured to return to the priesthood by his fellow priests, the more insecure I felt.

My husband reassured me, "I will never leave you no matter how hard they try to get me to go back." I believed he truly meant what he said. But I lived in constant fear that he would change his mind. I was afraid that with so much pressure and perseverance from his fellow priests, he would eventually break down and return to the priesthood.

His fellow priests would tell my husband things such as: "For the love of God Andy, please come to your senses. Return to the church where you belong. There is no shame in that. You will not be the first one or the last one that has made a mistake and then returned. The church needs you, Andy. The people need you."

After a while, my husband became tired of hearing the same sermon and felt annoyed by the pressure his fellow priests were inflicting on him to return to the priesthood. But still, he listened to them politely because it was not in his nature to be unkind or rude.

One month after we were married, I found out I was pregnant. My husband and I we were both ecstatic that we were going to have a baby! He had not been sure that he could ever have children due to a bad case of the mumps when he had been a teenager. "This is such an amazing and incredible news!" My husband exclaimed when he found out that he was going to be a father. We hoped that with this turn of events, the visits from the priests would cease, but soon our hopes were dashed. The fact that I was carrying his child, did not stop them from pressuring my husband to return to the priesthood.

When all of their tactics had failed to break my husband's will, the priests came up with a new strategy. They had one more card to play and they took a chance. Their new approach was to work on me, hoping that I was a more vulnerable link.

The priest chosen to try the new approach was well-known and was loved in Honduras. He had been a missionary there for a few years before Father Andrew's time. I had not met him, but I knew of him. His name was Father Mario. He was maybe in his late 40s, very tall, good-looking and charismatic. After he left the missions in Honduras, he had been assigned to become one of the superiors of the Franciscan province. This assignment required Father Mario to reside in New York City in their main monastery.

When Father Mario came to our apartment, I warmed up to him immediately. He spoke to me in Spanish and his name was familiar to me. I was very surprised that he came to talk to me and not to my husband. He was definitely very smooth, extremely charming and very smart. Father Mario asked my husband, "Andy, may I speak alone with your lovely wife?"

My husband replied, "Of course, Mario."

Father Mario began his mission by appealing to my love for my father and feelings of guilt for marrying a priest. "I know your father," he said, with an expression of sadness on his face. "José is a remarkable man, a very charitable one and a great Christian. I can imagine how sad and disappointed he must be feeling to know that his daughter is living in sin."

I did not know how to respond to that comment, but Father Mario seemed to know what I was thinking. "Don't be so sad," he said sympathetically. "It's not too late to do the right thing. God is merciful, and He will forgive your sin, if you do the right thing."

Trying to sound stronger than I felt, I asked Father Mario, "What is the right thing to do?"

"It's very simple." he replied. "You can separate from Andy. Then he will have no choice but to go back to the priesthood."

"What about my child and I?" I asked Father Mario in exasperation.

He quickly explained what seemed to be a carefully thought out plan. "If Andy returns to the priesthood, we will take care of you and your baby. We can establish you in New York and find a younger and more suitable husband for you and a father for your child."

Because of my respect for men of the cloth, I did not tell Father Mario what I really thought of his offer. I was also too shy to be rude. I simply said. "I do not want to give up my husband and I do not want another husband." How was Father Mario going to go about finding me another husband? I had no idea. His offer was so outrageous that I did not bother to ask for any details.

After Father Mario left that day, my husband noticed that I was clearly sadder and more upset than usual. He asked me with deep concern, "What's wrong, Chita? What did Mario talk to you about?"

I hesitated to tell him about Father Mario's offer, but he insisted on knowing; so I told him what Father Mario had proposed. My husband could not believe what he heard! He shook his head in disbelief and shouted very frustrated, "That's it! They have gone too far this time persecuting us." After composing himself, my husband lovingly embraced me and reassured me with a soft tone of voice, "Don't worry, darling. I will put a stop to this nonsense. I will do what I should have done in the first place."

A few days went by and no priests came to visit us. "Thank God," I said to myself, "I think they finally got the message." But I was wrong. A priest that I had never seen before came to try his power of persuasion. I do not know exactly what he said to my husband. They had been talking in private for a few minutes, when I heard my husband say something very loud. I had never heard my husband speak to anyone in that tone of voice. The man I knew was always soft-spoken and had the patience of a saint. But this time he had lost his tolerance and the priest left in a hurry.

After the priest left, my husband hugged me and filled in the blanks about their conversation. "I got rid of him," my husband said "by firmly telling him: I have reached the end of my patience with you guys. I am NOT going back. My wife is not an old shoe that can just be thrown out. I am not going to abandon her or my child. Please leave us alone! Please leave us in peace! And please tell the others to do the same thing."

I found amusing my husband's old shoes analogy. I forgot when was the last time that I had laughed. My husband chuckled, and said, "This is it, Chita. I don't think we will get any more visits from them."

Still laughing, I replied, "Que Dios le oíga." (May God hear you.)

The harassment from the priests had finally stopped, but peace in our lives was no way near yet. My mother-in-law continued to be very nasty. In addition, most of my husband's family and friends had stopped talking to us. However, they made no secret of their judgment and condemnation.

A few weeks after we had arrived in Boston, we started receiving hate mail on a daily basis. Most of the letters were from family members and friends who lived in the United States. But there were also letters from parishioners in Honduras and a few from El Salvador and Nicaragua. In the course of a year and a half, we had received almost two thousand letters. Following is an example of the content of the letters:

Dear Father Andrew,

I just heard the unbelievable news that you had left the priesthood! For the life of me, I cannot understand how you could have done such a despicable thing.

How can you face your family and friends after abandoning your priestly commitment and violating our trust? May I remind you that you took sacred vows and to not honor them is a guaranteed one-way trip to hell.

God punishes sinners and He will certainly punish you. And you will also drag into hell the young girl you took home as your bride.

But it is never too late to repent and ask for the Lord's forgiveness. I pray that He will help you come to your senses and do the right thing before it's too late. I pray that you find the strength to resist the ways of the world, make amends for your sins and go back to the priesthood, where you belong ….

This was the common gist in most of the letters. Another common insinuation in some of the letters were accusations of my husband's motives for going into the priesthood.

Maybe you have been a phony all this time. Maybe you never had a vocation for the religious life. Maybe you went into the priesthood only to avoid being drafted by the Army. Maybe you became a priest because you didn't want to work. You wanted to be supported by the church. Maybe you went to the priesthood to hide because you don't have the guts to live in the real world.

The accusations went on and on …. However, the pile of hate mail had a positive aspect. There were some letters expressing unconditional support, gratitude and prayers. Most of these kind letters had been sent by the young people my husband had helped to educate. Some of them were either in a convent or seminary in Honduras studying for the religious life, and a few of the young men were studying for other careers with the scholarships that my husband had helped them to obtain. Some letters of support also came from some of his former parishioners, begging Father Andrew to return to Honduras married or otherwise.

Even though, neither the pressure from my husband's fellow priests or the persecution from people had been able to separate us, they certainly had succeeded in taking all the joy out of my life and killing my spirit. All the happiness I had experienced a few weeks before had been replaced with feelings of sadness, insecurity, awful guilt, and fear of being condemned to hell forever. I guess that when one is told the same thing, hundreds of times, by hundreds of different people, one eventually starts believing it.

In my mind, what at one time had been the purest of loves now was the most terrible of sins. A time that should have been the happiest of my life, turned out to be the worst. I was constantly consumed by negative emotions. I was married to the man of my dreams. I was expecting his baby. These were wonderful reasons to rejoice. But I had allowed the darkness of my feelings to conceal the light of these amazing blessings.

My husband could sense that something was very wrong. I went from happy and energetic to almost comatose, and from funny to serious. But I did not want him to know how I was really feeling. I was aware that he was bearing the weight of his own heavy cross and trying to deal with his own struggles. I did not want to add any more burden to the heavy load that my husband was already carrying.

About two months after we were married, my husband asked me, "Honey, are you sorry you married me?"

I forced myself to smile and replied, "Of course I am! I am sorry I married you for two reasons: the cold weather and my mother-in-law."

My husband knew I was kidding, and he laughed. But as the saying goes, "Every joke has an element of truth."

At this point, my husband and I were just beginning to pay the price for giving in to our forbidden love. Our purgatory was to be continued for several years, but fortunately we had periods of relief along the way.

CHAPTER 10

In addition to feeling like an outcast from the church and society, along with financial hardship and a nasty mother-in-law, adapting to another culture and learning a new language were big challenges for me. I was transplanted almost directly from a small village in Honduras to a big city in the United States. These two extremes made the challenge even greater.

Because of a lack of resources, I had to learn English on my own. The English classes that I had been taking at the Berlitz School only lasted one week. The weekly tuition was more than my husband's weekly salary. My mother-in-law had offered to help pay for the classes, but she retracted her offer when the scandal of her son leaving the priesthood began.

When I came to the United States, I experienced a big cultural shock. There was an enormous difference between the customs in the United States and the customs in Honduras. Due to my ignorance about these differences, during my first few months in the United States I acted in ways that were very embarrassing. I can laugh at these incidents now. But at the time, they were not funny at all.

In Honduras, we soak white clothes with soap; then hang the clothes outside in the open air to be bleached by the sun. When I came to Boston, I would hang wet clothes outside in the middle of December, thinking that the sun would bleach them. I was very surprised when the clothes would get frozen instead.

When we had the first huge snowstorm, my mother-in-law gave me a shovel to clean snow in front of her apartment building. But I did not know that the owner of each building was responsible for shoveling the sidewalk in front of his or her building. I ended up shoveling half of the street. It took me more than three hours.

But the funniest and silliest thing I did was wearing my wedding dress to my doctor's office. I was dying to wear my wedding dress since I did not have the occasion to wear it in Honduras. But since I did not have any place to go, I wore it to the Beth Israel Hospital (one of the largest teaching hospitals in Boston), for a medical checkup. I had to take a train and a bus to get to the hospital. Fellow passengers were staring at me, giving me funny looks and others were giggling. I could not understand why these people were acting so strangely. "What's the matter with them?" I wondered. My wedding dress is beautiful, and it looks great on me. I wish someone had told me that what I was doing was completely inappropriate.

My mother-in-law saw me leaving the house wearing my wedding dress. She also knew that I was going to the hospital for my monthly checkup. But she did not say anything. I guess she decided to let me go ahead and make a fool out of myself. I do not remember if my doctor asked me anything about the wedding dress. I do not remember seeing him laughing either. Maybe he assumed I was on my way to have a shotgun wedding since I was already pregnant.

Nine months after we arrived in Boston, we could count on one hand the number of people who did not reject us. But fortunately, the arrival of our first baby opened up new doors and new possibilities to us. We became the happy and proud parents of a precious baby boy on August 28, 1964. We named him Francis after Saint Francis of Assisi and Joseph after my father.

I had no idea what to expect when I went to the Beth Israel Hospital to deliver my baby. I never imagined how intense and unbearable the pain would be. Without knowing what I was myself getting into, I requested to have natural childbirth. Since my English-speaking skills were still very weak, I told my husband to make my wish known to the doctors and nurses, which was a big mistake. At that time, husbands were not allowed in the delivery room. So even if I wanted to change my mind and ask for pain medication, I did not speak English well enough to make myself understood. My only choice was to bear the pain.

I am not sure whether I requested to have natural childbirth as a gesture of solidarity with other women in my country, who do not have access to pain medication, or as a punishment for my sins. Maybe subconsciously I felt that I deserved to suffer and to be punished for marrying a priest.

Besides the very painful childbirth, which I foolishly brought onto myself, the loving and special care that I received at the hospital surpassed even my highest expectations. During my ten hours of labor, a young intern had been assigned to watch over me, and he never left my side not even to have lunch. Instead, he asked someone to bring him a sandwich to the room. He was so concerned about me that with one hand he was holding the sandwich, and with the other hand he was rubbing my stomach.

During that hospital stay, I met Amalia Trigo, a very kind Cuban lady who worked in maintenance. We bonded immediately and became lifelong friends. We spoke the same language and we shared the same culture. But best of all, Amalia did not judge me, and she was a very devout Catholic. I had been so lonely and homesick that her presence in my life was like a gift from heaven.

The birth of our son, Francis Joseph, brought us not only joy into our lives but some peace as well. My mother-in-law stopped being angry at us, at least for a while. She was thrilled with her grandson. Because her only son had entered the priesthood, she had lost all hope of ever becoming a grandmother. She viewed this new grandchild as a blessing and a miracle!

A couple of my husband's fellow priests started visiting us again, but for a different reason. They wanted to meet and bless our baby. Even Father Mario, who had made that obnoxious offer to me, had had a change of heart. He sent us a congratulations on the birth of your son card and a generous money gift for our baby. A few relatives and friends of my husband also started coming around.

Babies definitely bring out the best in people. Through our son, Francis, we experienced kindness in Boston as never before. Once in a while, Francis needed to be rushed to Massachusetts General Hospital because he had convulsions due to a very high temperature. At that time, there was no 911 emergency service. Instead, one needed to call the local police directly in case of an emergency. Not only did the police officers take me to the hospital with my sick baby, but they also stayed with us to ensure that the baby was taken care of. And in more than one occasion, the officers even waited to take us home.

The kindness shown to us by these police officers completely changed my perception of law enforcers. I used to think of them as abusers rather than protectors. I had always had a negative image of law enforcers because of the experience I had with them in Honduras. Most of the time, law enforcers themselves were the perpetrators of crimes rather than being the protectors. Not only were they easily bribed, but they had no qualms about stealing, raping or killing. I was about fourteen years old when in a town near my village, one of the commandants was assassinated. This commanding officer left at least a dozen women pregnant, and most of the pregnancies had been conceived through rape.

My respect and gratitude for police officers increased even more when a cousin of my husband by marriage, a member of the Boston police force, became one of our guardian angels and a lifesaver. He was among the few family members who did not condemn us when most people did.

His name was Officer William Ventura or Bill as we called him. The first time that Bill and his wife, Graciela, came to our apartment to meet our new baby, I was giving the baby a bath in the sink because we did not have a bathing tub. A couple of days later, Bill returned not only with a baby bathtub, but with a changing table as well. He probably noticed my worn-out clothes because he brought some new outfits for me too. I was thrilled to have new clothes for the first time since we had arrived in Boston. Up until this time, all of my clothes had been second-hand, donated by the kindness of one of my mother-in-law's friends.

Bill and Graciela were very generous to us during the time when we needed it most. But even more than the gifts, their acceptance of us; their true care and concern for our welfare meant the world to us. They were like a ray of sunshine in a very cloudy day. Officer Bill and his wife are now in heaven and they continue to occupy a special place in my hearts for being our guardian angels when we were surrounded by so much hate, judgment and persecution.

Six months after our first baby was born, we found out that I was pregnant with our second child. I believed the old wives' tale I had heard in Honduras that if a woman was nursing a baby, she could not get pregnant. Naively, I used that as a method of birth control. This news ignited again the wrath of my mother-in-law. She regressed to calling us all kinds of insulting names and being on a rage most of the time. "Bringing up children is not a bed of roses," she would scream. "And you pigs are multiplying like rabbits." She felt that we were not capable of providing proper care to the baby we already had, and another one was on the way.

It was true that we already had more challenges than we could handle. Financially, we were still in a very bad situation. My husband's take home salary was barely $40.00 per week. We were still paying the debt to my mother-in-law for the plane fare from Honduras to Boston and also for the hospital bill for my first pregnancy since we did not have medical insurance. At that time, the hospital bill for pregnancy care and delivery amounted to $235.00, and we were paying the hospital one dollar a week because that was all we could afford to pay.

We knew only too well that being a parent was a very difficult task. I was barely sixteen years old, and I already had a bad case of varicose veins. I had to wear very thick and uncomfortable elastic stockings. I was not overweight by any means. This condition had been caused by being on my feet all day long and most of the night. Our precious baby boy turned out to be colicky. For the first three and a half months of his life, I would walk around holding him in an attempt to stop his constant crying.

Dealing with the pain of having a colicky crying baby was terrible, but dealing with my mother-in-law's reaction every time the baby cried was worse. She blamed us for the baby's crying. And she accused us of not taking proper care of him. "You have to be doing something wrong with that baby," she would shout over and over again. "You know very well how to act like pigs, but you don't know a darn thing about taking care of a baby."

After hearing my mother-in-law's accusation so many times and not knowing any better, I assumed she was right. I thought of myself as an unfit mother. I was already consumed with guilt for the unpardonable sin of being married to a priest, and now I had something else to feel guilty about.

I gave birth to my second child on November 25, 1965 at 7:30 a.m. I went alone to the hospital since Frank needed to stay home to take care of Francis, who at that time was fifteen months old. Because we could not afford to pay a taxi, and naively I believed that this second labor was going to be as long as the first one, I took public transportation to the hospital. It took me at least one hour and a half to get to the hospital. I had to change trains twice and take a bus too. To make things worse, I left the house at 6:00 a.m., which meant that I was traveling during rush hour. By the time I arrived at the bus stop, I was agonizing with severe labor pains. There were no seats available in the bus, and no one volunteered to give up their seat. I had to travel standing up the whole time.

As the pains became more severe, my panic increased, "Oh my God!" I told myself, "I am going to give birth in this bus and die of embarrassment in front of all these people." Fortunately, I was able to get to the hospital just in time. My second baby was born on the way to the delivery room. We named him Anthony in honor of my husband's father, and James after my paternal grandfather.

The saying "God doesn't give us more than we can handle" turned out to be very true in this case. We had spent sleepless nights wondering how we were going to manage with two babies, since we could barely manage with one. But we were pleasantly surprised when our new baby, Anthony James, not only looked like an angel, but also behaved like one. He slept through the night from the very beginning and hardly ever cried.

Being blessed with such a patient baby somewhat helped me feel better in my role as a new mother. My husband also helped me to eliminate some of my feelings of inadequacy by writing the following letter.

November 6, 1965

To my Dearest Wife,

I am writing to you in English to better express myself, these few sentiments which have for some time resided in the most recessed part of my heart. They are sentiments of love, admiration and respect for a young lady, now a woman for some time.

I think that nothing in life can compare to the dedication of a mother for her children. It is a nobleness and sacrifice of the highest order, and the purest expression of love. To find this in a mature woman is to be expected and surely natural, but in a young mother is extraordinary, wonderful, and admirable to the highest degree.

This I have found in you, my dear beautiful wife. For though you are young in years, you have shown a nobility and courage found only in few women, not only in these days but through the centuries.

May our two sons realize and give due respect to their incredible mother. And may they never dishonor her in any way, either by words or actions. May God grant them the ability to appreciate in you those rare qualities found in a human being: nobleness of character and courage.

These are my sentiments for you, who already has given me two beautiful sons; beautiful and sensitive as their mother, beauty from beauty.
God bless them and you, my dearest wife.

With all the love of your humble husband,
Frank

My husband brought me this letter to the hospital the day after our son, Anthony James, was born. This gift from the heart meant more to me than any card, bouquet of flowers or any other gift he could have given me.

Shortly after our second son was born, we received amazing and unexpected news. Some of the same priests, who had harassed my husband to go back to the priesthood, were now our greatest advocates. They were working on getting a dispensation from Pope Paul VI for us to be permitted to get married in the Catholic Church. It was a very long process, and a lot of red tape was involved. It took two long years for the dispensation to be approved by the Pope, but it was finally granted.

Frank and I were extremely happy and grateful when we received the fabulous news that we could get married in the Catholic Church. Both of us thought the same thing. "Thank God that our children will not have to suffer the humiliation of having two parents who are outcasts of the church."

Even though we were still in great financial difficulty, Frank insisted on buying me a new dress for the special occasion. I ended up buying a lovely beige color suit. However, history seemed to have a way of repeating itself in our case.

We were ready to get married! We had the dispensation from the Pope, the new outfit, and even the witnesses, only to find out that we could not get married in Massachusetts. I was only nineteen years old, which at that time was considered underage. Our civil marriage in Honduras was also not recognized here in the United States, the marriage certificate needed to be translated from Spanish to English, and it required the proper seal to become official. We were advised to go to the state of New Hampshire (one of the states next to Massachusetts) to get married, because the legal marrying age there was eighteen years old.

We called the rectory of Saint Joseph's Church in Salem, New Hampshire, and explained our predicament to the pastor. He gave us an appointment to get married on November 2, 1967, which is All Souls Day in the Catholic Church. My husband and I wondered if the priest had an ulterior motive to force us to get married on the Day of the Dead.

I waited for my church wedding with the same anticipation as I did when I was fifteen years old. I felt again the thrill of reaching for something that I had considered an impossible dream. But I was even more ecstatic because my mother and baby sister, Alma, were coming to the United States for the first time, and my mother was going to be present at the religious ceremony.

Since I had left Honduras, I had not seen any family members, and I missed them very much. During the four years I had been in the United States, I had kept in touch with family through letters. I would also send them beautiful pictures of the babies. Because I did not want my parents to worry about me, through my letters I had painted an idyllic life that I was supposedly living in the United States. It had never occurred to me that the truth would come out sooner rather than later.

When my mother saw me after four years, she was horrified. "Oh my God!" she exclaimed in disbelief. "You are nothing but skin and bones." She surveyed my whole body with her eyes. Then she asked, "Why didn't you come home? Maybe this cold weather doesn't agree with you."

I reassured my mother that I was fine and happy. But she was not convinced, especially since she was coming from a culture that views being too thin as a sign of sickness and poverty.

After her initial shock, my mother went on to explain, "We told you that if you left our house and things didn't go well, you wouldn't be allowed to set foot at home again. But neither José nor I meant that. You could have come home, and we would have welcomed you. We had no idea you were in such bad shape. Why did you lie to us?" She demanded to know.

I explained to my mother, "I didn't want to worry you." I reassured her that I was happy with my husband and my babies.

"But why do you look like a skeleton?" She asked.

"I don't like the food too much and I have been somewhat nauseous with the pregnancies; so, I lost a little weight, but I am happy and healthy." However, no amount of explaining could convince my mother that I was okay, and she was clearly upset because I had not been honest with her and my father.

When my mother saw me in action, caring for two babies and waiting on my mother-in-law as if she was an invalid, she was alarmed even more. With a tone of sadness and concern, she warned me, "You are killing yourself with your own hands. The babies need to be taken care of, but there is nothing wrong with this old lady. She could very well take care of herself. If you don't change your ways, you are going to get really sick and end up in an early grave."

I agreed with my mother that my mother-in-law could take care of herself. By this time, I had realized that the hand of God, or her demise, would not be coming any time soon. However, I had made her so dependent on me that I did not know how to reverse that situation. I felt that my only choice was to continue taking care of her as if she were another child.

Since I was too busy during the day, I would do house cleaning at night after everyone had gone to bed. I wanted everything to be nice and clean in the morning to avoid criticism from my mother-in-law. Another one of my nightly rituals was to wash clothes by hand and hang them to dry in the basement. Many times, I would stay up until 3:00 a.m. doing the washing and housework.

Hard work was not strange to me. I considered my situation normal, but I was very tired. I did wish things were different. I would have loved to live alone with my husband and children, but I did not voice my wishes to anyone. "Putting up with my mother-in-law is a small price to pay to be married to the kindest man in the world," I told myself. Besides, I was about to get married in the church. How could I complain about anything?

Our scheduled wedding day finally arrived. My husband, my mother, our two witnesses and I took a very early bus to New Hampshire. When we arrived at Saint Joseph's Church, we were greeted by a somewhat elderly and arrogant bishop. He then proceeded to ask us to follow him to his office at the rectory. As soon as we entered his office, the bishop informed us in a curt and disgruntled voice, "Your marriage ceremony is going to be here." Addressing my husband, the bishop continued, "You already made solemn vows at the altar, and you broke them. You certainly don't deserve to approach the altar again to take new vows."

Neither my husband nor I responded to the bishop's unkind remark. It seemed that turning the other cheek had become a way of life for us.

I was about to take my coat off for the ceremony when the bishop said to me clearly annoyed, "Do not bother doing that. This will be very short!" I buttoned my coat again and kept it on.

I have no recollection at all of the brief ceremony. I was too embarrassed, too hurt, and too disappointed to register it in my mind. After the ceremony, the bishop abruptly gave us the record of our marriage on a three by eight-inch piece of paper and told us, "You can leave now. You are all set."

My husband and I did not exchange any of our thoughts during our long bus ride back home, but I am sure we were both thinking the same thing. "How could a supposed representative of Christ on earth be so unkind?" It was obvious that even though we had received the dispensation and the forgiveness from the head of the Catholic Church, the Holy Pope, some clergy within the church had still not forgiven us.

Nevertheless, we were very happy and grateful to have been married by the Catholic Church. Now our marriage was blessed by God. We were even considering having another baby, since according to the church our first two babies had been the product of sin, and we wanted to have a baby now that we were in the grace of God.

Although, before we could bring another baby into the world, we needed to improve our financial situation. My husband had worked briefly for the post office in Boston before entering the seminary. He had applied to work there again when we had first arrived in Boston. He also did very well on the postal exam, but there were hundreds of applicants ahead of him on the long waiting list, and he had been unsuccessful in getting a job.

Someone gave my husband the idea of writing to Senator Ted Kennedy explaining the situation and enlisting his help to get a job at any of the post office in Boston. My husband did not believe in using his political connections to receive special favors, but since our situation was so critical, he reluctantly took the advice. When Senator Kennedy found out that Frank had been a missionary in Honduras and needed to get reestablished in Boston, he was very sympathetic and helpful. Immediately, my husband was hired to work at the South Station Post Office as a clerk for registered mail.

Shortly after our financial situation improved, I became pregnant with my third child. Before I had children and thought about becoming a mother, I wanted all of my children to be boys because I was conditioned by the macho mentality of my people. But after seeing my beautiful baby sister again, I had been praying for a baby girl. Throughout my nine months of pregnancy, I would often go to Saint Anthony's church in downtown Boston to pray for a baby girl without knowing that the sex of a baby is determined at the moment of conception.

Nevertheless, my prayers were answered, and our beautiful and adorable baby girl was born on November 28, 1968. We named her Marie Bernadette. Marie after my mother, but gave her the French version, and Bernadette after Saint Bernadette of Lourdes. We were absolutely thrilled to have a daughter! And to my delight, she turned out to be light-skinned, with blond hair, blue eyes and absolutely beautiful, the way I had always wanted to look.

Marie Bernadette was ten months old when we decided to move away from my mother-in-law's crowded apartment. While looking for a new place to live, we would take a bus or a train because we had no car. After several months of searching, we finally found a house that we liked and could afford. We bought a small house with 20,000 square feet of land in a small town called Stoneham, which is located thirteen miles north of Boston. It was there, in this pretty little town, that the new chapter of our lives began.

CHAPTER 11

Moving to Stoneham, Massachusetts, drastically changed our lives for the better. No one knew about our past, and we had the opportunity of starting a new life without anyone judging us. It was so refreshing not to be persecuted by anyone and to be accepted and welcomed by our neighbors.

Our house was sunny and spacious. It had seven rooms, but it was not fancy by any means. We could not afford to buy furniture for several years, since we could hardly make our mortgage payments. But between the few pieces of furniture we already had and some furniture that the previous owner left behind, we were able to set up our new home without feeling deprived.

We found Stoneham to be a beautiful little town with warm and friendly people. It was the perfect place to raise children. After having no space to play in Boston, now our children had a fabulous yard with several huge trees, where they could run around freely. At any given time, at least a half dozen of the neighborhood kids would gather in our yard to play with our children. Now I even had the space to plant flowers and have a vegetable garden. I felt as if I had a little piece of my country in the United States.

And best of all, now we had wonderful neighbors. During the six years we lived in Boston, we had not been able to get acquainted with one single neighbor. But in this charming little town, several of our neighbors came to our house to welcome us and to offer their help and friendship. Some of them even became like family to us. Thelma Meaher and her husband, Jonathan, were the nicest of our neighbors.

They had seven children of their own, and they practically adopted me; they always treated me with loving kindness and made me feel as another one of their daughters.

Their oldest daughter, Katie, and I were of the same age, and she became my best friend and confidante. I missed speaking my native language with someone other than my husband, and Katie fulfilled that need. We could speak to each other in Spanish because she was a Spanish and French teacher. Thelma and Jonathan's youngest daughter, Rosemary, was closer in age to my oldest sons, and she became like a big sister to them.

Thelma was a very active and well-respected member not only in the Catholic Church, but of the community as well. Up until the time I met her, I had been living in a shell with no social life; but through the kindness of this remarkable lady, I was able to leave my cocoon. She took me to several organizations, which provided me with the opportunity of meeting new people and becoming involved with the church and the community. With Thelma's guidance and encouragement, I became a member of Our Lady Sodality of Saint Patrick's Church, which is the only Catholic Church in Stoneham. I also joined the Mothers' Club of Saint Patrick's School, the parochial school my children were attending. In addition, I became a volunteer at the Stoneham Boys' Club, where my boys used to go for sports and other interesting activities; such as theater, music, chess, etc.

By the time we moved to Stoneham, I was able to express myself; however, it was in broken English. Since we could not afford formal English classes in Boston, I had to learn English by myself. Pronunciation was my biggest challenge and there were no electronic dictionaries to help me with pronunciation. I can remember several very embarrassing situations that now I can laugh about, but at that time they were not funny at all.

I had been in Boston for a short while, and I went to a convenience store to buy some peanuts. I did not know how to pronounce the word "peanuts" and my husband was at work; so I could not ask him. I looked it up in the Spanish/English dictionary; but when I went to the store, I could not find peanuts. Then I went to ask the store clerk, who was an old man, "Do you have peanuts?" But since I could not pronounce the word correctly, instead I asked, "Do you have penis?"

The old man started laughing and replied, "I hope so."

That did not make any sense to me; I knew right away that I had said something wrong. I ran out of the store awfully embarrassed and with no peanuts. Until this day, I refuse to pronounce that word.

Another time I went to a meeting at the Boys' Club in Stoneham. It had been raining that evening and I was looking for a hook to hang my coat. There were several people at the meeting already and with a loud voice I asked, "Any hookers around here?"

Everyone started laughing and one wise guy yelled, "If you find one, let me know."

I immediately realized my mistake and started laughing too. I either had to learn to laugh at myself or close my mouth forever.

Fortunately, when we moved to Stoneham, I had the opportunity of taking English as a second language classes through the Stoneham Adult Education Program. The instructor was a very kind young man and a wonderful teacher. Shortly after completing English classes, I obtained my driver's license.

Due to the lack of frequency of public transportation in Stoneham, we were forced to buy an old model used car for transportation. The car was in constant need of repairs. Fortunately, my husband knew something about mechanics because he had plenty of experience repairing his old jeep in Honduras.

But in spite of finding the transportation to be challenging, moving to Stoneham was a great decision. However, I still had to deal with two very serious issues that I brought with me from Beacon Hill. The first one was my mother-in-law, and the second one my obsessive guilt feelings for being married to a priest.

When we moved to Stoneham, my mother-in-law came to live with us. She did a fabulous job placing a huge guilt trip on us. "I took you in when you were outcasts and penniless. You cannot leave me now when I need you the most," she would constantly remind us, while we were looking for a house. We felt we had no choice, but to bring her along to live with us.

She absolutely hated living in Stoneham or "in the country", as she called it, mostly because everything was far away. She had lived in a city her entire life, and she found living in the country not only boring but restrictive. She complained all of the time, and she did not want me to have any friends. Her attitude toward friendship was very negative. She would constantly tell me, "You don't need any friends. Friends only take advantage of you, especially in your case because you are such a fool." She was referring to my lady friends, since I did not have any friends of the opposite sex.

Even if I talked on the telephone for a few minutes to a neighbor, my mother-in-law would give me a hard time. "Telephone is for emergencies only," she would say, "and not to chew the rag about stupid things."

Whenever I went out, even when I went to church, my mother-in-law would complain. "God wants you to take care of your children and not to go out gallivanting around." I thought that teaching my children about religion and values was a way of taking care of them.

Because I had been brought up in a culture where I was taught to respect my elders, I tolerated my mother-in-law's controlling behavior. There is an old saying, "Old dogs cannot learn new tricks," but I was able to teach her a good lesson once in a very respectful manner by making up a story.

Since I was responsible for preparing her meals and I wanted to please her, I would ask my mother-in-law before preparing every meal, "What would you like to eat?" She would respond depending on her mood. The rare times when she was in a good mood, she would tell me exactly what she felt like having. But if she was in a bad mood, she would rudely say, "Poison, I want to die." Her "poison" reply occurred more often once we had moved to Stoneham. But I found a way to stop that nonsense by telling her the following story:

Once upon a time, there was a very crabby old lady in Honduras. She had a very kind, but simple young girl as her servant. Wanting very much to please the old lady, the simple servant would ask her before preparing her meals, "What would you like to eat?" In one occasion, the cranky old lady rudely responded, "Poison." And since the young servant was so obedient, with pain in her heart, she gave poison to the old lady.

My mother-in-law had attentively listened to the story. When I finished telling it, she curiously asked, "And what happened?"

Pretending to sound sad, my reply was. "What do you think happened? The crabby old lady died, of course." Needless to say, I never heard the word poison come out of her mouth again.

Unfortunately, I did not have any other word of wisdom or magic cures to change my mother-in-law's constant controlling behavior and criticism of me. I felt very frustrated, at times depressed, resentful, and angry for having to live under such circumstances. But even my husband was not aware of my frustration because I never told him how I was feeling.

I kept all of these negative feelings to myself, partly because I did not know any better. "I went from the frying pan to the fire," as the saying goes. First, I was abused and controlled by my mother and afterwards by my mother-in-law. Frankly, I could not see a way out of my situation. And since it had been a way of life for me, being abused seemed somewhat normal. I also think that unconsciously, I felt that I deserved to be punished for having fallen in love with a priest.

In addition to feeling controlled by my mother-in-law, feeling guilty was also a way of life for me in those days. Even after getting married in the Catholic Church, did not eradicate the heavy burden of guilt that I was carrying for being married to a priest. As an attempt to alleviate my conscience, I started having telephone counseling sessions with priests from different parishes in the area. I would call a church and ask, "May I please speak to a priest?" Then I would go on and on telling the priest my long story and expressing my obsessive feelings of guilt. "This guilt is consuming me. It is draining all the joy out of my life and preventing me from moving on," I would tell each priest. Most of them were kind and sympathetic.

When I revealed that I was already married by the Catholic Church, all the priests would say the same thing, "You have no reason to feel guilty about anymore. You are already in the grace of God." But no matter how much reassurance of God's forgiveness different priests would give me, I could not forgive myself.

This mental torture went on for a while until a very wise priest asked me a simple question, "Are you bigger than God?"

I quickly replied, "Of course not."

His next question was, "Well, if that's the case and God has forgiven you, who are you not to forgive yourself?" The priest went on to explain that by not forgiving myself I was rejecting God's gift.

His explanation made a lot of sense to me. I do not recall what my answer was at that time. But from that moment on I was able to make peace with myself and my past. And for the first time in years, I began to experience true peace and joy.

After the heavy burden of guilt was lifted off of me, I was then able to set new goals for myself. My next goal was to obtain my high school diploma. My main motivation for wanting to continue my education was not only to fulfill a young girl's dream, but I was also thinking about the future of my children.

I knew that at some point, if I wanted to help my children with their academic work, I needed to improve my own level of education. I came to that realization when my oldest son, Francis, was about seven years old and he asked me, "Mommy, what do you want to be when you grow up?"

I replied, "Honey, that's a very good question. I need to think about that."

I enrolled in a correspondence program to get my high school diploma. It was a five-year program offered by La Salle Extension University, based in Chicago. I had every intention of finishing the program much sooner than the time allowed, but unexpectedly I got pregnant again. The news of my fourth pregnancy infuriated my mother-in-law, and somewhat diminished the time I could spend studying. But in no way did it lessen my motivation to achieve the educational goal I had set for myself.

My books were the first items I packed when I went to the New England Memorial Hospital in Stoneham to have my fourth child. On September 30, 1971, I gave birth to another precious and healthy baby boy. I decided to call our new baby Andrew, after his father's religious name and Linus after my maternal grandfather.

Linus in Spanish is Lino, which is also the name of a fabric. Because of the double meaning of the name, no one in my family had named any of their children after my grandfather Lino. I can only imagine the thrill my grandfather felt when he found out that he had a great grandson in the United States who had been named after him.

Something completely unexpected and out character for my husband happened the day I came home from the hospital after giving birth to baby Andrew. We had a magnificent grape vine that produced enough grapes to give away (after saving some for us) and to make jelly for the whole year. When I came home from the hospital, I noticed the grapes were ripe and a lot of them were already on the ground. After putting the baby to sleep that afternoon, I took a big bucket and went to the garden to pick up the grapes.

I was coming back to the kitchen through the basement stairs, when I heard the baby crying and my mother-in-law yelling all kinds of nasty things towards me. "Can you hear that baby crying you lazy, good for nothing?" And her favorite expression toward us, "You know how to act like pigs, but you don't know how to take care of a baby!" My heart sank and rather than continuing to the kitchen, I put the bucket of grapes on the stairs and sat there for a while to compose myself.

My mother-in-law was still yelling at me, when I heard my husband coming down from our bedroom on the second floor and going straight to his mother's bedroom on the first floor. I could not believe my ears! He yelled at his mother like never before. With a very loud and angry tone, I heard him saying:

"How can you be so unfair and ungrateful with a girl, who is practically your slave? YOU SHOULD KNEEL AND BEG GOD FOR FORGIVENESS! THE WAY YOU TREAT A GIRL WHO

HAS BEEN TAKING CARE OF YOU BETTER THAN ANY DAUGHTER WOULD, IS NOT ONLY UNFAIR, BUT SINFUL."

My mother in-law did not say a word, and her son continued, "If weren't for Cándida, where do you think you would be right now? Probably vegetating in a nursing home. You do realize that besides taking care of you, Cándida has been cooking for your brothers and sister? If she never came to this country, they would never have known what it's like to eat a nice and warm home-cooked meal. And you have the gall to call this girl lazy?"

Frank continued his monologue for a while, and he finished by saying, "I have to go to work now mother, but I hope you think about what I said, and for God's sake change your attitude."

I was flabbergasted and still sitting on the basement stairs. When I finally mustered the courage to go to the kitchen, my husband was taking his lunch out of the refrigerator and was on his way to work. He kissed me goodbye, but did not say anything about the angry talk he just had with his mother. I did not tell him either that I overheard the entire incident.

I went upstairs to take care of the baby. After returning to the kitchen, I noticed that it was supper time. Usually, I would ask my mother in-law, "What would you like to eat?" But this time, I did not have the courage to go near her room. I assumed that she was more furious than ever with me because of the way her son had finally put her in her place. So rather than start cooking, I decided to take care of the grapes first. A few minutes later, my mother-in-law came into the kitchen acting as if nothing had happened. And with a soft and sweet voice she offered, "May I help you pick grapes?"

Trying not to show how surprised I was, I answered her, "Thank you very much, that would be very nice."

Then she went on to ask about the baby. The incident was never brought up by either one of us, but from that day forward my mother-in-law had a change of attitude.

By the time Andrew Linus was a year old, my two oldest sons were attending Saint Patrick's School. Francis was in first grade, and

Anthony in kindergarten. The school was looking for volunteers among the parents to work as reading or math tutors. I signed up to volunteer in the first-grade classroom that Francis was attending.

The first-grade teacher, Sister Shawn Marie, was a wonderful nun and a fabulous teacher. All students and parents loved her. She had the gift of making everyone feel special, unique, and welcomed in her classroom. I was pleasantly surprised when she asked me to teach Spanish to her first-grade students. "Any parent can help with reading and math, but you have a unique gift to offer," Sister Shawn Marie kindly told me.

Immediately I started teaching Spanish to a group of twenty-two first graders without knowing what to expect. To my amazement, these small children were like sponges absorbing the new language, and they loved learning it. A few months after, they were able to understand simple phrases, answer basic questions, count to one hundred and even sing like angels in Spanish with perfect pronunciation.

I continued teaching Spanish as a volunteer in Saint Patrick's School for another year. By this time, three of my children were students there because my daughter, Marie, was now of school age. The tuition was not that expensive, but it was still a financial hardship for us. We were hardly getting by with the salary my husband was making as a postal office employee.

Without being aware of our financial predicament, Sister Irene, the principal of Saint Patrick's School, made me an offer that I could not refuse. "How would you like to teach Spanish three times per week to our junior high school students in exchange for the tuition of your three children?" I was more than delighted to accept the principal's generous offer. This was definitely an answer to our prayers. Even though Stoneham had wonderful public schools, we preferred that our children were educated in a parochial school.

I worked in Saint Patrick's School teaching Spanish to junior high school students for the following three years. In addition to the teaching experience and free tuition for my children, working in Saint Patrick's School came with extra bonuses. Some of those benefits would last a lifetime.

It was while teaching at Saint Patrick's School that I became friends with Lee Duncan, the school's guidance counselor and reading specialist. She was one of the most extraordinary human beings I have ever met. I admired her deeply, and she had a great deal of influence in my life.

What first attracted me to Lee was her sunny disposition, her unconditional acceptance of others, and her willingness to celebrate their differences. Lee also had the great ability to challenge people to reach their full potential as human beings by elevating their self-esteem. She did wonders for me; I definitely needed someone like her in my life.

One of Lee's many accomplishments while working at Saint Patrick's School was founding a mothers' group. The purpose of the group was not only to provide support for mothers, but also to help them with their emotional and spiritual development. I had the good fortune of being a member of Lee's group. And it was through her guidance and inspiration that I dared to pursue and achieve personal and professional goals that I had always considered were out of my reach.

Lee was diagnosed with polio when she was ten years old, and was confined to a wheelchair for the rest of her life. But no one ever thought of Lee as being physically challenged. She was more productive and contributed more to the world than most people who have never been afflicted with a serious illness.

After working fifteen years in Saint Patrick's School as a counselor, Lee went on to work for an additional 25 years as a rehabilitation counselor in a State Agency. During a quarter of a century, Lee counseled hundreds of clients and also taught them vocational skills. But more importantly, Lee modeled and inspired her clients to live happy and productive lives in spite of their physical limitations.

I remember complimenting Lee for the magnificent work she was doing with her clients, but she was so modest about her accomplishments and quickly responded, "My clients have inspired me as much as I have inspired them." Her generosity with praise toward others, made her even more endearing and remarkable. In spite of having been afflicted with polio, Lee lived to the age of 75 years. She will be forever missed by the many people whose lives she touched.

Teaching Spanish at Saint Patrick's School was definitely rewarding in more ways than one, but I was not bringing home any money. I needed to have an added part-time job to help make ends meet. I worked outside the home while three of my children were in school. My husband was home during the day because he worked evenings at the post office. He hardly ever had enough sleep since he had to take care of his mother and of our youngest child, Andrew, while I was working.

My other part-time job was doing housekeeping. I worked for a sweet and very kind Italian lady named Mrs. Francini. She was in her late 80s, but appeared and acted younger than her age. Cooking and watching soap operas were two of Mrs. Francini's passions. We never lacked for topics of conversation; she would always tell me all about the soap operas she was watching.

I enjoyed listening to Mrs. Francini's stories, but at times, she would suddenly start crying over someone who had died in a soap opera. She would also worry endlessly if one of the soap opera characters was ill or something bad was going to happen. Very soon, I realized that Mrs. Francini was not distinguishing fiction from reality. I explained to her many times, "Don't worry. It's not happening for real. These people are only acting." Whether she understood me or not, I was not sure. But the poor sweet lady continued to suffer and worry over things that were only happening in soap operas.

One day, I found Mrs. Francini more distressed than usual. She was concerned about a young woman who was almost nine months pregnant and was alone, sad, and lonely. Mrs. Francini went on and on explaining to me, "The poor thing is almost nine months pregnant, and all of her family is in another country. She has a ten-month old little girl. I don't know who's going to watch the little girl when she goes to the hospital." Then she added something that completely threw me off, "Maybe you can help her. You know what it's like not to have family in this country. Don't you?"

I thought Mrs. Francini was talking about a character in one of her soap operas, and I asked, "How can I help someone in a soap opera?"

"No," she corrected me, "this girl is not on television. She's my neighbor."

Thanks to Mrs. Francini's tender heart, I met the most wonderful couple in the world, the Russos. Clara is from Switzerland and her husband, Mariano, from Italy. Immediately after Mrs. Francini introduced me to them, I started working as a childcare provider for their two adorable children, Maria and Carmelo. Since my children were almost grown up, I missed having a baby, and I loved caring for them. This job not only provided the extra money we needed to make ends meet, but it also fulfilled my desire of having a new infant.

Coming from a country where I personally had witnessed that childcare providers, cooks, and housekeepers were treated as low-class citizens, I was absolutely amazed that Clara and Mariano always treated me as an equal and as a very dear friend. Their kindness and generosity went beyond anything I had ever experienced. In addition to paying me a good salary for my services, they would shower me with gifts, cards, compliments and gratitude.

Whenever the Russos had a party in their very elegant home, I was always included as one of their guests. I always felt somewhat uncomfortable during these parties because all of their guests were professional people, who had important professions and spoke several languages. I was probably their only guest who barely had a high school diploma and spoke English with a heavy accent.

At this point in my life, I was still struggling with a very low self-esteem, and it was through Clara and Mariano that I learned the most important lesson of my life. They helped me realize that the worth of a person is not based on his or her educational level, social status, or possession of wealth, but in the character of the person and ability to love.

My husband and I were the humblest, most economically disadvantaged and the least educated of all of Clara and Mariano's friends. But they chose us to be guardians of their precious children in case anything happened to them. I was completely surprised when

Clara asked me, "Would you and Frank be willing to be appointed as legal guardians of our children in case something happened to my husband and me?"

I was not only honored by my friend's request. I was astounded! "Why us?" I asked her, "since both of you have close family members and important friends?"

Clara then responded, "Most of these so-called friends are just acquaintances and they are too busy climbing the social ladder. You and Frank are the kindest people we know. Besides my husband and I, no one loves our children more than the two of you."

Clara was absolutely right. We loved Maria and Carmelo as much as our own children. I had cared for them since they were babies, and they had easily found their way into my heart. I have had the privilege of seeing them grow up and become amazing adults and very accomplished professionals. Maria has a very distinguished career in England as an international marketing specialist, and Carmelo is a TV producer for the Disney Studios in Los Angeles, California.

Fortunately, the need for my husband and I to become Maria and Carmelo's legal guardians was not necessary. But the fact that their parents had chosen us to be entrusted with their most precious treasures has done more for my self-esteem than a lifetime of psychotherapy.

Unfortunately, after forty-five years of enjoying and cultivating a deep and very special friendship with the Russo family, Mariano passed away. Besides his wonderful children, he left this world with an incredible legacy of love, kindness, inspiration and great example from the way he had lived his 95 years of life. I am eternally grateful to him and to his wife Clara for showing me where the true worth of a human being lies.

One would think that after my husband fell in love with me, I should have learned that lesson, but for wherever reason his love had done very little to improve my self-esteem. I guess that to reverse the negative programming of one's self-worth is a very difficult and slow process that can take years or even a lifetime to be resolved. In spite of all of the affirmation I had been receiving from different sources when I moved to Stoneham, at times I would still revert to negative thoughts about myself. "These people think that I am so wonderful because they don't really know me. As soon as they find out who I really am, they will change their minds." Those were some of the thoughts that would go through my mind.

I remember that when I completed the requirements for my high school diploma, which took four years of hard work, I did not give myself any credit. I gave all of the credit to my husband because he had helped me with homework.

Surprisingly, my negative thinking did not prevent me from taking advantage of all of the opportunities that had been available to me when I moved to Stoneham. In spite of my mother-in-law's opposition, I made some friends, went to work, became involved in the church and the community, continued my education and obtained my driver's license.

However, while I was beginning to improve the quality of my life and becoming more fulfilled as a woman, I was feeling somewhat disillusioned with my marriage. At this time, my husband had turned rather indifferent toward me. Putting up with my mother-in-law was getting somewhat easier, but it was still challenging at times. I knew for a fact that my husband had advised many couples in Honduras not to live with their parents or in-laws. So, I would ask myself, "Why doesn't he take his own advice?"

I lacked the security to express my feelings of frustration with his mother to my husband. I longed to spend time alone with him and our children, but that never happened. Every time we went somewhere, my mother-in-law always wanted to come along. Neither her son nor I, had the courage to tell her to stay home.

Meeting my physical and emotional needs had never been a priority for me. I needed time to rest, but it never occurred to me to take time off from my many responsibilities. More importantly, I needed to be reassured of my husband's love, but I did not know how to express that to him. To make things worse, both of us had lost sight of the fact that a marriage is like a flower that needs to be nourished in order to stay healthy and keep on growing.

CHAPTER 12

By June of 1977, Frank and I had been married thirteen and a half years, and it was about that time that we were to face the first real crisis in our marriage.

I had grown up with the erroneous believe that once a woman was married, she would never experience any romantic feelings for another man other than for her husband. On the other hand, my husband assumed that if a man was working hard to support and provide for his family, no other expressions of love to his wife were necessary. We were both completely wrong.

Frank had stopped telling me he loved me for at least a decade, and every once in a while, I would ask him, "Honey, do you still love me?" His reply was always the same. "Am I not working like a horse? What better proof of love do you need?"

That was not the answer I wanted to hear, of course, but at that time I did not know how to express my needs to my husband. Consequently, for a long time I felt not only abused by my mother-in-law's endless demands and complaints, but I also felt neglected by my husband. And since I had low self-esteem, I felt even worse.

The turning point in our marriage began when Frank had been reacquainted with a classmate of his from the seminary named Father Kevin, who was a few years younger than him. According to my husband, Father Kevin had always wanted to go to the missions, but his superiors wanted him to remain in the United States because he was intellectually very gifted, and they had other plans for him.

"Kevin would have made a wonderful missionary, and he wanted to go to the missions. But since our superiors felt that it would have been a waste of his talents, they kept him here in the United States and made him a superior," Frank explained to me. And with a trace of bitterness in his voice, he added, "On the other hand, our superiors sent morons, like me, without any preparation whatsoever, to sink or swim in a foreign country."

"Honey," I reminded my husband, "for someone that was sent to the missions without any preparation, you accomplished incredible deeds in my country. Some people have even called you a miracle worker."

"Thank you, Chita," he replied smiling. "You always know what to say to make me feel better."

Frank and Father Kevin had not seen or contacted each other during the whole time Frank had left the priesthood. Then Father Kevin happened to be the celebrant of a funeral mass for Frank's uncle. The two friends seemed genuinely happy to have found each other again. Frank introduced me to Father Kevin. I did not know why, but he seemed very surprised when he saw me. Then he said to my husband, still calling him by his religious name, "Andy, no one had told me that your wife was so beautiful! I have been to Honduras two times, and I have not seen anyone there who is as tall and as beautiful as your wife."

I immediately perceived that my husband had been bothered by what his friend had said about me. Trying to hide his feelings of annoyance, Frank replied with a soft voice, "Thank you, Kevin."

I asked my husband as soon as we were alone, "Why did Father Kevin's comment about me bother you so much?"

With anger in his voice, he quickly responded, "Who did he think I was married to, a plump and short woman, with a long black braid, and carrying a clay pot on her head? Did he think that I don't deserve to be married to a beautiful woman like you?"

I laughed at my husband's funny comments and reassured him that he was overreacting. "I don't even think that Father Kevin meant what he said; there is no need to get defensive about it, honey," I told him, still laughing.

I guess that in the presence of whom my husband had considered a handsome young man in his seminary days, he was feeling somewhat insecure. But he was remembering Father Kevin as he had been in their younger days. Now Father Kevin was somewhat plump, which accentuated the rather square shape of his face. He had also lost his abundant blond hair, and his hair transplant was so obvious that rather than enhance his looks, it emphasized his vanity. His charisma, along with his eloquent verbal communication skills and brilliant mind were Father Kevin's best attributes now.

A few days after their initial meeting, Father Kevin called Frank to invite us to dinner at the rectory of the church he was stationed at in the North End of Boston, a beautiful Italian section of Boston, very close to the waterfront. I declined to attend dinner, but I strongly encouraged Frank to accept the invitation. I wanted to give my husband the chance to catch up on their lives with his friend. I also did not want to go through the trouble of finding someone to watch our children. We could not afford to hire a babysitter, but we had some very nice neighbors who had graciously offered to watch our children whenever necessary. But my mother-in-law would always complain about any babysitter we had.

The last time my husband and I had gone out had been to attend the wake of a dear friend. On that occasion, even before we had arrived at the funeral home, my mother-in-law had left us a message asking us to return home immediately. We assumed that one of the children had become very sick and we rushed home as fast as we could. When we returned home, we asked my mother-in-law, "What is the big emergency?" Very annoyed, she replied, "Andrew was crying because you left, and that useless girl you left watching your children could not make him stop crying."

That day I concluded it was not worth for me to go out with my husband ever again because of the hassle my mother-in-law had created the few times we had gone out. She did that because she wanted to go with us wherever we went. One of our neighbors made the observation that apparently my mother-in-law could not take care of herself, but yet she was able to go out. "I don't understand," my neighbor asked, "if your mother-in-law is okay to go out, why do you wait on her hand and foot as if she were an invalid?"

I thought about what my neighbor had said, and I explained to her, "When I came to the United States, my mother-in-law gave me the impression that she was very sick, and I took over taking care of her. By the time I found out she didn't have a terminal illness, I had already made her dependent on me. I didn't know at that point how to reverse that process. So she is like another child to me, but a very cranky one."

My neighbor shook her head and mumbled, "Obviously, you are not from this country."

Frank did attend the dinner with his friend and claimed to have had a fabulous time reminiscing about their seminary days. Soon, he decided to reciprocate Father Kevin's gracious invitation by inviting him for dinner at our house. I made a typical Honduran dinner, decorated the dining room table beautifully with fresh flowers from our garden, and instructed the children to be on their best behavior. I was delighted that Father Kevin seemed to enjoy the food and he was very complimentary of our children.

During the course of the conversation, Father Kevin found out that I was teaching Spanish in the parochial school in Stoneham. I was very surprised when he asked me if I would teach him Spanish. He explained, "One of my duties as a superior is to oversee the missions in Central America, and I am due to take a trip to Honduras in the near future. I want to be able to communicate with the people in their own language."

How could I refuse to do something that would benefit the missions, especially if it had to do with my own country? "I will be more than happy to teach you Spanish," I told Father Kevin. My husband also agreed that it was a wonderful idea, and he was in full support of the arrangement.

Father Kevin and I decided to meet at my house two times per week to start his Spanish classes. After the first session, he told me, "You are a natural born teacher, and you make Spanish seem so easy." He also wanted to pay me for the class, but I firmly refused to accept any money. Then Father Kevin asked my husband, "Andy, since your wife refuses to accept any money for the classes, would it be acceptable if I sometimes bring a gift for the family?"

My husband reassured his friend, "No gifts are necessary, but if you insist on doing so, I would have no problem with that."

The next time Father Kevin came to our house for a class, he brought a fancy box of chocolates for the family. But as time went on, the gifts became more extravagant. He would bring wine for Frank, chocolates for my mother-in-law, games or toys for the children, and flowers for me. We tried to put a stop to Father Kevin's generosity. We did not want any church money to be spent on us. But every time we told him to stop, Father Kevin would justify his generosity by saying, "Do not take this small pleasure away from me. I have a sister who has a terrific job, and she is very generous to me. I use the money she sends me to buy little things for you guys because it makes me very happy. You deserve it, and you are like family to me."

My children were thrilled with this newfound uncle for obvious reasons. And even my mother-in-law, who was usually very critical of all of our friends, practically adored Father Kevin. "I wish I had a son like Father Kevin. His parents are so lucky to have a son like him," she would often say. But even more than the gifts, Father Kevin ingratiated himself with my mother-in-law by spending time with her and showering her with compliments.

As far as myself, I had not felt that happy and alive in years. In addition to the flowers, Father Kevin would entice me with flattering remarks of praise and admiration. "You are so beautiful and intelligent! Andy is definitely a very lucky man. You are a fabulous mother, a great cook and an amazing person!" He also kept on emphasizing, "You are a born teacher! You make Spanish so easy to learn." I loved how Father Kevin made me feel.

However, my feelings of exhilaration soon turned into fear and guilt when he started sending me romantic cards by mail on a daily basis. Sometimes I would receive three cards from him on the same day. Some of the cards were created by him, which obviously took a great deal of time. My favorite card had a large photo of me in the center, and around the picture a bunch of adjectives, such as: beautiful, lovely, amazing, kind, adorable etc. The bottom of the card was decorated with beautiful flowers and the following sentence was written in big multicolored letters, "I love you more than anybody else."

I was afraid that Father Kevin was losing his perspective, and I felt very guilty because I was enjoying his attention so much that I had kept it a secret from my husband. But I also feared that I was losing my perspective as well. Shortly after I started receiving the inappropriate cards, I decided to express my apprehension to Father Kevin. "I am feeling very uncomfortable about the cards you are sending," I told him very nervous, but in a firm voice.

Before I could continue talking, Father Kevin replied, "I am so sorry, Cándida! I did not plan for this to happen, but I have fallen in love with you. I fully realize that I am not as good as Andy, but I love you more than anyone else."

I was astonished by what I heard and even more surprised at the willingness of Father Kevin to make a full confession about his feelings so quickly. Having always had a very low self-esteem, I felt extremely flattered. But very soon my conscience overcame my ego, and I decisively told Father Kevin, "What you are feeling isn't right; I have been very wrong also for accepting your cards. But this has got to stop now. Please do not send me any more cards or talk to me about your feelings ever again." I also added, "If you cannot do that, you will have to stop coming to our house. My husband is a wonderful man, and he doesn't deserve to be betrayed by us."

Father Kevin listened carefully to what I had said. After what seemed to me like a very long pause, he broke the silence by saying, "I accept your conditions, Cándida. I cannot bear the thought of not seeing you anymore. I will do anything you say."

After we came to this agreement, we continued with the Spanish classes for about a month. During that time, Father Kevin stopped sending cards and talking to me about his feelings. But it was very difficult for me to feel comfortable again in his presence not only because I knew how he felt about me, but also because of the way I was beginning to feel about him. Once more the old monster returned; I was confusing gratitude, for the way he made me feel, with love. However, I wanted to preserve the friendship, mostly because my whole family was so fond of Father Kevin. I knew very well that to do that I needed to put a lid on my emotional involvement with him and I needed to act as normal as possible around him.

At some point, toward the end of the month after we had continued with the Spanish classes, Father Kevin took my family and me to meet his parents, Phil and Susanne. They were a lovely and friendly couple; we warmed up to each other rapidly. As a matter of fact, in some way, Phil reminded me of my own father. I found Susanne to be very likable as well, but I was surprised that she was not the typical mother of a priest, the religious woman one would expect. Soon after meeting her, she made the comment, "Kevin is wasting his life away in the priesthood. We didn't want him to go to the seminary, but he didn't listen to us."

Father Kevin cooked a fabulous lobster dinner with all the trimmings for the special occasion. He had also purchased all kinds of Italian pastries for dessert. We knew he was a gracious host, but we had no idea he was also a fabulous cook. My mother in-law could not praise him enough for his cooking skills and complimented his parents for having such a wonderful son.

Father Kevin's parents lived two blocks away from Revere beach. After dinner, we took the children to walk around the beach and Father Kevin made sure they had a great time. He played frisbees with them, bought them ice cream, etc. During the whole time, I was feeling very uncomfortable around Father Kevin. But I guess that I did a pretty good job of hiding my feelings because neither my husband nor my mother-in-law noticed anything different in my behavior.

Two days after meeting his parents, Father Kevin came to my house for another Spanish class. I had prepared the class as usual and had the materials ready on the dining room table. I was about to begin the class when Father Kevin interrupted me. "I am sorry, Cándida," he said, "I cannot concentrate on learning Spanish today because I have something very important to tell you.

I closed the book, and smiling said to him, "Okay, Father Kevin, I am all ears."

Without any hesitation, he declared, "I am sorry Cándida! I cannot go on like this. I love you too much, and I cannot pretend anymore. Please marry me! We can go to Chicago and start a new life there, you, the children and me. I love them too and we can get custody of them."

To say that I was shocked and speechless upon hearing Father Kevin's proposition is an understatement! Now I knew for sure that he had lost not only his objectivity but his mind as well. I could not believe that a priest, who had an important leadership role within his church, was willing to risk so much. I do not remember exactly what I said. I think that I replied, "Us, getting married? That's absolutely insane!" I remember him distinctly saying, "Please think about it!"

Then Father Kevin quickly got up and was heading toward the door ready to leave without saying goodbye. I followed him to the living room, which led to the outside door. I was concerned about his state of mind and as he was about to open the door, I asked him, "Are you okay to drive?"

"I have to be okay," he replied with a sarcastic tone, "I need to go to the radio station to tape Saint Anthony's novena. I also have the 5:00 p.m. mass tonight."

Without thinking I asked another question, "Do you think you should go to confession before performing your priestly duties?"

He made eye contact and told me abruptly, "I don't need you to preach to me. With all due respect, Cándida, my spiritual life is none of your business."

Father Kevin had never talked to me that way before. I was very surprised that my concern had offended him that much. Making eye contact, I was ready to apologize to him for the remark. But before I could utter a word, he grabbed me, pulled me close to him and kissed me passionately on the lips. I should have pulled away, which would have been the right thing to do, but I did not. I was caught by surprise in a moment of weakness.

We were immersed in the ecstasy of the long and forbidden kiss; so neither of us realized that my mother- in-law had opened the door of her bedroom, which led to the living room. My heart almost stopped when I heard her yell, "Oh Madonna mía!" (An exclamation of shock, which translates into Oh Mother of God!) Then she let out a mouthful of insults to both of us. To Father Kevin she yelled, "I considered you a saint and you're the devil himself; you certainly had me fooled." And with fury in her eyes and pointing at me, she shouted, "You ought to be ashamed of yourself! I would never think that of you. You're nothing, but a putana (prostitute)."

Trying to avoid eye contact, we listened to my mother in-law's litany of insults without saying a word. When she finally got tired of insulting us, she went into her bedroom and slammed the door. Father Kevin could not get out of the house fast enough. I rushed to my bedroom upstairs to beg God for forgiveness while wishing the earth would swallow me whole. I had never felt so embarrassed in my entire life!

I waited until my mother- in-law was really hungry to talk to her about the kiss. She was so used to my bringing her meals to her room three times a day that even if there was food already cooked, she would not help herself. I dreaded facing her, but I finally mustered the courage of going into her room to talk to her. I began by apologizing profusely for what had happened and reassured her that it would never happen again. She was still very angry and commented, "My son is so stupid, and he has such a blind trust in you." Then she added, "You could have another man's child and the poor fool would think it's his."

She went on and on …. I finally decided that it was time for me to defend myself, even though I was feeling very guilty. Very firmly but still with respect, I told my mother-in-law, "That's enough Doña Alicia! Now you're going to listen to me. Nobody can get pregnant with a kiss and that's all it was. I am not a putana, and if you ever call me that again or tell your son what you saw, I am going straight back to Honduras." After a long pause, she finally decided, "We have a deal."

Then my mother-in-law asked me something about the children, and I knew that was her way of changing the subject. I forced myself to give her a fake smile and sweetly asked her, "What do you feel like eating tonight?"

"You know that I am always ready to eat your delicious chicken soup," she replied. After I fed her, we continued with our nightly routine which consisted of back and leg massages for her poor circulation and then getting her ready bed.

Later that evening, I was completely exhausted with all that had happened on that day – the last thing I needed was to deal with another stressful situation. Then I received a very surprising telephone call from Susanne, Father Kevin's mother. After exchanging greetings with Susanne, she explained the reason why she was calling. "Kevin confided to me his feelings for you and his wish to marry you. I want you to know that my husband and I would be in complete support of your relationship with him." In order to sound more convincing, she added, "We never wanted our son to go to the seminary in the first place."

I could not believe what I was hearing! Neither did I knew what to say to Susanne. I do not remember exactly what I said. But I distinctly remember that even before the telephone call ended, I had started thinking, "Is it possible to have a mother-in-law who would be that nice and supportive?" Then I started rationalizing, "If I marry Father Kevin, I will not have to put up with my difficult mother-in-law anymore." The idea of getting away from her was a tempting proposition. Besides, at this time I was not sure whether she was going to keep her part of our agreement. I was also afraid that even if she did not tell her son about the kiss she had witnessed, she would constantly throw it in my face which would promote my feelings of guilt and shame.

After a long and sleepless soul-searching night, I finally concluded that I needed to enlist my husband's support in order to deal with this dilemma. In addition to feeling guilty, I was very confused. I knew that I needed to stop seeing Father Kevin, but I did not have the strength to do it on my own. I realized that while I did not love Father Kevin intensely, I did have some romantic feelings towards him. I loved the attention he was giving me, but I did not know that I was confusing gratitude with love. Furthermore, my greatest fear was that I had lost my objectivity because I wanted to get away from my oppressive mother-in-law almost as much as I wanted to get away from my abusive mother when I was a girl.

I was fully aware that I would be taking an extremely high risk by telling my husband about my predicament. My experience in my country had been that a woman gets blamed for everything no matter what. No man in my culture could possibly understand or admit that neglect in the marriage can cause a woman to have romantic feelings towards another man. And no woman in her right mind would confess something like that to her husband because it would cost her marriage or even her life. I was counting on the fact that a priest, even if he left the priesthood, would always be a priest. And I needed my husband's priestly advice and support to deal with this particular problem.

I revealed the secret to my husband the very next day. It was probably the most painful confession he had ever listened to, and the most difficult one I had ever made. It was a Saturday morning at about 7:30 a.m. We were alone in our bedroom. Our children and my mother-in-law were still sleeping.

With a trembling voice I began by saying, "Honey, I am so sorry, but I have a problem, and I need your help."

"What kind of problem?" my husband asked. Then after a very long hesitation, I continued, "Well, Father Kevin claims to be in love with me, and I am afraid that I have become emotionally involved with him." My husband could not believe what he was hearing and asked me to repeat it again. The second time I repeated the same thing but a little louder, and I added a few more details.

After taking about a minute to process what I had told him, which seemed like an eternity to me, a wave of fury and rage came over my husband's face like I had never seen before! He made a fist with his right hand. I was sure he was about to hit me. But instead, he bit his fist and angrily delivered the following soliloquy: "How can someone, who claims to be my friend, be such a Judas? How can he betray me like this? That bastard is fully aware that I have failed one sacrament, but he is more than willing to help me fail another one! If it weren't because I do not wish to stain your good reputation in any way, I would have him thrown out of the Franciscan Order right now."

At this point, I interrupted my husband by pleading, "Honey, please forgive me, and please do not blame him alone. I must have encouraged him in some way, unconsciously, of course, for things to have gotten so out of hand. I am willing to accept my share of the blame."

To my surprise, instead of getting angry, my husband embraced me and told me tenderly, "I do not blame you, Chita! You are only tempted to respond to his advances because you have not been getting the attention from me that a beautiful woman deserves. Please forgive me for being such a jackass. I have been neglecting you for a long time. I never meant to do that, but I am so tired working nights. I will make it up to you. I promise!" Then he kissed me tenderly on the forehead.

At that very moment, I fell in love with my husband all over again. I had expected reproaches from him, but instead I received love, compassion and understanding. I immediately told him to please call his friend to let him know that he was no longer welcomed in our house.

Frank called Father Kevin that afternoon, and I overheard his side of the conversation. My husband bluntly told his friend, "Kevin, you are no longer welcomed in my house. Please do not call or show your face around here ever again. I expect you to have the decency of honoring my wishes and have no further contact with my family or with me ever again."

I have no idea what Father Kevin said to Frank, but he honored Frank's wishes. He had no further contact with us, with the exception of one single time.

It was very difficult explaining to our children and my mother-in-law why Father Kevin had stopped visiting us. The children did not ask many questions, and my mother-in-law pretended that she was surprised by asking for Father Kevin every once in a while. Our explanation was always the same, "Father Kevin was transferred to another parish, which is very far away from here. It's too far for him to come see us." Frank and I agreed to use this excuse.

A few months after ending the relationship with Father Kevin, I received one more card from him. It was a Halloween card with a witch on the cover and a magic wand. Inside the card, written in his own handwriting was the following message:

Cándida, my darling,

I wish I had a magic wand; so I could make you appear and be with me forever. I miss you terribly.

Love you always,
K.

I did not answer Father Kevin's card, but I had to use every ounce of will power I had to refrain from calling him. I felt very bad for him, and honestly, I was missing him too. A few times, I had even picked up the telephone to call him, but then I would come to my senses by reminding myself, "If my husband finds out, he is going to be very upset. I cannot inflict any more pain on him or any more guilt on myself."

My husband never saw Father Kevin again, and I only saw him once about ten years later. However, I had to deal with the guilt I felt for my moment of weakness and for causing my husband to end a friendship so abruptly with whom he had so much in common. I made my mission then to make it up to my husband and to rekindle in our marriage the flame that at one time had burned so brightly.

After this experience, there was definitely an ongoing change in my husband's behavior and attitude. He treated me with the intense love and devotion that he originally had shown me, which brought back the magic to our marriage. By now we both realized that marriage is like a flower that constantly needs nourishment and care. We were both willing to do our part to recapture the love that had brought us together in spite of so many obstacles and to keep our marriage happy and healthy.

My mother in law never mentioned the kiss incident again. In fact, she was soon to surprise me with an unexpected level of emotional and financial support. I kept my part of the agreement as well, and found a way to make it up to my husband for losing a friendship that had connected him with his past.

CHAPTER 13

*I*t seemed that guilt had been my constant companion for years, and I hated it. It first appeared when I became aware of my romantic feelings toward Father Andrew, and it stayed with me for at least six years after I married him. Now I was feeling guilty for hurting my husband by using him as my confessor with my dilemma with Father Kevin. I also felt guilty and responsible for being unable to save Father Kevin's friendship with the family.

My husband never held that cruel and painful confession against me. If anything, from that day on he tried very hard to be the sweet and kind man I had fallen in love with, and he started sending me romantic messages again and reassuring me in many ways that he still loved me.

At some point, my husband had even stopped feeling angry at Father Kevin and admitted he missed his friendship. He had other friends at work, but no one who knew about his past. One day, I was telling him about missing my family in Honduras; then he confided to me, "My whole life I have missed having a brother or sister, but I have accepted that. Now I miss having a friend who shares my past, someone I can talk to about old times the way I did with Kevin."

After that revelation from my husband, I decided to make amends for the way his friendship with Father Kevin had abruptly ended. I had no idea how I was going to make it up to him, but I was determined to find a way. Fortunately, the opportunity presented itself.

It came to my attention that Brother Joseph, a missionary who had been working with Frank in Gualaco, during the entire nine years he had been in Honduras, was now back in the United States in the Boston area.

There is a significant difference between a brother and a priest in the Catholic Church. Priests can administer sacraments, such as: celebrating mass, hearing confessions, performing marriages, baptisms and anointing the sick. Brothers cannot administer sacraments, but outside of that, they are eligible to minister in any other work within the church. They also need to take the same sacred vows as a priest: poverty, obedience and chastity.

I was very happy to learn that Brother Joseph (or Brother Joe as we affectionately called him) was not only back in the United States, but that he had been assigned to a church in the North End, the Italian part of Boston. That was really good news for me. "This is my opportunity to make amends to my husband." I told myself. I knew it was not going to be easy because my husband and Brother Joe had not communicated for fourteen years. Nevertheless, it was worth for me to take on the challenge of reviving their friendship.

Brother Joe and Frank had been more than fellow missionaries and best friends while they had been in Honduras. They were more like brothers, but they had not communicated since Frank left the priesthood. Their relationship ended because Brother Joe felt angry at Frank for having left him alone in Gualaco without any warning. At that time, Brother Joe had no idea that Frank was leaving the priesthood because my husband had not confided in him.

I did not know Brother Joe personally. We had not met in Honduras because I had never gone to Gualaco, and he had never come to Las Limas even though my father and he were great friends. My father had invited him many times to visit us, but unfortunately, Brother Joe was trapped in Gualaco for lack of transportation. No horse or mule was strong enough to transport him over the mountains due to his heavy weight.

Brother Joe weighed over four hundred pounds. He had become quite a celebrity in Gualaco and surrounding communities because people in those areas had never seen a person that big. Some people, who lived farther up in the mountains, would walk for one or two days just to go to Gualaco. These people wanted their children to see someone who they considered to be a wonder of nature, a human being who weighed as much if not more than one of their local pigs.

The weight of the pigs was estimated by how many gallons of lard a pig could produce. So people applied the same method to calculate Brother Joe's weight. They would look at him and would try to calculate how many gallons of fat he was carrying. The pig sellers and buyers were pretty accurate in their calculations, and the consensus among them was that Brother Joe was good for about ten gallons of lard.

Brother Joe was a big man for certain but not only in size, as he also had a big heart. Besides being well-known because of his weight, he had the reputation of being a healer, and he certainly deserved that status. He had learned medicine while assisting doctors in a hospital in Juticalpa for several years. His knowledge of medicine came very handy in Gualaco. He was able to save many lives, not only by dispensing medications but by performing minor surgeries as well.

Along with Father Andrew, Brother Joe was one of the most dedicated missionaries that Honduras had ever had. In addition to running the medical clinic and doing all the cooking at the rectory, he was very active working as a teacher to the orphans that Father Andrew had brought to the rectory.

Brother Joe and Father Andrew were well suited to work together because they shared the same philosophy on how to serve God's people. Both of them had strived very hard to put into practice the teachings of Saint Francis, the founder of their religious order. Both of them believed in using a holistic approach to meet the needs of their congregation.

Even though I had never met Brother Joe personally, I had a great deal of respect for him. I knew that Frank did too. I had already made up my mind to go to any lengths to bring these two friends together. Fortunately, having them make peace with each other ended up being much easier than I had anticipated. I contacted Brother Joe by telephone and invited him to our house. Much to my surprise, he was delighted to accept the invitation! When my husband and Brother Joe saw each other for the first time in fourteen years, it was such a touching, tearful, and joyful reunion. The two friends embraced each other like long lost brothers.

Frank tried to ask Brother Joe for his forgiveness for having deserted him in Gualaco without any notice, but Brother Joe interrupted him by saying, "There is no need to ask for forgiveness, Andy. I forgave you a long time ago." From that day on, Brother Joe became a part of our family; he spent all of his free time at our house and participated in all of the activities we did as a family.

Among his many attributes, Brother Joe was a fabulous chef. He had graduated from Cornell University with a degree in Culinary Arts. He took me under his wing as a student and taught me how to cook many types of food. One of his many specialties was pastries. I love Italian pastries, and I learned to make all types with his help. However, I stopped making these pastries after a while because I did not want to weigh as much as my mentor. By this time, Brother Joe had been back in the United States for several years and had reached the weight of six hundred pounds.

Brother Joe was very impressed at what a fast learner I was, and one day he commented to Frank, "This girl is brilliant! It's a shame she never had the opportunity of going to college. It seems like such a waste not to develop this much talent." He also added, "You know Andy, if she had stayed in Honduras, she could possibly have become one of her country's leading scholars. Remember that her father was deeply involved in education. José had enough connections to open doors for her."

Frank listened carefully to Brother Joe's remark. After a moment of reflection, he answered, "You are absolutely right, Joe."

I was very grateful to Brother Joe for the seed he had planted on my behalf. It fell on fertile ground, and it grew into a gigantic tree, seeing that I eventually reached my dream of graduating from college and even pursuing a higher education.

This conversation between Brother Joe and my husband took place sometime in June of 1978. Several weeks later, my family surprised me with some beautifully wrapped presents. I was stunned by the surprise because it was not my birthday nor Mother's Day! I carefully unwrapped the presents and discovered a big thick, five-subject notebook from my children with the inscription, "To a mommy who is too smart and will do well in college."

My mother-in-law gave me a school bag with my initials and a little card with the phrase, "If you can't do it, no one can!" The last present I unwrapped was a big dictionary from my husband with a long inscription covering one whole page. The inscription basically said:

You are going to need this dictionary Chita when you go to college. Have no doubt that you are capable of reaching the highest academic achievement. Remember that you are your father's daughter.

Your humble husband, who loves you so much and believes in you.

Frank

I was shocked and immensely happy with the surprise my family had given to me. I hugged them one by one and thanked them for their very thoughtful gifts.

I was absolutely thrilled with the idea of going to college! Other than marrying the man I loved and becoming a mother, going to college had been one of my biggest dreams. I doubt this dream would have been fulfilled if I had stayed in my country. My father was indeed very involved in education, but at that time in Honduras, getting a higher education was a privilege reserved for men only. As a matter of fact, I only knew of two women from San Esteban who had gone to college.

After having no hope for so long of ever going to college, I could not understand how this could be possible now. I knew we could not afford tuition. I had not taken any entrance exams, and I was not even sure that I was college material. In my mind, the fact that I had obtained my high school diploma did not guarantee that I had academic ability. The courses and even the tests, were taken by mail, and I could ask for help whenever I needed it. "But there will be no one in college helping me to take the tests," I told myself, adding fuel to my insecurities.

I bombarded my husband with questions about the logistics of the plan for me to go to college, and he tried to reassure me that everything was in place. He went on to explain, "My mother already offered to pay for your tuition. I already picked up a registration package from Bunker Hill Community College, and I was told that the only exam you need is an English placement exam."

My husband could sense my feelings of confusion and insecurity, and he lovingly reassured me, "Everything is going to be all right, Chita. You will do fine. You are brilliant! You have nothing to worry about." I wish that I had been as confident in my ability as my husband seemed to be. I felt anything but brilliant. However, all throughout my life I had never wasted an opportunity to improve myself, no matter how insecure I felt. I was determined to take on this new challenge and give it my best try.

After wrestling with my insecurity and winning a small battle, I really felt excited about going to college. I wanted to jump for joy and announce to the whole world, "I am going to college!" And that is exactly what I did. Besides telling the exciting news to anyone who would listen, I wrote at least a dozen letters to my family in Honduras notifying them of the great news.

Everyone was very happy for me, especially my father, who by this time had come to realize the importance for a woman to be educated. He made sure that Alma, my younger sister, had the opportunity of pursuing a higher education. However, in my brother's case there had never been a question about whether he would go to college or not because of his gender.

My experience in college was even better and somewhat easier than I had expected. I had wonderful professors and tutoring support when necessary. To my surprise, English was not my most challenging subject, but it was Algebra. However, I had a very skilled tutor, a Chinese young man, and I ended up getting an "A" with his help.

When I first started college, my goal was to get decent grades and get credit for courses. But when I received "A's" in the four courses I had taken during my first semester (English, math, psychology, and sociology), it gave me the confidence to raise the academic expectations I had set for myself. And I continued to receive straight A's in all of my courses.

Two years later, I graduated from Bunker Hill Community College with an Associates' degree. That was only the beginning of my long academic history. The following two years, I attended Salem State College in Salem, Massachusetts, which at that time specialized in teachers' training. I had decided to become a teacher because I seemed to have a natural ability for teaching, and the long vacations were also a big incentive. I wanted to be home with my children as much as possible during their school vacation.

In June of 1982, I graduated Summa Cum Laude from Salem State College with a Bachelor's Degree in Arts and Science. I worked extremely hard to reach this goal. Sometimes, I would only get two hours of sleep at night because I was up at all hours doing projects or studying for exams. It felt like such a great achievement to graduate with the highest honors! My parents came from Honduras for my graduation, which was an added bonus!

Salem State College honored my parents by giving them a nice reception because they had come all the way from Honduras to witness their daughter graduate. My father gave a heartfelt speech during the reception. Being a poet, he certainly had the gift of words, and in perfect English, he delivered a short but very moving speech.

After congratulating me and the other graduates who were present at the reception, my father thanked the college for being involved in such an important mission as education. Then he went on to thank the professors and to exalt the teaching profession to the highest degree. "Teachers are needed for someone to achieve any professional goal, no matter how small, noble, or sophisticated the goal may be." Then he concluded his speech by saying, "The most famous people in the history of the world, such as Jesus Christ, Plato, and Confucius were teachers and had a profound effect on the culture of their time and even today. All teachers have the same opportunity as these great philosophers to shape history and to help make our world a better place."

With this conclusion, my father received a standing ovation from the professors, students, and all of the people who had been present at the graduation reception.

One of my professors at Salem State College, Rick Reed, had been to Honduras and had spent a month at my father's ranch. This professor decided to write an article about my graduation and my background, which emphasized how far I had come academically. He published the article along with a picture of my father and I on the front page of several local newspapers. My mother had not been around when the picture was taken. She had not been intentionally left out, but no one could convince her otherwise.

Because of this article, I received hundreds of congratulatory cards even from people I had never met before and about a half dozen bouquets of flowers. I also received congratulations from some of my husband's fellow priests from different parts of the United States. I later found out that through Brother Joe a clipping of the article about my graduation had circulated in several rectories of the Franciscan priests and brothers.

But the highlight of my graduation was the reception that my mother-in-law had for me in the most elegant night club in the Stoneham area, called Montvale Plaza. It seemed more like a wedding reception than a graduation party. The hall had been beautifully decorated with fresh flowers, and organ music was playing as the guests were arriving. In addition to family and friends, anyone who had contributed to my education in some way, such as teachers and mentors, had been invited.

The celebration began with a thanksgiving mass followed by a fabulous dinner and live music for dancing. My mother-in-law was eighty-eight years old at that time, but she was able to dance the afternoon away with my father.

Toward the end of the reception, I gave a short speech thanking each person or group of people for having contributed to my academic success and for attending the reception to share in the celebration. Then in addition to thanking my mother-in-law from the bottom of my heart, I presented her with my graduation cap and gown, along with the gold color rope, which was the symbol the college had used to distinguish the Summa Cum Laude graduates.

I kissed my mother-in-law, and with my heart overflowing with love and gratitude I told her, "Please wear the cap and gown for the rest of the party. After all, this is as much your graduation as it's mine! Not only did you provide the money for my tuition, but you were my biggest cheerleader and supporter." Turning to the guests, I continued saying, "She probably told me a thousand times in the course of the four years, 'If you can't do it, no one can.' She has certainly been my biggest cheerleader." After putting the cap and gown on my mother-in-law, along with the gold tassel, everyone present clapped, cheered, and gave her a well-deserved standing ovation. It was such a magical moment to see my mother- in-law clearly bursting with joy and pride!

By this time, my mother-in-law and I had bonded as if we truly were mother and daughter. She loved to send greeting cards to my husband and I for every occasion, and her choice of cards had changed. Instead of saying to "My son and his wife," now the cards were addressed to "my daughter and her husband." I guess miracles never cease. Who could have ever imagined that my relationship with my mother-in-law would change that much?

I have no idea about the exact moment when we really bonded with each other because it had been a slow process. The fact that she had so much confidence in me and played an active role in my education erased any feelings of resentment that I had toward her. At some point even before I started college, she asked me. "Do you mind calling me mother, rather than Doña Alicia?"

It took some getting used to calling her "mom." But I readily agreed. Soon taking care of her became a labor of love, rather than a responsibility I was stuck with.

Shortly after that, my mother- in- law and I started sharing some deep secrets. One day she told me, "I guess God has forgiven me because He sent me another daughter." Upon hearing that, multiple questions went through my mind. "Forgive you for what? Did you have another daughter?" Then she confessed to me the terrible pain and horrible guilt she had been carrying for fifty years.

"I did have a daughter," she said "before my son was born. I was about four months pregnant when my husband and I decided for me to have an abortion. It was during the Great Depression and we reasoned that we could not afford to have another mouth to feed. I didn't know that the fetus was already alive, and I went to see someone, who was illegally performing abortions. I almost died in the process. The pain was worse than giving birth to ten children. But the emotional pain was a thousand times more painful when I saw that I had aborted a beautiful baby girl that was still alive."

I listened with horror and incredible pity to my mother in law's terribly sad story. We both hugged and cried for a long time. I tried very hard to make her feel better by telling her, "You didn't know that the baby was alive. You already paid the price for the unfortunate incident by almost dying in the process and by carrying this heavy load of pain and guilt all these years. God has forgiven you for sure; so please forgive yourself." I think she took my advice because she dried her tears, made eye contact with me and said, "Thank you Candita, this is the first time I feel at peace in fifty years."

I have no idea whether her son knew or not about his mother's terrible secret. I never told him, of course. My mother-in-law never mentioned the incident again, and neither did I. She seemed happier during the last few years of her life. I have good reason to believe that we both experienced peace and forgiveness for what we had considered to be unpardonable sins.

Shortly after my graduation and even before I put together a resume, I received some job offers. I accepted, what I thought of as a dream job, teaching Spanish at Stoneham High School, which was about a quarter of a mile from my house. I wanted to work near home so that during lunchtime I could come home to give my mother-in-law a nice and warm lunch. I was absolutely ecstatic when I was hired for this position, but I had no idea then how challenging this position would turn out to be.

Sometime after my graduation and before the beginning of the school year, I went into a deep depression, and I could not figure out why. Everything was going so well for me. I had just accomplished an amazing goal, one of the most cherished dreams of my life had come true, but I still felt depressed. I confided to one of my friends about my state of mind, but I did not receive any sympathy from her. "You are almost living a fairy tale life. What do you have to be depressed about?" she asked me, obviously annoyed. After much reflection, I concluded that I was feeling unworthy of all the attention and praise I was receiving.

I expressed my feelings of unworthiness to my husband and he asked me, "Why do you think you are not worthy of being congratulated and praised for your success?"

Without even thinking about it, I answered, "I do not think that I deserve to have graduated Summa Cum Laude. My teachers probably gave me all those A's only because they liked me. They were always complimenting me for my beautiful handwriting and for being so kind and polite." (Most of my essays had been handwritten because I only had an old typewriter that was not working as well, and I could write faster by hand.)

My husband thought about what I had said for a while, and then he asked another question, "How many teachers did you have in the entire four years?"

I knew the exact number because of my number of credits. With the exception of two courses, I had a different teacher for each course. I quickly replied, "I had at least forty-five teachers."

And then my husband applauded and said, "Bravo! You did better than Jesus Christ himself! He was the son of God, and not everyone liked him, but 100 percent of your teachers completely adored you; they admired your handwriting and gave you free 'A's. Does that make sense?"

I had to agree with my husband that my reasoning did not make any sense. At that point, I fully realized that my excellent grades had been the product of my drive, my hard work, perseverance, and determination. Therefore, it was perfectly acceptable to enjoy my success. Then I remembered something that I had read somewhere. "The talents you have are God's gift to you, but what you do with them is your gift to God." And for the first time in my life I felt that I had given God a gift by the way I had used the talents He had given me. Soon the cloud over my head that had been depressing me was completely lifted.

Now I could not wait to start my new position teaching Spanish at Stoneham High School. I had made the mistaken assumption that academic achievement equated teaching ability, but I would soon find out otherwise.

Discipline turned out to be an overwhelming challenge for which I was not prepared at all. I do not know why, but in those days no attention was given to prepare teachers for classroom management skills during teaching preparation. I did not take a single course that had to do with discipline. I did my student-teaching in a fifth-grade class under the supervision of Mr. Austin, a young teacher, who had no control whatsoever of his class. Consequently, I had not witnessed classroom management skills being demonstrated. I was also unprepared to motivate students to learn a second language and lack of motivation was the second biggest challenge that I was about to encounter.

They say ignorance is bliss, and that was certainly true in my case because I had no idea about the nightmare that was waiting for me in my new position. I hardly could wait to begin what I had expected to be a wonderful and rewarding experience.

CHAPTER 14

I was looking forward to beginning my new job at Stoneham High School with the same anticipation that children wait for Christmas. But the summer of 1982 seemed to drag on forever. I met with the lady who was going to be my supervisor and she turned out to be an ex-nun. I did not tell her about my past, but I felt very comfortable with her because I reasoned we had a lot in common. She was very nice, personable and even thoughtful in the beginning, but after a while I found her to be very difficult to please.

I began, what I thought was my dream position, with great confidence, but I soon had a rude awakening. All of the book knowledge, and even some teaching practice, did very little to prepare me for what actually takes place in the classroom of a high school. I had no problem with teaching techniques or the subject matter. After all, I was teaching my native language, and I knew it well. But classroom management was another story. The students took advantage of my easy-going nature, "Mrs. De Vito is such a big pushover," was a common remark among students. "It's pathetic the way Mrs. DeVito lets you guys take advantage of her," was another frequent saying of some my female students to the boys.

To make things worse, three of my children were attending the same high school, and during lunch time they listened to the negative comments some students were making about their new Spanish teacher.

In addition to discipline problems, I was also unprepared to motivate students to learn a second language, and lack of motivation was the second big challenge that I encountered. Most of the students had no desire or interest in learning a foreign language. "We are not interested in learning English; why should we bother to learn another language," was the mentality of most of them. The few students who were willing to learn Spanish and respected me, were being ridiculed by the majority. One student in particular stood out among the rest. His name was Charles Carriero, who is now a Research Physicist and Principal Investigator at Boston College's Scientific Research. Because he was the nicest and brightest student that I had that year, he was teased the most.

The discipline problems went on and on throughout the school year, but asking the principal or vice-principal for help never occurred to me. I guess I was afraid that if they knew I lacked classroom management skills, they would think of me as an incompetent teacher. Since I could not let that happen, I had no choice but to make the best of a bad situation.

Even though I was making a decent salary for the first time in my life, my inability to control my classes quickly depressed and exhausted me. Now I could afford to buy new clothes, but I was too tired and too depressed to go to any stores. I remember that some students even made fun of me because I wore the same green suit too often, and they started calling me "parrot."

My morale was already at its lowest point when on October 10th of the same year, I received one of the biggest emotional blows of my life. My dear mother-in-law, who was now like a real mother to me and had been with us for twenty years, died rather suddenly. Not only was I completely devastated, but I was feeling guilty as well. My mother-in-law had been in the hospital for two days, and I had been there with her almost night and day. But I was not with her at the actual moment of her death.

It happened on a Sunday morning. Frank and I had taken our children to church, and from church we went directly to the hospital. My mother-in-law was very happy to see her grandchildren, of course. She was talking fine and eating breakfast. After a short visit with her, she told us. "Please go home and feed the children." We went back to the hospital less than two hours later, but she was already dead when we arrived.

Since I was already an expert on torturing myself, that is exactly what I did. I could not get out of my mind that after everything we had gone through and finally bonded; I had not been there when my mother in-law needed me the most. "I should have been with her," I told myself over and over again. Even though I enjoy eating, I refused to eat anything from that Sunday until the following Thursday. Blinded by tears and tortured by regret, I would tell my husband the same thing. "I was not there when she died. I did not even ask God to be with her."

Finally, my husband got tired and impatient after hearing the same comment over and over again. So he scolded me by saying in a very angry tone, "Does God need you to tell Him how to do His job? For goodness sake, Chita! You were there for her for twenty long years! You were practically her slave. No daughter could have taken better care of her than you did. What is more important, twenty years of caring or being there for the few minutes it takes for one to die?"

I guess I needed to be reprimanded by my husband because it quickly brought me to my senses. I continued missing my mother-in-law, but the guilt was finally gone. Then I started eating again and even made up for the meals I had missed.

Now that my mother-in-law was gone, and I did not have to work near my home, I contemplated leaving my hellish teaching position several times. But being true to my masochist tendency, I was able to endure a difficult situation for a whole year. However, when the teacher whom I was replacing returned to school, I was overjoyed. Now I had an excuse to get out of teaching without feeling like a failure.

Nevertheless, I did not get out of teaching altogether. I was offered another position within the Stoneham Public School system, but not as a classroom teacher. This new position consisted of teaching English as a second language to students who were newcomers to the country. I figured that I would be working with small groups and that students new to the country were less likely to need discipline. So I gladly accepted the position for the following school year.

As I already mentioned, three of my children were attending Stoneham High School the same year that I was teaching Spanish there (1982 to 1983). Francis was a senior, Anthony a sophomore and Marie a freshman.

Francis graduated ranking number one of his graduating class. He was given a full scholarship to the college of his choice. My husband and I were very proud of our very gifted son and assumed he was going to apply for admission to some of the most prestigious universities in the Boston area. Later on, we found out that the only institution Francis had applied to was Saint John's Seminary in Brighton, Massachusetts, because he wanted to study for the priesthood.

With all of the opportunities he had, my husband and I were surprised and somewhat disappointed that our son had focused on only one institution without investigating other possibilities. But fortunately for him, he was accepted at Saint John's Seminary.

When I first found out that my son wanted to become a priest, I had the suspicion that his main motivation was to finish what he thought his father had left undone. So I explained to him, "If you want to become a priest to follow in your father's footsteps with the idea of finishing something you think he left undone, you are going into the priesthood for the wrong reason. Your father did more for the missions in nine years, than some priests accomplish in a lifetime." Then I added, "Please don't make that mistake."

Francis felt insulted at my insinuation and reassured me that his decision to enter the seminary had nothing to do with his father leaving the priesthood. "I am not that shallow," he said, "I am going to the seminary because I feel a calling for the religious life." I accepted my son's explanation as to the reason of why he wanted to become a priest, and I offered him my complete support in his pursuit of a religious vocation.

Even after Francis' explanation as to why he wanted to become a priest, I was still not absolutely convinced that my hunch was wrong, but there was something I knew for sure. My son had inherited the best qualities of my husband and me; he was an improved version of both of us. I was sure if he persevered in his pursuit of a religious vocation, he would make an amazing priest. Since he was a small boy, Francis showed signs of great kindness and incredible generosity. I will never forget an incident that happened when he was only about six years old.

We had a large strawberry patch in our property that was already there when we bought the house. Francis and I picked a large bucket of big and ripe strawberries. A nice lady driving her car down our street stopped by to admire the beautiful strawberry patch. Without asking me, Francis told the lady, "If you like strawberries, please take the whole bucket." The lady looked at me, and I reassured her that it was fine. She gratefully accepted the gift and left with a big smile. Francis and I continued to pick another bucket of strawberries, but I made the mistake of storing them in the basement. About three days later, I found the wonderful strawberries completely spoiled. I felt so bad, and I told Francis, "What a shame! We lost all those beautiful strawberries." He quickly replied, "No we didn't! We saved the ones we gave away." He was absolutely right and that made me feel better.

Francis started out his life as a cranky baby, but he turned out to have a delightful personality with the capacity of an easy laugh. I used to tease him, "If you become a priest, you are probably going to laugh while performing funeral masses and that would definitely be inappropriate." But his nice disposition has served him well.

I used to feel sorry for Francis when he was a baby not only because he was colicky, but also because physically he looked so much like me. Since I considered myself an ugly duckling, I figured that I had an ugly baby. However, he turned out to be some people's description of a great looking guy, tall, dark and handsome. When the church announced that he was going to the seminary, a lady remarked after mass, "Your son is too handsome to be a priest. Why are you sending him to the seminary?"

I smiled and responded, "Thank you, but it's his choice, not mine." Then I asked her. "Why do you think priests should not be good looking?"

Without hesitating, she responded. "They would have less women after them."

The summer before Francis entered the seminary, I decided it was about time for the whole family to take a trip to Honduras. Twenty years had passed since my husband and I had left Honduras, and my husband had not shown any interest in going back. I had taken a short trip to Honduras only once after being in the United States for thirteen years. I brought my two oldest sons with me, who were 12 and 11 years old at the time.

My husband loved Honduras, and I could understand there were several reasons why he had not been back. To begin with, we could not leave his mother alone, nor did we have the financial means to afford the trip. However, now we had the means to take a trip together as a family, but he refused to go. I suspected there was another reason why my husband did not want to visit a country he loved. I pressed for an explanation and he finally admitted, "I am terrified of being rejected by my former parishioners. I cannot expose myself to be hurt like that."

It took some convincing on my part that his congregation would be happy to see him again. "I am quite sure that after two decades, the scandal caused by our marriage has probably been forgotten, but I bet that all the good you did is still remembered," I reassured my husband and he finally agreed to take the trip.

Thank God my hunch was right. What happened during that trip was beyond our wildest dreams and expectations! My husband was received as a hero not only in Gualaco, but everywhere he went! During the six weeks we were in Honduras, groups of people came by to see him or invited him to their homes on a daily basis. Everyone was very happy to see him. The outpouring of love and gratitude my husband received from so many people was absolutely unbelievable!

Some of the homeless children that Father Andrew (Frank) had rescued were now productive adults, and a few of them even had the best jobs in the country.

My husband was surprised and happy beyond description! At some point, he expressed his gratitude by saying, "Thank you, Chita, for convincing me to come. And thank God that in His great mercy, He has allowed me to see the fruits of my labor after feeling like a failure for twenty years."

My husband's presence was not the only cause for celebration during this visit to Honduras. My father, who was never interested in having parties, now decided to host a party every night for the six weeks we were there. This was my father's way to make it up to me for not allowing me to attend any parties when I was a young girl.

The parties consisted of entertainment provided by accordion and guitar players, along with food and drinks. The women in the village took turns helping my mother and me with food preparation. We would alternate serving tacos, burritos, enchiladas, pupusas and nacatamales (a type of meat pie wrapped in banana leaves). The drinks were made from any fruit that was in season, usually oranges, passion fruit, limes and pineapples. There was an open invitation to the entire village, and practically everyone in the village attended the parties on a nightly basis.

In the beginning of our visit to Las Limas, these parties were fun and exciting! I was glad to see everyone, and I loved listening to accordion music. I also loved having the opportunity of dancing with all the local "caballeros" (gentlemen) both young and old. However, after about two weeks, these parties became a burden rather than entertainment. The constant preparation for the evening party, along with lack of sleep because the parties would continue until the early-morning hours of the following day, soon became exhausting.

In order to add some variation to the parties, we had piñatas for the children, games and running competitions. For the young girls we had some kind of pageant with the opportunity for every contestant to be a winner. The judges would decide on the best trait of each contestant and declared all of them winners on that basis. I had brought some beautiful long gowns for that purpose and the girls were allowed to keep the gown, each one had chosen, as the winning prize.

We also had a version of the newlywed game for couples and a game called "Carrera de Cintas a Caballo" (Ribbons race on horseback) for caballeros. It is a fun game! The girls make a pretty ribbon with their names and hang all of them on a high clothesline. All the caballeros line up on their horses and the aim of the game is for them to get the ribbon of the girl they love or at least like. The names of the girls are hidden; so some caballeros end up very disappointed, if they choose the wrong ribbon. They have to give a prize to the girl, whose ribbon they take out. If a caballero does not have a prize ready, at least he has to give a kiss to the girl in front of everyone. That can be a problem, of course, if a caballero does not like the girl.

All these events were fun, but the planning took time, effort and creativity. We were all exhausted. I considered asking my parents to stop the parties, but my husband discouraged me from doing so. He was sick and tired of the parties himself, but he was thinking of the people. "In such a small village," he said, "the opportunities for entertainment are so rare, and everyone including children and old people are having the time of their lives. So please, Chita, let the parties continue." After hearing my husband's point of view about the parties, I did not have the heart to take away the enjoyment of our family and friends in Las Limas.

Toward the end of our stay in Las Limas, there was a procession for "Santiaguito," a very popular saint of the Pech Indians. They keep the statue of their saint in a church at a town called Santa María del Carbón; but every once in a while, they take it in processions to the villages around San Esteban. These processions are like a big celebration for the saint; most of the people in the villages join the processions and go from house to house, usually walking. People take turns carrying the statue of the saint on their backs, and it is transported in a small wooden box, called "nicho" in Spanish. During the procession some people carry candles, flowers and wreaths. The whole crowd sing hymns of praise and a few of the men play musical instruments.

I attended the procession in Las Limas for Santiaguito and even took a turn carrying the statue, which was not too heavy. When we arrived at one of the houses, someone came towards the crowd galloping on a majestic horse. I was not very curious to find out who the rider was until I heard him saying. "Buenas tardes señora del Padre Andrés!" (Good afternoon Mrs. Father Andrew.) I looked at him with an expression of fear and surprise. Besides being somewhat older and having some gray hair, Alejandro looked the same. He was still carrying two guns, one on each side of his belt, along with his security blanket, an ammunition belt full of bullets. I did not know how to answer his strange greeting. I simply responded. "Good afternoon Mr. De la Vega!"

Alejandro and I exchanged glances, but I could not read his expression. I still remembered the threat he had made twenty years earlier, "If you ever marry someone else, I swear to God that I will kill you when you return." I tried very hard to hide my fear by casually making my way into the crowd. I was saying my prayers and my knees were shaking! But to my relief, Alejandro stared at the crowd for a little while; then took off without saying goodbye.

"That was so strange!" I wondered. "Why did he come if he wasn't going to join the procession? Why did he call me Mrs. Father Andrew? Was he trying to remind me of my sin that I had married a priest? Does he still have any feelings for me?" I found out the next day the answers to some of my questions.

The following day, a distant relative of mine on my mother's side of the family, who worked at Alejandro's house, shared with my mother and me a detailed account of the incident, "Don Alejandro went on a shooting rampage last night inside the house. He was very angry at his mother, and I overheard him yelling to her. 'Because of you, I lost the only woman I ever loved.' Then he took both guns out and emptied them aiming them toward the kitchen ceiling. His mother and everybody else ran out of the house and spent the night next door."

I never saw or heard from Alejandro again. But five years later, I found out that he died from a massive heart attack, leaving a string of broken hearts including: his five children, the mother of his children and his own mother.

Two days before returning home to Boston, my family and I left Las Limas and went to Tegucigalpa. The flight for the United States was leaving from there. We stayed at my sister's house, and she had a big surprise for us. Another party! "That is just what we need!" I thought with dread. However, this party was different. I experienced what it would have been like to be on Fantasy Island, a popular television show from the 1970s and 1980s where people's fantasies came true.

One of the guests at the party was Sebastian, the tall and handsome young man who I had a crush on when I was fourteen years old. He was the man who broke my heart by playing with my feelings. He claimed to be interested in me when I first met him. But then, he stopped seeing me at once after meeting my cousin, Graciela. I had not seen Sebastian in twenty years, but I had not forgotten him either. The memory of him had remained fresh in my mind for two decades because he had been the first man to break my young heart.

When Sebastian came to the party that evening and I saw him, I honestly did not recognize him. He was only a shadow of the tall and handsome young man that I remembered. He seemed much shorter now; he had a puffy red face and a beer belly. He recognized me immediately, gave me a long embrace, and seemed delighted to see me. I tried very hard not to show how surprised I was that he had changed so much. Although he deserved it, I did not want to hurt his feelings.

We talked for a few minutes, and when the "mariachis" (a Mexican band) started playing, Sebastian asked me, "May I have the honor of this dance?"

I replied, "Gladly!" He had met me as a shy and terribly insecure young girl, and now I wanted him to meet the educated and confident woman I had become. As we were dancing, he gazed into my eyes, and in his best imitation of a romantic voice told me, "You are so beautiful! I never forgot you! I never for one moment stopped loving you."

I listened to his litany of lies without saying anything. So Sebastian went on and on with the lies.... "The biggest mistake of my life was to let you go, but if I have to wait another twenty years, I will wait for you."

After that last comment, I could not take any more of his lies. So looking directly into his eyes I firmly told Sebastian, "That's enough! It's my turn to talk now." I could sense that I was about to explode like a pressure cooker. Therefore, I suggested for us to go to the patio and talk. Now I had the opportunity of telling Sebastian everything I had wanted to say to him for twenty years. "You can wait until hell freezes over," I began saying. "You are twenty years too late. Do you think I am beautiful now? Didn't you tell the whole village that I was not as pretty as my cousin Graciela? I am still the same person. Obviously, you don't know anything about true beauty, the one that doesn't fade with the passing of time."

I forgot what else I said to Sebastian, but I recited a litany of grievances as if defending the young girl, who twenty years earlier had been too shy to express and defend herself. It was indeed a dream come true! On the show Fantasy Island, people had to pay a lot of money to make their fantasies come true, but I had my fantasy come true free of charge.

Sebastian's reaction to my harsh words was a combination of apology, denial, and pleading for forgiveness. "Please forgive me!" he said, "I am so sorry! I had no idea that I hurt you because you never told me you had any feelings for me, and I do not remember telling anyone that you were not as pretty as your cousin."

Then, "Why did you abandon me so quickly?" I asked, "Why after claiming to love me you disappeared from my life without an explanation?"

Sebastian avoided my questions by proposing, "It is not too late for us! We could still be together and enjoy an unforgettable love affair! If you want, I could even go to Boston." That proposal not only insulted me, but infuriated me even more. However, I welcomed the opportunity of letting him know that I was a woman of character, unlike other women he knew who were married and continued having affairs with him.

"I am not a loose woman," I replied angrily. "I am faithful to my husband, and I feel insulted by your insinuation that I could be otherwise." To let him know that I meant what I said, I abruptly left the patio and went back to the dance floor. Sebastian followed me and asked me to dance a few more times after that, but I continued to refuse and finally told him, "Please leave me alone; I heard enough of your garbage."

My supposedly beautiful cousin Graciela was also there at the party. I had not seen her in twenty years as well. I remembered her as a strikingly beautiful girl. In addition to being endowed by nature with the body of a ballerina, she had fair skin, dreamy hazel eyes, and shiny black hair. However, by now some of her beauty had faded away. I had been envious of Graciela's beauty when I was growing up. But now finding out that I had nothing to be envious about, did not give me any pleasure. The rivalry between us had stopped when I got married, and I was very happy to see her. Graciela did not end up marrying Sebastian. They had plans to get married at one time, but he broke up with her shortly before their wedding day. She is now married to a wonderful man from South America, and they have three handsome sons.

I was told the day after the party that even though Graciela was married to someone else, she was obviously jealous because Sebastian had paid attention to me the entire evening. I also learned that Graciela and Sebastian had a big fight that night.

Looking back at what I thought was a fantasy come true, I should have thanked Sebastian for leaving me when he did, instead of arguing with him. He was now a married man and the father of about eight children with a number of women. But obviously, he left his wife at home and was looking for a new conquest.

After my encounter with Sebastian twenty years later, I appreciated my husband even more. Frank was sleeping during the whole time my fantasy was taking place. He was exhausted from all of the parties we had in Las Limas and from his newfound celebrity status in Honduras.

I was exhausted myself and thankful that this was the last party. I had discovered the wisdom of an old saying, "Even a good thing is not good in excess."

This was the only trip that my husband and I were able to take to Honduras as a family, but it had lifelong benefits. So much healing had taken place, especially in the life of my husband. He was able to see the fruits of his labor and stopped feeling like a failure. As for me, I put to rest the pain of having been rejected by a man who was not worth even remembering.

CHAPTER 15

When we returned home from our unforgettable trip to Honduras, our oldest son, Francis, began his studies for the priesthood at Saint John's Seminary in Brighton, Massachusetts. Even though the seminary was only about twenty-five miles away from our home, when Francis left for the seminary my husband and I experienced the sadness of empty nest. However, he was allowed to come home for a day visit on weekends, and he always brought home at least half a dozen seminarians with him.

Most of these seminarians were from Puerto Rico, and they did not have any family in the Boston area. Our house became their home away from home. Pretty soon I felt like a foster mother to this group of wonderful young men; I loved playing that role because I enjoy cooking and feeding people. Whenever there was a family get-together at the seminary, my husband and I attended not only to provide moral support to our son, but also to the other seminarians who did not have family nearby.

At the same time, I started my new teaching position in the Stoneham school system. My new teaching job had its challenges, mostly with travel time because I had to be at a different school every hour. But it was very fulfilling, unlike the chaotic situation of my previous position. Not only was I teaching English as a second language to students new to this country, but I was also helping their parents make the transition to a new culture. However, as the saying goes, "All good things come to an end." The following year my position was no longer funded because of budget cuts.

Fortunately, I had no problem finding another position immediately. I was sure that I had landed another easy and rewarding job when I was hired as a social worker by a nonprofit organization in a town with a heavy Hispanic population and not too far from my house. I was appointed to this position because of my bilingual skills, but I did not have any type of training or even orientation to be a social worker. My first and biggest mistake was being unaware that I was supposed to keep my personal and professional life separate.

I gave my home telephone number to all of my clients, and all at once after that my telephone was ringing at all hours of the night. To make things worse that was not my only mistake. If a client claimed to need money for food or for an emergency, I gave him or her all the money I had in my purse. It was not that much money because this job was a very low-paying job. But I would give all the money I was carrying, and I had nothing left to even buy a cup of coffee. If I could not find shelter immediately for a homeless person, it is not hard to guess what I did. I took that person home, of course. I even took some female clients home sometimes only because they claimed to be lonely.

Even though this job did not pay well, it had some benefits in addition to the satisfaction of helping people in need. I learned how the court system works because one of my responsibilities was to be a translator for the trials of clients who did not speak English.

I will never forget the first time I served as an interpreter in court. Because my supervisor was not available that day, I was sent to court to be an interpreter without any training, of course. I welcomed this new opportunity, but I felt nervous because it was the first time that I was witnessing a trial. As a matter of fact, it was the first time I had been inside a courthouse. I was instructed by the judge to translate everything as exactly as I could and to use the first person only. I had some experience working as a translator before, but never in a court system. When I noticed a tape recorder near where I was sitting, I became even more nervous because I knew then that every word that came out of my mouth was going to be recorded.

The trial was for three young women from Puerto Rico, who had gone to a party in Boston and had hitchhiked a ride to another city about 30 miles away. They had no money to pay for a taxi and public transportation was no longer in service because it was 3:00 a.m. According to them, they accepted a ride in a stolen car without being aware that the car was stolen. When the police caught up with the stolen car, the driver, along with his three passengers, were arrested. These young women had been in jail for five weeks already when their trial finally took place.

As the trial continued, I felt as if I were the defendant since I was translating in the first person. The prosecuting attorney was trying to put in question the moral character of the defendants and asked each one of them, "Are you married?" One of the women answered, "No, but I have three children and no husband." The other two women answered in the same way. I knew they were giving too much information and their answers were somewhat incriminating, but I could not offer them any advice. Neither could I alter their answers in my translation.

During the two hours of being interrogated by attorneys, the defendants seemed stoic and maintained their composure. Both attorneys were going back and forth presenting their arguments. Finally, the judge heard enough and in exasperation said to the defendants, "I think the three of you are as guilty as sin, but I do not have enough evidence to convict you. You are free to go."

As soon as I translated the verdict, the young ladies started crying, hugging me and thanking me for their freedom. I explained to them, "Your wonderful attorney is the one responsible for your freedom not me. All I did was to translate for you." But no matter what I said, I could not convince them otherwise. One of the young ladies commented, "Our attorney may be good, but we couldn't communicate with her until you came along."

As I was walking back to the parking lot after the trial, I noticed that my left shoulder was still wet from the young ladies' tears. I was wearing a dark blue suit, and I could see their tears streaming down to my shoulders. At this point, I became very emotional and decided to share the good news with someone. There were no cell phones then; so I had to look for a public telephone. I called my husband and woke him up from a sound sleep because he worked nights. When my husband answered the telephone, I told him excitedly, "Honey, we won! We won!

My husband asked half-asleep, "What did we win?"

I replied, "The trial, the trial about the stolen car."

Completely confused, my husband asked, "Which stolen car? We didn't steal any car."

Finally, I had to get a hold of myself and explain everything to him from the beginning.

I served as an interpreter in court several more times, but I did not allow myself to get that emotionally involved again; at least not in a courthouse.

This social worker position also provided me with the opportunity of serving as an interpreter in hospitals. I had the privilege of witnessing the miracle of birth, without experiencing the physical pain. Some of my clients, who had no one else, asked me to be their labor coach and interpreter when delivering their babies. I was so happy the first time I helped with the delivery of a baby, and I could not contain my joy. A cousin of my husband, who was a rather negative person, happened to call me that day, and she asked me, "What are you so happy about?"

Cheerfully, I answered her. "I served as an interpreter today for the delivery of a baby."

She then asked me sarcastically, "Why do they need an interpreter to deliver a baby? They certainly didn't need one when the baby was conceived," she added.

Another good outcome of my social work position was that I lost weight without even trying to. I had gained about fifteen pounds after my four pregnancies. For several years I had tried many times to lose weight without having much success. I was very surprised that now I did not seem to have a problem losing weight, but I did not understand why. After a while, it finally occurred to me what the secret was. I would sit at the dinner table to eat with my family. Then I would start thinking of the clients who probably did not have enough to eat, and I would stop eating at that point.

Within six months into this position, not only did I begin to look like a skeleton, but also my house had become like a homeless shelter. In addition to that, I was on call twenty-four hours a day taking sick people to the hospital, reporting missing children or young people, trying to find housing or employment for clients and doing translations as well. My life had become totally chaotic and a complete disaster.

Even my husband, whose life mission was to help people, could not take this lifestyle anymore and decided to put a stop to it. He told me in a very firm voice and rightfully exasperated, "We cannot continue going on like this Chita! Charity starts at home first. You have to stop this madness before all of us end up in the nut house!"

I knew that my husband was right. I was already thinking of finding a way out of this fiasco without letting my clients down and without feeling like a failure again. But before I could come up with an acceptable solution to the problem, I received the devastating news that my father was terminally ill. Upon receiving this terrible information, I had no hesitation resigning from this position so that I could go to Honduras to help care for my dying father.

In less than a year, my wonderful, handsome and brilliant father had been consumed by stomach cancer. For the first time in my life, I was glad that I did not inherit his striking good looks. I figured that the more physically gifted someone is, the greater the loss when sickness or old age robs one of one's beauty.

But even near death, the cancer was not able to diminish the strength of my father's spirit or dim the sparkle of his beautiful hazel eyes or the function of his intellect. I asked him just a few days before he died, "How do you want to be remembered?" I thought I knew what he would say, "I want people to remember me as a man of great charity." Because that was one of his most outstanding qualities, but instead the poet in him answered my question. "I want to be remembered as a human being who made his life's mission to cultivate beauty."

My father certainly fulfilled his mission in more ways than one. The ongoing theme in all of the poems he wrote was to exalt the loveliness of women and the beauty of nature. I remember when I was growing up that every time he went to the forest, he would bring me back an orchid plant. I ended up growing a beautiful collection of orchids of every color of the rainbow.

Even more than singing praises to women and nature, my father cultivated beauty in the hearts of people. He treated everyone with dignity and respect. Whether a candidate to the presidency of the country, or a simple peasant came to visit, he was always ready with a warm smile and a strong welcoming handshake.

My father had a well-deserved reputation of being extremely generous. If a beggar came to his house asking for money, and all he had in cash was 20 *lempiras* (ten dollars at that time), my father would give all he had without holding anything back. Whenever he slaughtered a cow, which was fairly often being a rancher, rather than hoarding or selling some of the meat as most rich people did, my father would distribute the meat among all of the needy people in the village.

But in addition to his generosity, my father was well-known and respected for his wisdom. He was considered the wisest man in the village, and very often people would come to his house to ask him for advice. Sometimes, he took it upon himself to solve people's problems without being asked to do so because he felt sorry for them.

I remember one particular incident when a woman from the village came to our house. She was crying and covering her swollen, black and blue face due to her husband's constant physical abuse. I forgot the reason why this lady had come to our house, but I will never forget the sad and sympathetic look of my father when he saw this poor woman. Right then and there, he decided to put a stop to the abuse. He was able to do that with a single conversation by telling a white lie to her husband.

My father paid a visit to the abusive husband and warned him with a voice of authority, "You better stop abusing your wife my friend, or she will blow your brains out one of these days." The abusive husband was perplexed to hear that! "She came to my house this morning and asked to borrow my gun. I may let her borrow it, if you don't stop hitting her," my father added.

The abusive husband believed what my father said because he knew that my father's word was as good as gold. This man not only stopped abusing his wife, but started respecting her as well.

I also remember another incident when my father's wisdom paid off. My paternal grandfather had a brother named *Don Justo*. This grand uncle was not as nice or popular as my grandfather, but he obtained his title of *Don* simply by being close to one hundred years old. *Tío* (uncle) *Justo* changed for the better in his last year of life, and one of his rituals was to get up every morning and go from house to house greeting people in the entire village. One day *Tío Justo* stopped doing that. Then my father decided to pay him a visit and took me along.

When we arrived at his little house, we found him in bed and fully covered from head to toe with blankets. After a short greeting, my father asked him. "What is the matter, *Don Justo*? Are you sick?"

He responded, "Not really, but I am almost 100 years old and I realize that God is probably going to take me at any time. I am feeling very old!"

My father told him, "Don't worry *Don Justo*. I have some medicine that even cures old age. I will go home and get it; I will be right back."

We came back to the house and my father went to his room to get the medicine. Soon he came out holding some kind of liquid in a small paper cup. We went back to *Tío Justo's* house, who was still in bed all covered up. My father reassured the old man, "This medicine is magnificent! Make sure you drink it all; so you get cured." Right after drinking the medicine, *Tío Justo* jumped out of bed with the energy of a young man, and told my father. "You are absolutely right *Don José*! That medicine works like a miracle! I feel great!"

We left *Tío Justo's* house and my father seemed very pleased with his accomplishment. Even at my young age, maybe nine years old, I did not believe in miraculous cures and I asked him, "José, what did you give *Tío Justo*?"

He smiled and whispered, "Tomato juice."

Thanks to my father's insight into human nature, *Tío Justo* lived for five more years during which he continued his ritual of greeting everybody every morning.

My father was always doing favors for people. Among the many favors some men would request of him was to ask the parents of their future brides for their daughters' hand in marriage. It was customary at that time in Honduras for a groom to ask the parents of his future wife for their consent to marry their daughter. The groom would usually send someone well-respected to make such a request. It was especially important to send someone very diplomatic and well respected especially when the parents of the bride were opposed to their daughter's marriage for whatever reason. My father was considered the perfect person to accomplish this somewhat delicate mission in some cases.

There were also a few extreme cases when the groom was too timid to propose marriage to his desired bride, and my father was also entrusted with that task. So even though, he never did get married himself, he had the opportunity of proposing marriage to these young ladies on someone else's behalf. One potential bride in particular was so mesmerized by my father's poetic and flowery marriage proposal that she did not realize that he was proposing for someone else. So, before my father could finish his carefully prepared speech, the poor young lady leaped with joy and blustered out, "Oh yes, I will be more than honored to marry you, *Don José!*"

My father then had the very unpleasant task of explaining to this simple young lady that he was proposing marriage on behalf of someone else. A couple of days later, she went around telling her girlfriends, "I accepted to marry *Ramiro* because *Don José's* proposal was so beautiful. I couldn't say no to him."

It was very easy for my father to play the role of Romeo, because in reality he was a *Don Juan*, and he continued to be one throughout most of his life. At least two of the women he had children with decided never to marry, and they remained single mothers for the rest of their lives. These poor women were publicly declared enemies. They fought with each other for most of their lives for a man who was not interested in either of them, and they wasted their lives waiting for a lover who would never return.

Aside from being a *Don Juan*, my father was the most remarkable man I have ever known, with the exception of my husband. Losing my father was one of the most profound heartaches that I had to endure in my entire life. It took many years for me to be able to remember him without anguish in my heart. My only consolation was that his wish had been granted. He would often say, "Old age terrifies me; I want to die before I get too old."

My father lost his courageous battle with cancer on September 5th, 1986. He was barely 70 years old. Besides his poetry, he left a lasting legacy through his incredible kindness, honesty, generosity and many talents. Many years later, people still remember him as one of the most humanitarian, brilliant and wise persons that ever lived in *Las Limas*.

This was a very low period of my life. In addition to dealing with the terrible sadness and emptiness of losing my father, I was also feeling completely insecure and disillusioned with my career. To make things even worse, I was cursed with an "all or nothing" mentality. Because of my lack of success in my two previous positions, as a high school teacher and as a social worker, I had no confidence in my capacity to be effective at any job.

The only area I felt confident at was in my academic ability. Consequently, when my husband suggested, "Chita you should go back to college to get a master's degree," I was delighted. However, I did not agree with my husband immediately because I knew tuition was very expensive and we could not afford it. But there was another reason; I also had an internal voice that kept telling me, "You are becoming a professional student because you are not good at anything else."

Reluctantly, I went with my husband to the Department of Foreign Languages at Boston College to inquire about the master's degree programs. When I heard the cost of the tuition, $7,000.00 per semester at that time, I realized that it was completely out of our reach.

My husband suggested we take a home equity loan on our house to pay for the tuition, but I absolutely refused getting ourselves into that kind of debt.

Just when I was losing hope of ever being able to continue my education, a miracle happened. The director of the foreign language department at Boston College called me to offer me a teaching fellowship. She explained to me that I would get tuition remission and a small stipend of $400.00 a month. I could not believe my luck! I was sure this offer had come from heaven! I gladly and gratefully accepted the proposal and decided to pursue a master's degree in one of my father's greatest passions, literature of course. I felt that this was my gift to him, my way of honoring him.

I started my teaching fellowship at Boston College on September 1986. During my first year, I was taking four courses in Spanish literature per semester and working twenty hours per week at the language laboratory. My main responsibilities were instructing students on the use of the language laboratory, and handing them the proper materials for their target language and level. I was also responsible for duplicating language tapes at students' requests.

It was a rather easy job, and the director of the language laboratory was a fabulous young lady, named Cindy, who was a pleasure to work with. I found the literature courses very interesting and not that difficult. I loved the subject, and I already had some knowledge of Spanish literature. Furthermore, I had amazing professors and a great deal of support from fellow graduate students.

The real test of my work capacity and endurance began during my second year at Boston College. I was asked to teach three Spanish courses, two at the beginner's level and one intermediate. In addition to teaching these three courses, I was also taking three literature courses.

After the fiasco I experienced during my first year of teaching at the Stoneham High School, I had no confidence in my ability to manage a classroom of 30-plus students. But I had never let my insecurities prevent me from taking advantage of any opportunity. When I was asked to teach three courses at Boston College, I rose to the occasion. Fortunately, I soon found out that teaching at college level was very different from teaching in a high school. I did not have to discipline anybody, which had been my biggest problem at Stoneham High School.

Because I knew how difficult and embarrassing it can be to try to speak a foreign language, I allowed my students to call me by my first name to make them feel comfortable with me while practicing the new language. I also made no secret that I had struggled with the English language for many years, and that in some ways, I was still struggling. I wanted to make sure my students knew that I understood where they were coming from. My tactic worked – it put them at ease.

I incorporated humor, drama, songs, and poetry into my classes whenever possible. I also had the policy of not interrupting the students while they were practicing the new language even if they made mistakes. Instead, I would take notes of common mistakes they made and later corrected the mistakes addressing the whole class. In this way, no one was afraid or felt self-conscious to practice the new language.

Three weeks after classes began, I decided to get some feedback from all students. I gave each student a blank piece of paper and instructed them to write their reaction to my classes and any suggestions they had on how to improve the class. I explained to the students, "Please be as honest as possible; the notes will be anonymous. That way, you can be truthful without worrying about any repercussions."

While this exercise was taking place, the students in the three classes seemed to be writing away, and the more they wrote, the more nervous I became. Without considering that students in college have the choice of dropping a class if they wish to do so for whatever reason, I told myself, "They are writing so much because probably they have many complains about my classes."

After I collected the notes from the three classes, I went to the Saint John's Seminary grounds, across the street from Boston College, to read them. But first, I had to pray and muster enough courage to read the 90-plus notes. "Please God" I prayed, "help me to accept the content of these notes whatever it is. With your help, I hope to become a better teacher."

To my bewilderment and delight, the feedback from my students was absolutely positive! Their comments were mostly related to the things they liked about my classes. And as far as suggestions, most of the students wrote, "Continue doing what you are doing," or "Do not change anything." Only a few students wrote, "Please speak a little slower when speaking in Spanish," which was an excellent suggestion, and I quickly implemented it.

One girl even admitted that she did not want to take a language class with a teacher who was a native speaker, but that my class was the only one she could fit into her schedule. She concluded the note by writing, "I cannot tell you how happy I am that things turned out the way they did. I love your class, and I want to continue taking Spanish with you."

Roughly 98 percent of my students in the three classes continued taking Spanish with me the following semester. One year later, after I started teaching at Boston College, I was nominated for a Teaching Excellence Award. I won the award, which included a $1,000.00 check. To say that I was awestruck by this surprise is an understatement! From considering myself a complete failure as a teacher, I went to winning a Teaching Excellence Award in a very short time.

Even more than the honor of the award and the monetary incentive, I was thrilled to realize that my failure at Stoneham High School was not due to my lack of teaching ability, but rather to my weakness in disciplinary skills. This awareness was great news to me since skills can always be learned and developed. I knew then what I needed to do so in order to become a more effective teacher at any level.

I was still in shock after receiving the award when my family was notified of another surprise just as amazing. Our oldest son, Francis, who was about to graduate from Saint John's Seminary with a degree in Philosophy, had been chosen to be sent to Rome to continue his studies in theology. The seminary had the policy of choosing one seminarian from every graduating class to be sent to Rome to study four years of theology. When our son was the chosen one, it was such a great and unexpected honor for my husband and me.

Before Francis left for Rome, sometime in August 1987, the seminary asked him to take an intensive course in Italian. He was also told to spend as much time as possible with family and friends because he would not be able to come home for at least two years. That sounded like an eternity to our family, especially to me, but I would never discourage my son from taking advantage of such an amazing and rare opportunity.

One week before his departure, my husband and I surprised our son with a huge going-away party held at the reception hall of an Italian restaurant. Many people came by to say goodbye to Francis and to express their good wishes. In addition to immediate family and close friends, among the many guests at the party were seminary professors and classmates, friends and teachers from his previous schools, and family members who we only saw during weddings and funerals.

Francis felt honored by the many wishes people were bestowing on him. He also felt sad about not being able to see his family and friends for two long years. No one was sadder than I because two years without seeing my son seemed like an eternity to me.

However, I soon discovered that one should not suffer as much as I did for the temporary separation of loved ones. Time will come in everyone's life when there will be a permanent separation from the ones, we hold most dear. This will cause great sorrow and there is nothing one can do to change the situation. So, if the separation is temporary; such as it was in my case when Francis went to Rome, the hope of seeing our loved one again should lessen somewhat the pain of the separation.

CHAPTER 16

I thought that saying goodbye to my son, who had the privilege of going to Rome to study, was one of the hardest things I ever had to do. Even the hope of seeing him again in two years, did not lessen my pain. Little did I know then, that in less than a year I would be saying goodbye to the love of my life forever.

My teaching fellowship at Boston College was going remarkably well; therefore, I decided to extend the program for another year. I wanted to teach Spanish for two more semesters at Boston College and also attend a summer study program in Salamanca, Spain to complete my master's degree.

When I was accepted to this program at the University of Salamanca, I was ecstatic! I had studied Spanish literature for two years, and I was finally going to visit the birthplace of many of the authors I had read so much about. I was also thrilled that I was going to have the opportunity of taking three additional literature courses with two Spanish professors who were considered giants in their field.

Upon the completion of my studies in Salamanca, my husband and I had planned to meet there; so that we could travel to the south of Spain for two weeks. We were particularly interested in going to Seville because Saint Theresa of Avila, a Spanish mystic, writer and reformer of the Carmelite order within the Catholic church during the 16th century, had made references in her writings about Seville being an enchanted place.

Sadly, three months before our planned trip to Spain, my husband died suddenly on April 18, 1988. He was barely sixty years old when he died, and I was left a widow at the age of thirty-nine. We had been married for almost 24 years. The tragic day occurred on Patriots Day, the same day as the Boston marathon.

My husband used to work nights at the Central Post Office in Boston. His shift began at 6:00 p.m., and he was going to work that day. The afternoon of April 18, my husband woke up earlier than usual. After getting ready for work, he paid some bills and then he wrote a letter to our son, Francis, who was in Rome. This was the first time since our son had been in Rome that my husband wrote a letter to him without my prompting. In hindsight, it now seems that somehow he sensed it would be his last letter to our oldest son, and he wanted to say goodbye.

During the last couple of years of his life, writing did not come easily to my husband. In addition to his being a diabetic, working nights was getting to him, and he was always very tired because of his chronic lack of sleep. I was very surprised when my husband wrote the letter to our son, and he did it in a very short time.

Frank began the letter to Francis, by thanking him for some postal cards he had sent to us from his seminary break in Greece. Then he filled him in on how the family was doing and described future plans that each member of the family had. The following is the conclusion of the letter.

> *I am okay; I think. I have to go to work now. Patriots Day is not a federal holiday for postal employees.*
>
> *Well, adios (goodbye) my son. We love you and pray for you. Carry on old chum and keep your chin up always.*
>
> *Your father who loves you very much,*
> *Frank*

My husband left for work that day at 4:00 p.m., and brought the letter with him to be mailed from his place of work. He assumed traffic would be heavy because of the Boston Marathon; so he left for work earlier than usual.

One hour and a half later, I received a telephone call from the emergency ward of the New England Medical Center in Boston, notifying me that my husband had been brought to the hospital and he was in serious condition. I was deeply distraught by the sad news, but I did not think the worst yet. I rushed to the hospital with my daughter, who happened to be the only one home at that time. I do not have any memory of driving there, but I guess traffic was not bad because we arrived at the hospital within a half hour of the call at exactly 6:00 p.m.

When we arrived at the emergency room, I was told that I could not see my husband because doctors were still treating him. I glanced at the room where he was at, and I saw at least eight doctors and nurses around him. I was still in denial about the seriousness of his condition. I figured that as long as my husband was still alive, there was hope he would survive.

After waiting for a while in the emergency room waiting area, I was told to wait with my daughter in another room, away from the emergency ward. We kept on waiting, hoping and praying for what seemed like forever. After a while, I finally lost track of time.

The next thing I remember was getting up from where I had been sitting and looking at my watch. By this time, it was exactly 10:00 p.m. I was about to leave the waiting room to find out what was going on, when I saw the whole group of doctors and nurses I had seen earlier working on my husband, coming toward my daughter and me. For an instant, I thought they were coming to tell us good news, but as they came near and I saw the look on their faces, I just knew the dreaded truth. One of the doctors announced sympathetically, "We are so sorry, Mrs. DeVito; we did everything we could to save your husband, but unfortunately, we lost him."

I was in shock and still in denial. Completely composed, I asked the doctor, "May I see my husband, please?"

"Sure," the doctor replied, "you can see your husband in about ten minutes, as soon as they finish cleaning him up."

A few minutes later, one of the doctors brought me to the room where my husband was. When I saw him for a moment, I thought he was sleeping. I touched his arms and they felt warm. But when I touched his face, the reality of his death finally struck me. At that moment, I finally grasped what had happened. The man I had loved since I was a child, my soul mate, my friend, the father of my children, was gone forever.

The pain I felt at the very core of my being at that moment was indescribable! I held onto the bed where my husband was laying down because my legs were feeling very weak, and I was afraid I was going to fall. But as I turned around, I saw a familiar face, which I was sure had been sent by God to sustain me. It was Father Roy, my spiritual director and a very dear friend of our family. But I could not figure out, "How did Father Roy know to come to the hospital at the most devastating moment of my life? How did he know we desperately needed him?" I had not called him; furthermore, he was stationed in a parish in the north of Boston, at least one hour away from the hospital.

I stayed for a while embracing my husband's lifeless body. A million things went through my mind and I was switching back and forth between denial and despair. My daughter was probably in the same room with me, but I was not aware of her presence. I vaguely remember Father Roy coming into the room and saying, "Frank is with God now, Cándida. Please let me take you home." After spending some more time in the hospital comforting us, he kindly drove us home.

I was still in shock and silent while Father Roy was driving. We were probably halfway home when I finally came out my trance. I asked Father Roy, "How did you know to come to the hospital? Who told you that we needed you there?"

With deep sadness in his voice, Father Roy explained, "I happened to call Saint Patrick's rectory (my parish) to speak to one of the priests. He told me that earlier tonight your son, Anthony, had called requesting prayers for his father because he was in serious condition at the New England Medical Center. Do not ask me why because I don't know myself. All I knew is that I had to be there."

After hearing Father Roy's version of how he had ended up in the hospital at the precise time when we needed him the most, I could no longer doubt the providence of God. He certainly sent us an angel when we were in desperate need for one. This was only the beginning of many incidents when I clearly experienced God working in my life at both joyful and painful times. The following is another one that stands out in my mind.

Our youngest son, Andrew, who at that time was sixteen years old, was out of town when his father died. He had traveled to Pennsylvania with the Baker family, Andrew's best friend and his parents because it was April school vacation week. At that time, there were no cell phones, and I had no idea where the Bakers and Andrew were staying at. I did not have an address; I only knew the name of the state.

The Bakers were very nice people and somewhat wealthy; they had taken Andrew along on other vacations many times before. Andrew had never called home during the whole time he had been away with them, and I never worried about him because I knew he was in good hands. It had never occurred to me that I may need to get in touch with my son in case of an emergency; so I never asked the Bakers for an emergency telephone number.

I felt completely devastated already with the loss of my husband, but the idea that Andrew was going to come home to find his father already buried was like a knife twisting in my heart. And I could not afford to keep my husband in a morgue for more than a week. In desperation, I called the police station in my hometown to ask if they could help me find my son. I explained the situation, but the officer who answered the telephone call replied without any sympathy, "Lady, are you crazy? Do you know how big the state of Pennsylvania is?"

With a disheartened voice I answered him, "I have no idea, officer, but thank you anyway."

My husband's wake was to take place Thursday and Friday of that week and the funeral was scheduled for Saturday morning, but Andrew was not due to return home until Tuesday of the following week. I was absolutely astonished when on Thursday morning, the first day of the wake, in the midst of a flood of telephone calls, Andrew called me. Even before I told him about his father's death, I asked him, "Honey, how did you know you needed to call home?"

Andrew answered, "I don't know; I just felt I had to call home to find out how everything was."

Then with dread and sadness I had to inform my son about his father's death. I do not remember his reaction, but I can imagine how devastating the very sad and unexpected news had been to my son. The Bakers were very understanding. They took Andrew home immediately, and they did not seem to mind having to cut their vacation short.

Having to tell Andrew that his father had died was bad enough, but for whatever reason, it was even harder breaking the sad news to my son, Francis, who was in Rome. I called Francis right after I returned home from the hospital the night his father died. It was the most difficult call that I ever had to make. My hands were sweaty; my legs felt weak and shaky. After a long pause and much hesitation, I was able to articulate the words that I knew would break my son's heart, "I am so sorry honey, but we lost Papa. He died tonight." Over the phone receiver, I heard Francis whisper, "Oh God, no... ."

The very next morning, the rector of Saint John's Seminary made all the arrangements for Francis to come home. I had missed him so much since he went to Rome. I was very happy to have him come home in spite of the awfully sad reason for his trip. I felt that my husband was giving me a gift beyond the grave, the joy of seeing our son again.

My husband was such a wonderful father to our four children. But because I was so busy with Francis being a colicky baby, he especially bonded with Anthony, our second son. A few days after his father died, Anthony made a comment that hurt my feelings, but I could understand where it was coming from. Anthony is the more religious of our four children and honest to a fault. Stricken by grief and in the presence of Andrew, his younger brother, Anthony told me, "I didn't want any of my parents to die, but if one had to die, I wish it had been you and not Papa."

Even though I was deeply hurt, and I could understand why Anthony felt that way. I did not know what to say, but Andrew jumped to my defense and responded, "Don't be an idiot! If mommy had died, how long you do you think Papa would last? They both would be dead, and we would have no one."

The whole experience of having one's whole life change in a single moment is devastating for a spouse, but it is perhaps even harder for children. Anthony probably needed my support more than the rest of my children, but I was too absorbed in my own pain to notice. However, I did not blame him for feeling the way he did about his father's death.

It is hard to believe that such a painful experience can also have a silver lining, but it does. This was a time of great spiritual and emotional growth for me. I learned that when God gives us a cross, He also provides the strength to carry it. I learned that I was much stronger emotionally and spiritually than I had given myself credit for. I was able to stand on my own two feet without falling apart, and I had plenty of support to rely on when needed.

My family and I received an overwhelming outpouring of love, kindness, and support from relatives, friends, neighbors, and even strangers as never before. The following examples are to name only a few:

I was too confused to deal with my husband's funeral arrangements by myself, and the pastor of our church, Father Mark, came to help me without asking. I did not have to cook anything for weeks because the wonderful ladies of our parish took turns bringing us delicious hot meals every night. I needed financial assistance because the cost of the funeral was more than we had in our savings, and through the generosity of my husband's co-workers, that need was met. The postal office employees had come together and made a very generous donation toward his funeral expenses.

I desperately wanted to know, "What happened to my husband before he was brought to the hospital, and who was the good Samaritan who helped him in his time of need?" Neither the hospital nor anyone else could provide me with that information. But during the second day of my husband's wake, the good Samaritan came forward and gave me a detailed account of the incident. I learned that my husband had arrived at his place of work; but then had collapsed in the parking lot. "Thank God that he was able to make it that far and didn't collapse while he was driving," was my first thought. I also felt immensely grateful for having the opportunity of thanking the good Samaritan in person.

Initially I was not sure what had caused my husband's sudden death, but the autopsy results later determined that it had been triggered by cardiac arrest. He had been under a doctor's care for diabetes for many years, but any coronary artery disease was never detected. I had a hope that my husband would have a long life, the same as his mother, but unfortunately, he died from the same illness as his father did and exactly at the same age.

During the two days of my husband's wake, the line of people who came to pay their respects extended all the way from the funeral home to the sidewalk and the line never stopped. I was deeply touched that most of my students from Boston College and some of the faculty members were among the people who came to offer their support. I will never forget that one of the students brought me a sympathy card with one of the most comforting messages that I received. It was written in her own handwriting, "Please remember that the separation with your beloved husband is only temporary. He would want you to be happy and to continue lighting up the world with your smile."

I could not believe the incredible amount of sympathy and support we were receiving! At my husband's funeral mass, there were more priests and seminarians at the altar than I had ever seen at one time. Some of them were Francis' friends, but most of them were Franciscan priests who had come from several states (Father Kevin was among them), also some of the young men my husband had helped to educate, and a nun he had sent to the convent also came to his wake and funeral all the way from Honduras.

The number of cards and letters of condolences I received from people from both countries, the United States and Honduras, almost equaled the same amount of hate mail we had received 23 years earlier when we got married. I could not believe that such a quiet and down-to-earth individual had touched so many lives. I had so many people to thank for different reasons, that I spent months writing appreciation cards, and I am sure that I was not able to thank everyone.

Through these cards and letters, I saw another dimension of my husband's loving kindness and the courage he was able to hide so well. The following is an excerpt of a letter I received about a month after his death.

... You cannot imagine how deeply sorry I feel for the loss of your beloved husband. I am here today because Father Andrew saved my life.

I don't know if I ever told you that my husband likes his drinks too much. It turned out that one day I scolded him because he was drunk. A wave of fury rushed to his head. He grabbed his gun and I swear he was going to shoot me. He placed the gun right at my temple and he was ready to pull the trigger. Blessed be God that Father Andrew was in a house nearby and I sent one of my daughters to get him.

Poor Father Andrew! He came rushing to my house with the speed of lightning. My husband still had the gun at my temple, and he was threatening to kill me. As soon as Father Andrew arrived, he commanded my husband, "Put that gun down, Samuel! You can't do that to the mother of your children. For the love of God and your family, don't make a mistake that you will regret for the rest of your life."

At first, Samuel ignored him, but Father Andrew continued to lecture him until Samuel acknowledged him. Father Andrew got close to him, gently wrapped his arm around my husband's shoulders, and with authority in his voice he told my husband in a loud whisper, "For God's sake Samuel! Give me that gun before you do something stupid!"

Not only did my husband give the gun to Father Andrew, but he also began to cry and apologized to me on his knees. Even though Samuel struggled to control his drinking, he never threatened me again after that day.

I believe that had it not been for Father Andrew, I wouldn't be writing to you today. You have lost a loving husband and the father of your children, but our world has lost a great man. We are accompanying you in your sorrow ....

The sender was Doña María Cristina, a very pious lady from my country. I have known her since my childhood, and I have great affection and respect for her. We had communicated several times over the years, but I had not been aware of the incident she disclosed in her letter.

There were also other letters I received stating my husband's great deeds. I did not think that it was possible for my love, respect and admiration for him to increase. But after his death I found out that Frank was even more amazing than I had thought, and I felt truly blessed for the privilege of being his wife.

Even though nothing could or would ever be the same after losing my husband, life had to go on. One week after his funeral, Francis went back to Rome, and I had to return to work. Since the ending of the spring semester at Boston College was approaching, it was a very busy time of the year, which was probably a blessing in disguise.

On my first day back to Boston College, after losing my husband, I found a lovely surprise waiting for me in my office. It was a beautiful floral arrangement with a heartfelt condolence card. The sender of such a thoughtful gesture was Professor Shay, one of the professors of the foreign languages department.

After expressing his deepest sympathy for my loss, Professor Shay was letting me know of a memorial mass he had arranged for my husband to be celebrated at the chapel of Boston College. He specified the date and time of the mass, and added, "Please invite your family and any friends to the mass; a luncheon will immediately follow after the mass."

Three of my children were able to attend the mass because Francis had already returned to Rome. However, the chapel was almost filled with students and faculty members from the college. Some seminarians from Saint John's Seminary, classmates of Francis, had also attended the mass.

Professor Shay kindly extended the lunch invitation to everyone present at the mass, but only my children and I could attend because everyone else had other plans. I imagine that since it was such a small group for lunch, Professor Shay decided to give us a very special treat. He chose to take us to a very elegant Mexican restaurant called, Las Brisas, which was located next to the New England Aquarium in Boston.

It was a beautiful May afternoon; spring flowers were in full bloom. After a delicious lunch, Professor Shay and I took a walk along the waterfront while my children went to the Aquarium. We talked about different topics, but mostly about my impending trip to Spain. I was debating whether to still make the trip or cancel it under the present circumstances. Then Professor Shay helped me make up my mind. "You have to go to Salamanca! Your husband would not want you to miss such a great opportunity," he said convincingly, and I agreed with him.

I thanked Professor Shay profusely for his words of wisdom, kindness, and support. Then taking both of my hands into his and looking me straight in the eyes, he asked me, "Is there anything else I can do for you?"

I replied, "No, thank you Professor Shay, you have done so much already."

Giving my hands a hard squeeze, he said without thinking, "Oh no! I have not done enough for you, considering how I feel about you."

I was puzzled by that statement, and I felt somewhat uncomfortable, but I did not say anything or asked Professor Shay what he meant. In order to change the subject, I told him, "I think my children have had enough of the Aquarium. Shall we go find them?"

He replied, "Of course!"

My children and I thanked Professor Shay profusely for his many kindnesses; then we said our goodbyes and went our separate ways.

The next day, which was Saturday, I was taking a walk around a lake near my house, and a mental tape of what had occurred in my life in the previous weeks kept on playing in my mind. As an attempt to distract myself from the pain I was feeling, I changed focus to my conversation with Professor Shay at the waterfront, but I still could not understand what he meant when he said, "Oh no! I have not done enough for you, considering how I feel about you."

However, I did not have to wait too long to find out. The following week I received more flowers from Professor Shay and a letter explaining his remark.

CHAPTER 17

*I*t has been said, "You can take the person out of the country, but you can never take the country out of the person." The same principle can be applied to one's culture. That was definitely true in my case as far as my concept of widowhood was concerned.

I remember that while I was growing up in Honduras, when a woman lost her husband and became a widow, even if she was still young, her fate was to continue caring for her children, dress in black and mourn her husband for the rest of her life. Even though I had lived in the United States for almost a quarter of a century, when I lost my husband I was sure that my fate would be the same as the widows I remembered from my country.

I even believed the message in one of my favorite songs, "Solamente una Vez," which means "Only Once." The theme of the song is that one truly loves only once in a lifetime. I believed that since I already had my time to love and to be loved, I could not hope for another turn. I was sure that I had reached the finish line as far as love and romance were concerned.

To my surprise, and much sooner than expected, I found out that my concept of widowhood was incorrect, at least in the United States. Professor Shay was the first person who helped me to become aware of the reality of second chances. One week after he had made that vague remark about his feelings for me, I found more flowers in my office from him and also a letter revealing his feelings. The following is the introduction to a two-page letter.

May 13, 1988

My dearest Cándida,

In spite of all the exams that I still have to grade, I feel the need to write to you these lines, maybe not as coherently as I would have liked. But I have to share with you about my feelings; feelings which I can no longer deny no matter how hard I have tried.

First of all, I want you to know that to have been with your wonderful children the other day and seen the legacy of your marriage to your dear Frank, was a great inspiration to me.

Now I have to confess that when I went to your husband's wake in Stoneham, my heart went out to you and became overflowed with tenderness for you. I would have loved to take you in my arms to comfort you as a father would have if his small child fell down and got hurt. But then I could see that it was your faith in God and the love of your family and of so many friends, which were sustaining you.

During the following days when you returned to Boston College, I came to depend on seeing you on a daily basis. I finally had to admit to myself that I had fallen in love with you like a crazy fool. Anyone who knows you cannot fault me for that. When kindness is combined with beauty, it makes an irresistible combination ... .

I read Professor Shay's letter over and over again. My first reaction to the letter was one of surprise and disbelief! I could not understand how someone could have fallen in love during a wake.

I felt apprehensive about the situation, and at the same time, I felt flattered. The literary quality of the letter, in my estimation at that moment, was the same as in famous romantic novels. I was especially flattered at being the inspiration of such a beautiful piece of literature.

I deeply admired Professor Shay as a scholar and for the fabric of his being. I had taken three literature courses with him, and I had found him to be an outstanding instructor, passionate about any subject matter he was teaching, and very fair and supportive of all of his students.

It was probably because he was so caring and compassionate that Professor Shay was assigned as academic advisor to the most needy and difficult students. One day he confided to me, "When you began your master's degree program, I was assigned to be your academic advisor, but later on the chairperson of the Foreign Language Department assigned himself as your advisor because you were an easy assignment."

I was immensely grateful to Professor Shay for the academic and emotional support he had given me. I was also grateful to him for helping me come alive again and to become aware that my concept of widowhood was not entirely correct. Regrettably, I did not have any romantic feelings toward him.

I tried to explain that to him in the following letter with the hope of causing him the least amount of pain as possible:

May 18, 1988

Dear Prof. Shay,

I wish to thank you from the bottom of my heart for the beautiful floral arrangement and for your lovely letter.

I have to admit that the content of your letter, your confession as you put it, was very surprising to me. But I am deeply grateful that you decided to share your feelings. I feel not only flattered, but honored to be loved by someone as special as you.

I see in you the best qualities of the two men that I have loved the most in the entire world, my late husband

and my father. Your physical features, your passion for Spanish literature and your gift with words remind me of my father. And your spirit, the kind and caring person you are, remind me of my husband.

But as you can probably understand, I am not ready to love again, and at this stage in my life, I am not sure if I ever will. All I can offer you is what you already have: my unconditional friendship, my eternal gratitude, and my deepest respect and admiration.

Thanks again for the memorial mass for my husband and for the delicious lunch at Las Brisas.

God bless you for being so thoughtful and kind.

With love and gratitude,
Cándida

I placed the letter in Professor Shay's mailbox at the college. I was not sure of his reaction because I did not hear from him for a while. We both had our offices in the same department, but I tried to avoid seeing him because I felt uncomfortable.

On the last day of the spring semester, I wanted to personally wish Professor Shay a great summer, but mostly use that as an excuse to get feedback about my letter. I stopped by his office sometime in the afternoon; he seemed very busy doing paperwork, and I hesitated to disturb him. I was about to leave the threshold of his office, when he looked up and saw me. "Come in," he said excitedly, "I am so happy to see you!"

I answered, "Likewise, Professor Shay."

Then he asked me, "Do you think you could call me Bob?"

Feeling somewhat awkward, I replied, "Okay, Bob!"

He smiled, expressing with his nice blue eyes how pleased he was.

"Could you get away from your paperwork and go for a walk?" I asked next.

"Of course," he said eagerly, "you know that I would do anything for you, Mayan Princess."

"What did you call me?" I inquired curiously.

"Mayan Princess," he replied.

"How did you come up with that name?" I questioned him.

He smiled and said, "Well, aren't you part Mayan? And I think of you as a princess."

Since that day, Professor Shay has always referred to me as a Mayan Princess. I admitted to him, "I really like the nickname you gave me, although I have always felt more like a servant than a princess."

We went for a walk that afternoon around the college campus. It was a gorgeous sunny afternoon! The pink, white, and purple azaleas at the college campus were in full bloom, and I commented, "What beautiful flowers!"

Professor Shay looked at me, and half smiling, he graciously replied, "Not as beautiful as you!"

I had forgotten when the last time was that someone had made me feel beautiful, and not knowing what to say, I asked a silly question, "Bob, are you sure you are not Latino?"

"Why do you ask?" He wanted to know.

"You certainly know how to flatter a woman and make her feel beautiful," I explained.

After making small talk, I finally mustered enough courage to ask Professor Shay, "Did you read my letter?"

"Many times," he answered.

"I hope I didn't hurt your feelings," I said, expressing concern.

"You couldn't hurt anyone's feelings, even if you tried," he responded and went on to explain, "I understand that my confession of love didn't come at the right time or the right place. I am trying very hard to channel my feelings for you in other areas."

I did not quite understand what Professor Shay was trying to tell me with this last comment. But I felt awkward asking him for an explanation. I was just relieved that he understood my situation and he was not upset at me.

After talking about such a delicate subject, we were both silent for a while. Then Professor Shay broke the silence by sharing a part of his past, "You know, it's so ironic, since my wife passed away six years ago, some of her friends have tried very hard to get me interested in them, but no one has been able to touch my heart the way you do. I guess I can now understand how it feels to love someone with no hope of ever being loved in return."

"So you have all of these admirers!" I replied trying to add a little humor to the conversation. Then I asked Professor Shay, "Do you have any children?"

With sadness in his voice, he answered, "No, my wife and I couldn't have any children. It has been one of the greatest disappointments of my life not being able to be a father."

Giving him a sympathetic look, and with sadness in my voice I responded, "I am so sorry! You would have made a wonderful father."

As if trying to hide his own deep sadness, Professor Shay said trying to smile, "I am a father; I think of my students as my children."

I smiled back and reassured him, "You're absolutely right. You are like a father to your students. And your students are very lucky to have you." Then I added, "I know that I feel very lucky for having had the opportunity of taking three courses with you."

Professor Shay started to say something, but quickly retracted what he was about to say. He was silent for a while; so I asked him, "Why are you so quiet? What are you thinking?"

Reluctantly, he told me, "I was just thinking that in your case, I don't want you to see me as a father, but rather as the man in your life."

Before I could think what to respond to that comment, Professor Shay continued, "You don't have to say anything. I was just thinking aloud, but I promise not to talk about my feelings again." Quickly he changed the subject to my impending trip to Spain, and I was relieved.

When we said our goodbyes that afternoon, I gave Professor Shay a big hug, just as I would hug a very dear friend. And I went home confident that I would never hear about his romantic feelings again. As far as I was concerned, the issue had been put to rest.

While I was driving home that afternoon, I was remembering my conversation with Professor Shay. My heart went out to him and his departed wife. They would have made wonderful parents, but they had been deprived of the joy of parenthood. Professor Shay referred to his wife as "a wonderful woman." Both of them had so much love to give, which made their situation even sadder.

I had two and a half weeks left between the end of the spring semester and my trip to Spain. Even though I had much to do, staying at home intensified my sadness. I kept on remembering how my husband and I had so many plans we would undertake when he retired. But other than the trip to Honduras, we never went anywhere. We had planned to go to Rome to see our son and to Mexico, the birthplace of the mariachis (our favorite type of music). We also had plans to take a trip to Portugal to see some of the girls he had sent to a convent, who were now full-fledged nuns working as missionaries.

When I thought about how death had crushed all of our plans and dreams, I made up my mind not to live in the future any longer. My husband and I kept on postponing our plans for a future that never came. So even though my trip to Spain was fast approaching, when I found out that my mother was in Mexico City visiting her grandson and ex-daughter-in-law, I immediately decided to take a one-week trip to Mexico before going to Spain.

Traveling to Mexico had been a fantasy of mine since I was a young girl. I had read so much about the miracles and apparitions of Our Lady of Guadalupe to a humble Indian, named Juan Diego. I had dreamed about visiting the Basilica of our Lady of Guadalupe, taking a boat tour in the floating gardens and listening to live mariachis. These were only a few of my main attractions for wanting to visit Mexico. I was about to fulfill one of my greatest desires and I felt ecstatic with the anticipation!

My trip to Mexico City turned out to be even more amazing than I had expected. In addition to being very happy to see my mother and other relatives, I loved the city and its people. I found the Mexican people to be extremely friendly, hospitable and kind. I remember going to a restaurant and not being sure of what food to order. Then the waiter graciously brought me an assortment of samples to try so that I could make up my mind.

My ex-sister-in-law, Lissette, introduced me to some of her neighbors, and they welcomed me into their homes as if I were a long-lost friend. One of her neighbors, named Manuel, happened to be a quadriplegic and a very gifted artist. I admired his work, and I bought a couple of paintings from him. But even more than his art, I admired Manuel's courage and spirit. In spite of being confined to a wheelchair, he had a full life. Besides cultivating his artistic talent, Manuel had a full-time job as a professor at a local university; he drove a car, was married to a lovely woman and they had three healthy children.

Manuel kindly offered to take me sightseeing, and I accepted his gracious invitation. He picked me up in his shiny red car one Saturday afternoon. I was surprised to see him alone; so I asked him, "Isn't your wife coming with us?" He replied, "Oh no, she is busy this afternoon; she has taken the children to a party."

Manuel was eager to please me and asked, "Where would you like to go?" The first place I wanted to visit was the Basilica of our Lady of Guadalupe, of course. After being in awe at the image of our Lady of Guadalupe and the magnificent basilica, I said my prayers. Then I told Manuel, "You are fully in charge of the rest of the tour; please surprise me."

As if Manuel read my mind, he brought me to Plaza Garibaldi, the home of the mariachi music and a heaven for mariachi lovers like myself. First, we went inside the plaza to sample all kinds of traditional foods. Then, we went outside the plaza to listen to mariachis. There were so many bands of mariachis congregated in one place. I was in my glory listening to all of the different bands. Each band was charging more or less the same price, ten dollars per song.

I had a hard time choosing a mariachi band to request my favorite song. I finally decided on a trio composed of two young men and a lovely young lady. When they sang my song, "Solamente una Vez," I could not stop the flow of tears that came to my eyes. I took some tissues out of my purse, dried my tears, and explained somewhat embarrassed to Manuel, "Do not mind me; I am a sentimental fool as they say."

As an attempt to lighten the moment, Manuel responded, "Sensitivity is one of the many traits I adore in women."

His charming comment made me smile. Then Manuel proceeded to take some pictures of me with the band. One of the players took off his beautiful *sombrero* (hat) and placed it on my head for the pictures. I thought that was really sweet! That kind gesture from one of the musicians certainly warmed up my heart.

As a grand finale to a lovely afternoon, Manuel took me to the famous floating gardens. I had been fine until then, at least most of the time. I had been distracted from my grief for a few hours. But while we were in the floating gardens, a wave of sadness and nostalgia came over me, and I lost my composure.

I did not want Manuel to see me so vulnerable; so I got up from where I was sitting with the excuse of wanting to take more pictures. I was wishing with all of my heart that my husband could be there with me to see the floating gardens. I would have given anything to have one more moment with him. I was sure that nothing could have made me feel better at that instant when a comforting thought came to my mind. I told myself, "Don't be so sad; heaven is surely more beautiful than these floating gardens, and my husband must be there." I have no idea where that thought came from, but it was certainly comforting and even made me smile.

I could not have asked for a better tour guide than Manuel; he had been extremely smooth and very charming the entire time we had spent together. Besides sightseeing, we ate, laughed, listened to beautiful music and also danced in Plaza Garibaldi. I would follow the rhythm of the music with my feet and Manuel with his wheelchair back and forth. After a fabulous and unforgettable afternoon, he drove me back to my ex sister-in-law's house.

The next day, I saw Manuel's wife, and after exchanging warm greetings, I asked her, "How was the party yesterday?"

She answered, "I didn't go to any party."

Then I said, "I am sorry, I probably misunderstood." Later in the conversation, after inquiring about her children, I also asked, "How is Manuel doing?"

And she quickly replied, "Manuel is resting today; he had a very busy afternoon at work yesterday."

It became quite obvious then that Manuel did not tell his wife the truth about taking me sightseeing. If I had known that he was doing something behind his wife's back, I would have felt very uncomfortable. After talking to her I realized that even when confined to a wheelchair, it cannot take away the tendency to be deceitful in some Latin American men.

Another vivid and very pleasant memory I have of my trip to Mexico is how I was carried away with the Mayan princess nickname Professor Shay had given me. Just before the trip, I had done a little research about the life of a Mayan princess and I came across a sample of the kind of dresses Mayan princesses used to wear. While I was at the marketplace in Mexico City, I saw a similar type of dress. It was a one-piece, ivory-colored long dress with hand-embroidered flowers of different colors. It came with an orange color belt that matched some of the flowers on the dress. I fell in love with the dress and I purchased it. I did not have much money, but to my delight, it was also inexpensive. When I bought the dress, I did not have an occasion in mind of when to wear it. However, after my trip to Spain, the occasion presented itself.

One unexpected turn of events happened during my trip to Mexico. I found out that my mother had amnesia as far as abusing me when I was growing up. On more than one occasion when someone complimented her on having such a nice daughter, my mother would reply, "Oh yes! Cándida has always been wonderful ever since she was a little girl. I never had to punish her because she was so good."

After hearing that comment from my mother several times, I confronted her. It was not easy because I was afraid of her reaction, and in those days I would revert to a frightened little girl in her presence.

But I mustered the courage of asking her, "You really don't remember punishing me?"

Looking at me directly into my eyes, she answered, "I didn't have to punish you because you were always such a good girl."

I did not say anything to my mother about her denial, but I thought, "I have an entire village as witnesses to the abuse you inflicted on me when I was a child, and now you don't remember that?" I have no idea of whether she really had selective memory or if she was just pretending. Later on, I did some research and I found out that it is possible for someone to block a very painful memory from their mind.

I decided then to give my mother the benefit of the doubt and not to mention the incident again. For my own mental and spiritual health, I had to forgive her and throughout the years we have developed a loving relationship. However, one can forgive but not forget. Nevertheless, every once in a while the thought goes through my mind that I wish my childhood had been different. But then I remember how blessed I was for having had such a wonderful father. I also find comfort on the fact that my painful childhood experience probably made me a more sensitive and caring person.

Besides that sad incident with my mother, I returned home from my trip to Mexico with beautiful memories and with the satisfaction of knowing that I was finally learning how to live in the present and not in the past or the future. I also became aware that I would miss my husband immensely for the rest of my life, but I no longer felt like a victim of life for making me a young widow.

Rather than focusing on the pain of losing my husband, I had begun to feel grateful for the blessing of having been married to such an extraordinary man for nearly a quarter of a century. Yes, my trip to Mexico had definitely been rewarding and even therapeutic. Besides fulfilling one of my dreams as a young girl, it started my emotional healing.

When I returned home, I found more sympathy cards and letters. Three months after my husband died, expressions of condolences were still coming. Some of the letters were from well-meaning people in

Honduras that being true to their culture, expressed more pity than sympathy. For example, some people wrote: "You poor thing! Now you are all alone on this planet. Your poor children! Now they have no father. Father Andrew was such a wonderful man! You will probably spend the rest of your life mourning him. What a tragic end to an incredible love story! You were so lucky, and now you are so unfortunate. We are praying for Father Andrew's soul. We hope he doesn't stay too long in purgatory."

I know that each one of the people who wrote this type of message meant well, and I thanked them for their expressions of sympathy. But I was glad that I had gone to Mexico to see my mother and not to Honduras. If I heard comments, such as the ones just described, before my healing began, chances are that I would have been very receptive to believe that I had been doomed by destiny.

My trip to Spain was fast approaching and I was busy getting ready, when suddenly out of nowhere I would be reminded that my husband would not be joining me as we had planned, and feelings of grief and regret would overwhelm me again. I had to accept the fact that healing from grief is a process and not something that happens all at once.

A dear friend of mine had written on a sympathy card, "Time will come when thoughts of your husband will bring a smile to your face instead of a tear." When I received that message, I did not believe that one day I would be able to remember my husband with joy rather than pain. But fortunately, time does have a way of healing even very deep wounds. However, one needs to go through the painful healing process for however long it takes to overcome the pain.

CHAPTER 18

The day before I left for Spain, sometime during the first week of June of 1988, I received an unexpected surprise from Professor Shay, another letter. After explaining his resolve not to write again and his need to do so, he wrote:

> *This past weekend I had started to prepare the background for the new course on Hispanic American Drama. As I was taking notes of the Mayans and the glories of that civilization, your face kept constantly appearing in my mind.*
>
> *I was seeing you as an exotic flower, a Mayan Princess from that past culture. The author of the book I was reading was speaking about astronomy and philosophical speculations of the Mayans, but I was thinking that in you we could find the merging of the best of the Christian civilization and the old traditions of the Mayans, in your beauty and spirituality.*
>
> *You are still here, and I miss you already. I want you to know that since falling in love with you, I feel like a "high school boy," rather than the middle age man that I am. I guess you must realize by now that you are an exceptional woman and have the capability of attracting a man of any age.*

I will be thinking of you while you are in Spain and anxiously waiting for your return. Please be sure that my love, thoughts and prayers will go with you.

With all my love,
Bob

I was very surprised to receive another letter from Professor Shay. Again, I was impressed with his gift for words and I was flattered by his compliments. I also felt bad for him because he was acting like a schoolboy as he had stated in his letter, and I knew he would soon be feeling hurt and disappointed. But I was too busy getting ready for my trip to Spain, and I did not pay much attention to the letter.

I left for Spain with a colleague of mine from Boston College, named Michael. We were around the same age and became great study buddies. After a long flight from Boston, we arrived at the *Madrid* airport. We met my son, Francis, and a classmate of his in a hotel in Madrid, and the following day the four of us traveled to Salamanca together.

It is hard to believe, but Francis and I ended up participating in the same summer program in Salamanca by pure coincidence. Having the advantage of being in Rome, Francis was given the opportunity of studying during the summer in any country in Europe, and he chose Spain because he wanted to improve his Spanish language skills.

Francis was aware that I was going to Spain to complete my master's degree program in Spanish literature, but he did not know the specific details. We were both very surprised when we found out we had signed up for the same program in Salamanca and also during the same timeframe. The only difference was that he would be studying Spanish and I would be taking literature courses.

We had the choice of staying with a family or in a dormitory in Salamanca. Francis had chosen to stay with a family, since he wanted to improve his Spanish. I decided to stay in *Residencia Covadonga*, alone, in a single room, because I did not want my grief over the loss of my beloved husband to affect anyone else.

This dormitory was located next to the beautiful Old Cathedral. I often went there to pray while my fellow graduate students went to the plaza or someplace else to enjoy the exciting nightlife of Salamanca. I was invited many times to join the group, but I always declined. In addition to not being in a celebratory mood, I did not have money to spend in cantinas or nightclubs.

The *Residencia Covadonga* had the capacity of accommodating several hundred students. The University of Salamanca is very famous, and students from all over the world go there to study. During mealtimes, one could hear a different language being spoken at almost every table. The dining room was enormous, and at least twenty different languages were being spoken at the same time.

I felt somewhat out of place in the dorm because most of the students were much younger than I was. However, after a while, I noticed there were a few ladies closer to my age. I gravitated toward them because I was lonely. Fortunately for me, these ladies were warm and friendly; and a few of us continued to be friends even after the program was over.

In addition to completing my Boston College Master's degree program, several life changing experiences happened to me during this trip to Salamanca. I met Carol Ann, a Spanish teacher from Rhode Island, who has become one of my dearest and most treasured friends. I met her through my son, Francis. He had come to the dorm to see me. We were in the dining room and he noticed that this beautiful, petite young woman was crying. He felt so bad for her and told me, "Please go and console that young lady; she has been crying for a while."

I went to introduce myself to Carol Ann, and I found her to be nice and friendly. I asked her, "Is everything okay?"

She replied, "Yes, I am just missing my Gina."

I assumed that Gina was her daughter, and I said sympathetically, "I can understand how you feel; I am missing my children too."

Then Carol Ann corrected me. "Gina is not my child. She's my dog."

Well, thanks to Gina, I came to know dog love.

In addition to teaching Spanish, Carol Ann's mission in life is to rescue dogs. Her love for dogs is contagious. When I met her, I did not dislike dogs, but I was not a dog lover either. Years later, inspired by her example, I rescued a precious Chihuahua named Rudy, who still lives with me.

I do not remember the names of everyone in that group I became friendly with while in Salamanca, but I will never forget Shawn because she was the life of every party. She brought joy and laughter wherever she went, but I mostly remember her for her kindness. Besides being tall, beautiful and very elegant, she had a heart of gold, an unbelievable charisma and a delightful sense of humor.

Shawn noticed how sad and withdrawn I was, and she lovingly took it upon herself to get me out of my cocoon. It was toward the end of the program and I was still buried in my shell. Without asking me first, she set up a blind date for me with someone she had met in one of her Spanish classes. His name was Leonardo Avila.

When she first told me about the blind date, I quickly declined. I firmly told Shawn, "No way José! I am 39 years old and I never had a date in my entire life. I am not going to start with a blind date now. Thanks, but no thanks,"

She would not take "NO" for an answer. She was persistent! Besides having a sense of humor that could make a dead person laugh, Shawn certainly had the power of persuasion.

She kept on telling me over and over again, "Your blind date is so charming. I am sure he will melt the ice around your heart and get you out your cocoon. You don't have to do anything. I will do your hair, your makeup, and you will get to wear, even keep if you want, one of my dresses."

We were of the same size and height, and Shawn certainly had an unbelievable wardrobe of fancy dresses to choose from. It was not done consciously on my part, but I probably figured, "This is my only chance of getting to wear such a beautiful and expensive dress." I finally agreed to go on the blind date, and Shawn was ecstatic!

My blind date with Prince Charming was scheduled for a Saturday evening. Shawn reserved a table for us in the garden section of a fancy restaurant in the plaza, within walking distance from the dorm. She also made arrangements with the restaurant ahead of time to pay for dinner. She told me several times before going to the restaurant, "This is your evening! Please spare no expenses. Order anything you want and all the drinks you want." And as I was leaving the dorm, Shawn added, "I hope you get drunk; I bet you never been drunk in your life. Let your hair down for once and have a grand time!"

The big event was supposed to take place at 5:00 p.m. that evening. At 2:00 p.m., Shawn had already started getting the princess ready for her ball. She probably knew that she had a lot of work ahead of her.

From her very extensive wardrobe, I chose a light blue dress with a wide silver belt and matching shoes to wear for the occasion. Both the dress and the shoes fit me perfectly. For a little while, I almost felt like Cinderella. Shawn washed and styled my long black hair by putting it up, which gave me an elegant look. She also spent a considerable amount of time applying my makeup.

Everyone was telling me how beautiful I looked, and I believed them. But when I saw my reflection in the mirror, I was horrified! I did not recognize myself with all of that makeup. Rather than feeling like a beautiful woman, I felt more like a clown ready to perform. I guess that going from wearing no makeup to suddenly being all made up, had a surprising and very uncomfortable effect on me.

Meeting my blind date was the biggest surprise of all. He had all the attributes that Shawn had described; however, he was a classmate of my son from Saint John's Seminary, and I already knew him. He came originally from Portugal; he was very charming and spoke several languages fluently. Leonardo was at least ten years older than his fellow seminarians. He began to pursue a religious vocation when he was about 30 years old. Four years later, he decided that priesthood was not for him. Before going to the Summer program in Spain, he had already made up his mind to leave the seminary.

Poor Leonardo! He was probably more disappointed than I was with the blind date. At 35 years of age, he was probably looking forward to meeting a young woman, a potential girlfriend, and he met a 39-year-old widow instead. From the time Shawn arranged the blind date, he never stop asking questions about the incredible woman he was going to meet. He never imagined, even in his wildest dreams, that he would have a blind date with the mother of one of his friends.

Leonardo graciously handled the whole incident as a true gentleman; he concealed his disappointment well. We ended up going out that evening and had a fabulous time! We ordered paella for dinner, flan for dessert and a big pitcher of *sangría*. Shawn not only reserved a table in the garden section of the restaurant, she reserved the entire section to give us more privacy. That made us laugh even harder! Here we were in this incredibly romantic setting: fabulous candlelight dinner, exotic drinks, soft music, beautiful flowers, but there were not even sparks of chemistry between the dating couple. We could not believe that with all of the thousands upon thousands of people in Salamanca from all over the world, we ended up being each other's blind date.

My perception of that blind date has changed throughout the years. At the time when it took place, I considered the blind date a total fiasco, even though I had a grand time. Now I think of it as a fond and funny memory. But most of all, it reminds me how kind and thoughtful Shawn had been. While I was going through my dark night of the soul, she tried very hard to bring me back to the land of the living.

There was also another time when Shawn went to great lengths to cheer me up. I met an Italian man during one of my trips to the cathedral, and he invited me to go out for a cup of coffee. I declined, of course, because I did not trust strangers. When I went back to the dorm, I made the mistake of telling Shawn about the incident, and she insisted, "You have to go! I can help you get ready!"

I replied again, "No way José!" Then added, "He could be a crook."

She laughed so hard and then told me, "Please do not take offense, but anybody can see from a mile away that you aren't wealthy. I am going to tell you something; you have a big problem trusting men, but if the devil came disguised as a priest, I bet you would go with him in a heartbeat."

I had to admit she had a point there. Throughout the years, I have pondered about Shawn's comment that I would trust the devil if he were disguised as a priest. "What is it about priests that inspire such trust and attraction in me?" I have asked myself that question many times. I concluded that I trust priests because supposedly they have high moral values and they are more likely to be faithful. But most importantly, I warm up to them because the first person that made me feel really special was a priest, and he had never disappointed me.

After much resistance on my part, Shawn finally convinced me to accept the coffee invitation with the good looking stranger when she volunteered to be a chaperone from afar. I could not believe she was willing to do that for me, but she did. Besides cheering me up and increasing my low self-esteem, the caring that I received from Shawn started my metamorphosis. I am deeply grateful to her. Thanks to her loving kindness, generosity and persistence, my life was changed for the better.

I have a repertoire of mixed memories of that trip to Salamanca, which includes a twist of faith in the life of my son, Francis, the potential priest. He met Rachel, a beautiful young lady from Massachusetts, and they ended up falling madly in love. Besides her delightful personality, she was tall, slim, with long black hair and green eyes. When Rachel started pursuing Francis, she did not know that he was a seminarian. It was love at first sight for Francis as well. Soon after meeting her, he lost his head along with his dream of a religious vocation.

While we were in Salamanca, I only saw Francis every once in a while. I tried to keep my distance; I did not want to give him the impression that I was trying to be his chaperone. I had no idea he was having serious doubts about his calling to the priesthood. I was very surprised when Francis came to the dorm one evening to tell me the news. He was considering leaving the seminary at once, which meant that he also had to stop his studies in Rome right then and there.

I gave him a perplexed look and asked my son, "Do you think that you might be making this decision too hastily?" Then he reassured me that he knew what he was doing. I explained to him how feelings can change and that a decision that important should be made after much thought and reflection. I could not change his mind; so I proposed him a deal, "Please go back to Rome for one year. If after that time you still want to leave the seminary, you will have my unconditional support." Reluctantly, Francis agreed to go back to the North American College in Rome for another year.

When the program in Salamanca ended, Francis, Rachel, another friend and I traveled to the south of Spain for two glorious weeks. We traveled by train and explored the beauty and attractions of Seville and *Granada*. We spent the last four days of our trip in *Málaga*, mainly enjoying the beautiful *Malagueta* beach. We also visited some of the top-rated tourist attractions to include the Picasso museum and the *Alcazaba*, a palace built by the Hammudid dynasty in the early 11th century. It is the best-preserved alcazaba in Spain. Following exploring Málaga, the four of us returned to Madrid so we could depart to our respective destinations.

After spending a blissful vacation with Rachel, Francis went back to Rome completely heartbroken. I felt bad for him, but I knew it in my heart that it was the right thing to do. He had already invested five years of his life studying to be a priest, and leaving the seminary was a big decision. "A decision this important needs to be made with much time, prayer and reflection," I emphasized to him.

During my long flight from Madrid to Boston, I decided to read again all the letters I had received while I was in Salamanca. Most of the letters were from Professor Shay and some were still unopened. The other letters came from a seminarian in Boston, a classmate of my son. I read these letters over and over again. I also was waiting for them with the same anticipation that a child waits for Santa Claus and I could not figure out why. Later own I discovered that I had some feelings, which were hidden even from myself.

When I returned home, I had to deal with another painful situation for which I was indirectly responsible. Professor Shay had written to me once or twice per week while I had been in Spain. However, I did not reply to him; his feelings were deeply hurt and rightfully so. Such a neglectful act and lack of common courtesy on my part was not done intentionally. I was deep inside my shell, dealing with my own grief. It did not occur to me that Professor Shay was anxiously hoping to receive an answer to his many letters.

He had left several messages with my children; so I called him the following day after returning from Spain. Professor Shay seemed quite surprised to hear from me and acted rather distant. I asked him, "Are you all right?

He answered my question with two questions. "How can I be all right? Do you realize how devastating it's to write to someone every week for six weeks and never receive a reply?"

I could hear the hurt and disappointment in Professor Shay's voice, and all I could say was, "I am so sorry! Can you forgive me?" After what seemed a long silence on the other end of the line, I broke the silence by asking, "What about a picnic lunch tomorrow? I will bring everything, and we can meet at Boston College at our favorite spot."

Professor Shay thought about the invitation for a few seconds and finally said, "Okay! I guess it will do me good to get away from all this paperwork for a while."

I thanked him for accepting the invitation, and we agreed to meet at 1:00 p.m. the following day.

After talking to Professor Shay, I felt very sad, and I was very hard on myself for being so thoughtless. I suddenly remembered a verse of one of my favorite songs, "If I give my heart to you, will you handle it with care?" Remembering that verse made me feel even worse. I realized then that I had not been handling Professor Shay's heart with care, and I wanted to make it up to him in some way.

I was up very early the following day so that I could prepare everything for the picnic. I made his favorite oatmeal cookies and packed a healthy and appetizing picnic lunch. However, I wanted to do something drastic to surprise him and an idea came to mind. Since Professor Shay was the one who gave me the nickname Mayan Princess, I thought I would dress as a Mayan princess for the picnic lunch. I really wanted to make it up to him for being so thoughtless.

Our favorite spot was a little park behind the Boston College campus. Professor Shay was already there sitting on a bench when I arrived. Even before I approached the bench, he stood up, walked toward me and had an expression of awe on his face! He stretched out both arms to embrace me, and at the same time, he said, "Oh my God! You look like a vision! Lucky are the eyes that are beholding such beauty!" He gazed in my eyes for a while and then earnestly asked, "May I please kiss the beautiful Mayan princess just this time?"

Not knowing how I could have refused such a plea, I nodded in agreement. Professor Shay held me close to him in a warm embrace and passionately kissed me on the lips. I kissed him back as an attempt to find some hidden chemistry on my part, but I found none. I gently pushed him away and said, "I am rather hungry. Can we eat now?"

Then he replied, "Before we eat, I have something to give you." He proceeded to take out from a paper bag a beautifully wrapped square box and a little card. I opened the card first and read the handwritten message on it.

To my Mayan Princess,

This bracelet represents my love for you. It has no beginning and no end.

With all my love,
Bob

I was deeply touched by such a sweet expression of love, but in good conscience, I could not accept the gift. I realized at that very moment there was no way out of this situation other than being painfully honest with Professor Shay about my feelings for him. "It makes no sense to prolong the inevitable any longer," I told myself.

After thanking him for the card and the gift, with deep sadness and regret, I said to Professor Shay, "The bracelet is beautiful, but I cannot accept it. You are such a wonderful man, and I love you as a friend, but regretfully I do not have any romantic feelings toward you. My friendship is all I can ever offer you."

He did not say anything, but the expression on his face spoke volumes. I felt awful for having to inflict such pain on someone who had shown me nothing but love and kindness. As an attempt to ease his pain and being somewhat sincere, I continued telling him, "Please do not take my lack of interest in a romantic relationship personally because it has nothing to do with you. I am not ready to love again. I am not sure if I will ever be."

I guess that as a teacher, I have the habit of over explaining myself. And I repeated the same phrase I had written on my letter to him. I also added, "I am sure that if I could fall in love again, you would be the number one candidate." The words felt honest, but a part of me knew that I was not even being honest with myself. Another forbidden love was on the horizon.

Nevertheless, my long explanation seemed to help Professor Shay to understand where I was at this point in my life. With an expression of dignity and sadness in his voice, he broke the silence by saying, "Thank you for the compliments and for being honest with me. I wish to continue being friends with you. I promise not to cross the line of friendship again. I want you in my life."

Professor Shay spoke with such sincerity and conviction. His promise gave me hope of being able to rescue our friendship and put the past behind us. That possibility made me feel better because I wanted him in my life as a friend as much as he wanted me.

As we were saying our goodbyes that day, Professor Shay tried once more to give me the bracelet. When I explained to him that I could not accept it, he suggested, "Please give it to your daughter. If you don't accept it, I want your daughter to have it."

After he said that, I felt it would be rude not to accept the bracelet. I gave the bracelet to my daughter and told her who the sender was. But I never revealed the story related to the bracelet.

Professor Shay and I have remained great friends. He has never remarried even though he has received several marriage proposals from friends of his late wife. I asked him a few years ago, "How do you manage to refuse those proposals without breaking the ladies' hearts?"

He answered me laughing, "I tell them that I am not capable of falling in love again, knowing the whole time that I would have married you in a heartbeat."

When Professor Shay said that, I started laughing too because I had given him the same excuse when he tried to give me the bracelet. For someone who considered herself incapable of falling in love again, a short time later, not only did I lose my heart to someone, but also my head and my objectivity too.

CHAPTER 19

*T*here is an old song in Spanish called "Muy Despacito," which means very slowly. It was composed by the immortal Mexican singer and songwriter José Alfredo Jiménez. The following is the main message of the song:

"Slowly, very slowly, you found your way deep into my heart, and now that I wish to get you out, there is nothing I can do about it."

I can relate to the song because that was exactly what happened to me with David, a seminarian classmate of my son, Francis. David had been in the Navy before entering the seminary. He was a few years older than his fellow seminarians, which made him 11 years younger than me. But for the four years he had been visiting us, I thought of him as a son because he was my children's friend. Furthermore, he acted much younger than his age.

David was not very sociable, and he did not have a very good relationship with most of his fellow seminarians. However, he was able to get along great with Francis, and he considered Francis his best friend. David also became friends with my three other children. He had things in common with them: such as sports, music and movies, but he had nothing in common with me.

During the four years that David visited my family, neither he nor I had felt interested in getting to know the other on a personal level. When he used to come to my house, usually with Francis and other seminarians, I would make big meals and sometimes I had nice conversations with some of the them. But I hardly exchanged anything more than greetings with David. He seemed to prefer the company of my children, which was fine with me.

David stood out among all of his fellow seminarians because he was the tallest, measuring six and a half feet tall. Having been in the Navy, he was well disciplined physically and had the appearance of a great athlete. Some of his other attributes were his abundance of blond hair and the most gorgeous blue eyes I ever seen, which I had never noticed in four years because they had been hidden under a thick pair of eyeglasses and a pessimistic attitude.

When Francis went to Rome, David kept in touch with him through letters. He also kept visiting my house with other seminarians. I was hospitable and cooked big meals as usual, but I did not try to get to know him in a personal level. As a matter of fact, I was not too fond of David because other seminarians had complained about how difficult he was to get along with. Besides his negative disposition, he always acted as if he had a chip on his shoulder.

It was not until my husband died that I saw another side of David. He was very supportive of our entire family, and for the first time I saw the soft side of him. I remember seeing him sobbing like a child when he read the letter that my husband had written to Francis the day he died. My guess is that very few people even knew he had a soft side

David was born in the Boston area, and his world seemed to be limited to the United States. During the entire time I knew him, he had never shown any interest in learning a foreign language or about other cultures. When I found out that he had registered to be in my elementary Spanish class at Boston College in the fall semester of 1988, I was very surprised.

Another seminarian, named Keith, friend of both David and my son, had also registered to take the same Spanish class with me. I knew for a fact that Keith was truly interested in learning Spanish because he had plans of going to the missions in South America. But as far as David's motivation for taking my Spanish class, I was not sure. I figured he had decided to take the class because his friend Keith would be attending it.

I already knew Keith, and I was very fond of him. Keith was in his mid- thirties, very mature, witty, extremely kind, and a great listener. Unlike the other seminarians, I did not think of Keith as a son, but rather as a friend because we could communicate at the same maturity level. Sometimes Keith and I used to go out for pizza or ice cream after our Spanish class, and we would invite David to come along. After a while, we were like the three Musketeers, always together. But initially, my primary friendship was with Keith.

It was very easy to like Keith because of his rare combination of attributes. In addition to the ones already mentioned, he was charismatic, generous and thoughtful. Every time he came over the house for dinner, Keith always brought either flowers or wine. Not that great looks are as important as one's character, but Keith also happened to fit in the tall, dark and handsome category.

When my husband died, Keith was always concerned about whether I was doing well or if I needed anything. He invited me to the movies a few times, just to get me out of the house on Sundays because he knew that I found Sundays especially difficult. Since I was home all day and not distracted at work, I felt the absence of my husband more intensely. Furthermore, Keith was always thinking of inventing practical jokes just to amuse me. I could not have asked for a more kind or supportive friend.

I did not have any intentions of falling in love with any of the seminarians, or anyone else for that matter. That idea had never crossed my mind. However, if one could have control about who to fall in love with, Keith would have been my number one choice. He had all the attributes any woman could wish for.

I cannot pinpoint exactly when my feelings for David changed from somewhat disliking him to start caring for him because it happened very, very slowly. I began to care for him when I discovered his soft side from the way he showed his solidarity with my family during our time of grief. But it was his need for love, his insecurity and vulnerability that caused me to open wide the door of my heart to him.

I distinctly remember an occasion when I found out how needy David was. He had been in a car accident and came directly from the scene of the accident to my office at Boston College, at about two in the afternoon. I was having office hours, and I had appointments scheduled throughout the afternoon. But when I saw David acting very distressed and I found out about the accident, I cancelled all of my appointments and took him out for lunch.

We went to a Ground Round Restaurant nearby Boston College (a type of steak and salad place). David was very hungry and while he was eating, he kept on saying, "I cannot believe that you cancelled all those appointments just for me." After hearing the same comment many times, I finally asked him, "David, don't you think you are worth it?"

He did not answer me. But the silence did the talking for him. He reminded me of myself, when I used to consider myself a nobody, and my heart ached for him.

I brought David back to the seminary after lunch, and I will never forget what he said to me as he was getting out of my car. Obviously, he was feeling better because he had a big smile, and with a boyish expression on his face he told me, "Thank you, Mrs. DeVito. It was worth getting in a car accident so I could be cared for by you."

I do not remember what I said exactly when David made such a revealing comment. All I remember was that a wave of tenderness and compassion came over me. Call it a mother's instinct or a woman's tender heart, but at that moment this young man whom I had thought of as a clumsy and spoiled giant, became like a little child in my eyes. I wanted to take him in my arms, hold him close to my heart, stroke his blond hair and lovingly tell him, "You do not have to get in a car accident to be cared for. You deserve to be loved and cared for just by being who you are, a precious child of God."

I said none of those things to David that day, but I think that unconsciously I took it upon myself the mission of doing for him what my husband had done for me. He made me feel special, as no one had ever done before.

Since that day, I was always trying to find ways to make David feel special, mostly by paying attention to him and by giving him sincere compliments. For someone who initially did not show much interest in learning a foreign language, David was doing remarkably well in my Spanish class. I often complimented him on his ability to learn a foreign language.

During that time, I needed to make a video of one of my Level One Spanish classes about the four seasons of the year and about all of the clothes and footwear relevant to each season. I used David as a model to dress in various layers of clothing for all the seasons of the year. Then I had volunteers from the rest of the class name each piece of clothing in Spanish and take it off from the model. After wearing a coat, scarf, hat and boots, David ended up wearing a T-shirt, shorts and sandals. He looked absolutely ridiculous initially wearing everything all at once, but it was a fun class and he felt like the center of attention.

Two months after David started taking Spanish classes with me, the last Friday in October to be exact, I received a strange telephone call from him at about 10:00 p.m. He had never called that late before; so I was afraid something was wrong. I asked him, "Is everything all right?

He replied, "Yes, Mrs. DeVito, everything is just fine."

My next question was, "Do you want to talk to Andrew?"

"No," he said, "I am calling to ask you for a date."

I took that as a joke, and I asked him laughing, "A date for what?"

David quickly replied, "A date to go out, like a man and a woman."

Of course, I didn't think he was serious. Then I asked him jokingly, "David, are you crazy? Have you been drinking? What is happening to you?"

David assured me, "I am not crazy, Mrs. DeVito. And I am perfectly sober."

I could not believe what I was hearing, and after a short pause, I replied. "Okay, David, if you are not crazy or drunk and you are serious, the answer is NO. I cannot go out with you because you are my student. You are also my children's friend, and I think of you as a son."

Then David responded, "That's not a problem! If you cannot go out with a student, I can always drop off from your class. And as far as you thinking of me as a son, I know that. I used to think of you as a mother too. But the more I got to know you, the less I saw the mother, and the more I began to see the beautiful woman you are."

Still thinking that David was just looking for some attention, I said to him, "Let's drop this foolishness now and come over for lunch tomorrow if you want. I think Andrew will be home."

"I will be there with bated breath," he quickly replied.

Andrew was the only one of my children who was in the country at that time. Francis was in Rome. Anthony was studying theater arts in England and Marie was studying Spanish in Seville, Spain.

The next day after David's strange telephone call, I told Andrew, "Please be home for lunch because David is coming."

Andrew answered me obviously annoyed, "I have my own plans; I am going out."

I called David at the seminary to change plans because Andrew was not going to be home, but he had already left the seminary, and there were no cell phones in those days.

When I found out that Andrew was not going to be home for lunch, I changed plans. I had planned to go apple-picking to an orchard in Salem, New Hampshire the following day, which was a Sunday, but I decided to go Saturday instead. After that bizarre telephone call from David the night before, I thought it would be best for us to go out. When I invited David to go apple-picking with me, "I would love to," he replied with the excitement of a child waiting for Christmas.

It took us about forty-five minutes to drive to the apple orchard. Neither David nor I mentioned anything about the crazy telephone call from the night before. When we arrived at the apple orchard, I bought two empty bags to put the apples in, one for him and one for me. We went our separate ways walking through the orchard to pick the best apples. When the bags had been filled, we met in the parking lot. We were about to leave the orchard, when David asked me, "Mrs. DeVito, would you like to play a game?"

I responded, "What kind of game?"

"I will pretend to be Adam, and you pretend to be Eve. The aim of the game is for Eve to get Adam to eat the forbidden apple," he explained.

I accepted the challenge and picked the biggest apple I could find. Then I started running after David to get him to eat the apple. I chased him all over the apple orchard for about ten minutes, and I finally caught up to him. I was trying to get him to eat the apple, but we both fell down and ended up rolling down a hill. We laughed and laughed like two children. I do not remember playing like that when I was a child; neither do I remember laughing as much ever. We both had a lot of fun!

We went back to the house, and Andrew was still not at home. I told David that he could watch television while I made dinner, but he decided to make some phone calls instead. Andrew finally came home, and the three of us had supper together.

While we were still eating, I received a telephone call from Keith. The first thing he said was, "I cannot believe it! I have to hear it from your own lips."

I had no idea what he was talking about; so I asked him. "What do you need to hear from my own lips?"

Keith replied, "I need to hear from your own mouth about you and David." He went on to explain that David called him, probably while I was preparing dinner, and told him about the game we had played at the apple orchard. He also quoted David saying, "Mrs. DeVito and I are in love."

I explained to Keith that nothing had happened at the apple orchard, other than playing a game, and his comment was, "It was probably a game to you, but not for David." Then he asked, "What are you going to do about it?"

I tried to convince David and myself that it was only a game, but it turned out to be a very dangerous one. It had begun so innocently, but two months later, around Christmas time, we no longer could fool ourselves. David confessed that he was in love with me, and I admitted to him that the feeling was mutual. It was such a bittersweet experience! I felt young, happy and alive again. We probably had those feelings longer before we admitted them even to ourselves.

Falling in love with the intensity of a teenager took me by surprise. I was extremely happy but deep inside, I knew better. "I have fallen in love with the wrong person again," I told myself over and over again. Along with my feelings of exhilaration, the guilt was not far behind. However, there was a big difference this time; David was not a priest yet. I could find reasons to rationalize and even justify why it was okay to be in love with David in spite of our 11-year age difference.

On one hand, David reassured me, "Falling in love with you is the best thing that has ever happened to me. Loving you is changing me into a better person. Even my parents have noticed that I am kinder, more patient, more happy and easier to get along with."

On the other hand, I told myself, "Loving David is the deepest, most pure love I have ever offered anyone, other than my children. This time, I am not in need of being rescued from a bad situation or to be supported financially. My love for David is completely unselfish, and it is saving him from a life of loneliness, misery and insecurity."

Thinking that I was offering this completely unselfish love for the first time in my life and that I was rescuing David from his own negativity, unhappiness and insecurity, led me to lose objectivity at what I was doing or what I was about to do with my life. By Christmas time of the same year, David and I started planning our future together. We kissed passionately for the first time, and David exclaimed, "Oh my God! We have so much chemistry; we can blow out the whole City of Boston!"

He was thinking that he would leave the seminary immediately. But I gave him the same advice I had given my son, Francis, "Do not make a hasty decision about leaving the seminary." So even though David was no longer sure that he wanted to become a priest, he went back to the seminary for another semester. He also decided not to enroll in my Spanish class again because he knew that I would not date a student. "Anyway, I only took Spanish to be near you," he admitted.

We continued to see each other in my house a couple of times during the week. He would come over for supper; then we would talk and kiss until the early morning hours of each day. David would go back to the seminary and I would go to sleep for only a couple of hours before going back to work at Boston College.

We were crazy about each other and kissed nonstop for hours, but even though the temptation was always there, we never crossed the line to have full intimacy for several reasons. My values did not allow me to engage in sex before marriage, and in some ways, I felt that I needed to be faithful to my late husband. I was also afraid of an unwanted pregnancy, but mostly, I feared that David was immature enough to tell my children or even his mother if we were to be intimate. On the back of my mind, there was another reason that is kind of hard to explain. I put my role of a mother first and of a woman second. I figured that if I respected David by not having intimacy with him, that my own son, the seminarian, would be respected as well by another woman if he were to find himself in this type of situation.

Even though love is blind, David's immaturity was obvious to me. On several occasions, other seminarians had mentioned that he needed to grow up emotionally, and I could see that for myself. At times, he was very sweet, caring, and thoughtful; then, suddenly, he would do something that would reveal his lack of maturity.

I remember having a severe toothache one day and telling him, "David, I need to go to the dentist; I have a toothache that is killing me." Instead of offering to help me, he proceeded to tickle me very hard, thinking that tickling me would cause the pain to go away. I became very angry instead, and we had a big fight that day.

A few days before this incident, David got very angry at me for having my hair cut too short. When he saw my new haircut, he became very serious. Then he exclaimed with anger in his voice, "That haircut makes you look like a shrewd businesswoman. It takes away from the beautiful exotic look you had with your long hair." I felt very upset when hearing this silly comment and I yelled at him, "If you love me for my hair, I am going to go bald; so you won't have anything to love, okay?"

Fighting and making up again was the common trend in our relationship. I tried to break up with David almost every time we had a fight, but after hearing his heartfelt apologies, I would take him back again. In spite of being on rocky ground several times, we thought that we could make our relationship work. Only a couple of months after declaring our love for each other, we decided to face the challenge of informing our families that we were in love.

I started by telling the news to my son, Francis, because I knew that he would be the easiest and most understanding of my children. I gave him the news over the telephone because he was still in Rome. He was very surprised, of course, but after the initial shock, he commented, "I support whatever makes you happy." Then he gave us his blessing.

After I told Francis the news, David wrote to him. The following excerpt comes from that letter, dated February 19, 1989.

> .... I find it very bizarre to say, I am in love with your mother, but this is how I feel ... Neither your mother nor I had planned to fall in love. It just happened. I hope you can understand that.
>
> Being in love transforms your whole being, outlook in life and even disposition. Even my mother noticed how much I have changed, and she likes the new and improved me .... Now I personally know the meaning of the lyrics of the song, You are my Everything. I very much agree with the theme of the song that being in the presence of the one you love, everything else fades. Your mother is everything to me and I cannot imagine my life without her. Neither can I imagine anyone not loving her because she is certainly one of God's best creations.

David received a very kind reply to his letter from Francis reassuring him that their friendship would continue on the same as before.

When I told the news to my other sons, Anthony and Andrew, neither one expressed any opinion or showed any emotion. They did not seem to care one way or another. However, in my daughter's case, it was another story.

I broke the news to Marie, and she exploded! I had never seen my daughter so upset. After lecturing me about the big mistake I was making, she asked a rhetorical question. "You think that David is such a prize because he is young, tall, and good-looking, but what does he really have to offer you? Nothing! Can't you see that?" Then my daughter continued lecturing me, and with a mixture of anger and conviction in her voice, she concluded her argument. "You are the prize, not him! You are still young. You're beautiful, a great person, well educated; you have a great job, and you have people who love and respect you."

I was speechless and surprised that my daughter thought so highly of me. After a short silence, she pleaded with a softer voice, "Please think about what you're doing! Please don't throw your life away!"

I did not know what to say, and she did not give me a chance either. She stormed out to her room and I was left in the living room reflecting on what had happened. I certainly had a mixture of conflicting emotions. At the same time that my daughter was scolding me, she was also paying me some of the greatest compliments I had ever received from her. I had never thought of myself as a prize, and I knew my daughter was being sincere. I also knew for a fact that she was being brutally honest. Even then, I respected my daughter's opinion very much because she was very mature for her age, and I knew she had a good head on her shoulders.

My daughter was only 19 years old then. Not only did she have the audacity to stand up to me, but the wisdom to know what was going on. I admired and respected her for that. I also appreciated that she was looking out for my wellbeing. I seriously thought about everything she had said, and I believed her. But I did not have the courage to break up with David for good; I loved him too much.

A few days after my daughter had tried to talk some sense into me, David and I had one more serious argument. He made an embarrassing scene in the seminary when Gabriel, a seminarian from Portugal, was helping me study for an exam in Portuguese. I was under a lot of pressure because I needed to do well on that exam in order to complete my master's degree program at Boston College. Gabriel graciously offered to tutor me in Portuguese and prepare me for the exam. That day, we were having a tutoring session at one of the tables in the dining room of the seminary. When David saw us, he rushed to the table and in an enraged voice he accused Gabriel, "It is obvious that more than tutoring is going on around here. Do you really want to help Cándida with her Portuguese or do you just want to be near her?"

Poor Gabriel! He did not know how to respond to such a ridiculous accusation, and I was too upset to say anything. Keith was also in the dining room. He heard the bizarre comment and quickly intervened by saying to David very angrily, "When are you going to grow up? This woman is under tremendous pressure because she has to pass that exam in order to graduate this semester, and instead of helping her, you are adding more pressure on her with your damn foolishness."

This time David went too far. I had finally had enough of his nonsense and decided to break up with him right at that moment. I told him firmly, "We are finished for good and I am not taking you back again. This time it's different. I am determined to get you out my life and out of my heart." After ending my relationship with David, I was deeply sad, but I also felt relieved because I knew it in my heart that it was for the best.

The next day, David showed up at Boston College at the end of the day. I was walking toward my car when he followed me. He attempted to take my briefcase and said, "May I help you carry this?"

I continued walking very fast and abruptly told him, "No thank you. I can carry it by myself." But he forcefully took my briefcase anyway. After putting the briefcase in my car, he started apologizing for the argument we had, and pleaded with me to take him back.

I was feeling confident about my decision, and I told him in a loud voice. "No way, David! I am done fighting with you." Then he handed me a card. First, I refused to take it. But when I saw the pleading look in his big blue eyes, I broke down and accepted the card. The card contained an apology for the argument and a copy of a beautiful song, called "Love by You," written by Joan Armatrading.

The following lyrics express the theme of the song:

... You are my lifeline... Baby come back to me
Don't leave this guy lost in space
You're the one who could
Guide me out of this maze

"This song expresses perfectly how I feel about you," David said. After reading the card and the lyrics of the song, I could not do it. I went back on my word and took David back. He came home with me that afternoon, and we kissed in the living room for hours.

After this last incident, my relationship with David improved somewhat. I truly believed that he was changing and maturing. He wanted to leave the seminary then, but I encouraged him to at least finish the semester. When David proposed for us to take our relationship to the next level as soon as the semester was over, I foolishly agreed in spite of having very strong reservations. Not only did I agree to marry him, but also to start all over again by having children in the near future. He wanted to be a father, and I was willing to do anything to make him happy.

Chapter 20

By April of 1989, David was still sure that he wanted to leave the seminary and continued talking about marriage and children. I had my reservations not only about marrying him, but also about starting all over again having children. My youngest son was already 17 years old at that time.

When I told some close friends what I was planning to do, they said, "You should have your head examined; thinking of starting all over again having children? That's insane!" I knew that my friends were right, but my love for David was so strong that I felt capable of doing anything for him. The best way to express what I was feeling at that time can be found in a verse from a popular and beautiful Spanish song which says, *"Por él sería capaz de empezar otra vez"* ("For him, I would be capable of starting all over again").

Since we had tentative future plans to get married, David felt that he could no longer withhold the truth from his parents, though he was terribly worried about his mother's reaction to the news. He confessed, "The main reason I have stayed in the seminary is because my mother would surely have a nervous breakdown if I ever left. She claims she cannot see me as being anything other than a priest."

After a long pause and a sigh of anger and frustration, David continued, "I hate my parents' double standards. My sister has plans to marry a classmate of mine from the seminary and that's fine with them. They are so happy about their daughter's upcoming wedding. It's okay for my classmate to leave the seminary and marry my sister according to my parents, but it's not okay for me to leave the seminary and do what I want with my damn life."

David had a good point there. I listened to him sympathetically, but I did not respond. I was afraid of saying something that might give him the impression I was pressuring him to leave the seminary. While he was ranting and raving, I was crediting myself for not pressuring my own son to join the seminary. It was Francis' own choice to study for the priesthood.

David finally told the news to his parents, not only about his intentions of leaving the seminary, but also about marrying me. His parents were shocked to say the least and were very disappointed, of course. David called me after he broke the news to his parents. "They were very upset;" he said, "however, they took the blow better than I had anticipated, even though they begged me to reconsider my decision."

I was friendly with Jane, David's mother, and we had planned a trip to Rome together in June of the same year. I do not remember whether she called me, or I called her, but we agreed to meet and talk things over, both about the trip and the situation with her son.

We met in a restaurant at a halfway point from my house and hers. I was very nervous driving there because I did not know what to expect from Jane. But I was pleasantly surprised to find her easy to talk with and very understanding as well. She acknowledged that she had noticed a big change in her son's attitude in the last few months. "He is much kinder and more considerate now. He is less angry and has a better disposition. Falling in love with you has certainly changed him for the better."

I was happy and relieved to hear that from David's mother. However, call it a woman's intuition, but I was sure that her kind words would be followed by a but. "You are a wonderful person;" she continued, "please know that it is nothing against you, but I want my son to be a priest. I cannot imagine my son as being anything other than a priest."

I thanked Jane for her frankness and reassured her that I had her son's best interests at heart and mind. "If David wants to be a priest," I said, "I will completely support his decision. I will never try to do anything to discourage him from pursuing a religious vocation, if that's what he wants." I meant what I said. I reminded Jane that I was the mother of a seminarian also and that I could understand how she felt.

My meeting with Jane turned out well. She was a wise and very kind woman. She was able to express her hopes for her son's future without hurting my feelings. She was also able to perceive my sincerity when I told her, "I have your son's best interests at heart and mind." We left that day on good terms, decided to continue being friends, and still take the trip to Rome together.

While David's parents were pressuring him not to leave the seminary, Marie, my daughter, and Keith kept on pressuring me to come to my senses about marrying David. However, it seemed they were all fighting a losing battle. Keith continued to be a constant and supportive friend, even after suspecting for sure that I had completely lost my mind. Many times I remember him saying to me, "Have sex with David, and you will see how quickly you will get him out of your system. You want a real man in your life, not a boy."

I did not consider David a boy. I thought of him as my Prince Charming and gave him the nickname "Rey de mi Universo" (King of my Universe). He in turn used to call me "Diosa de las Manzanas" (Apple Goddess). He invented that nickname because of the association of teachers receiving apples from their students.

Keith's advice was not well taken. My moral values and my respect for David would not have allowed me to engage in premarital sex. However, another friend had given me the same advice many times and she even offered me the keys to her apartment for David and I to meet. In a moment of weakness, I accepted the keys from my friend and planned with David to meet at her apartment and finally unleash our passion for each other.

When I arrived at my friend's apartment, David was already there. His car was parked in front of the building. I parked my car next to his. We greeted each other nervously with a warm embrace and a long passionate kiss. I knew David was always hungry; so I suggested getting something to eat before going into the apartment. We walked holding hands to a pizzeria nearby. I sweetly asked David, "What kind of pizza would you like, Rey de mi Universo?"

He answered in a rude manner, "I don't care. Get whatever you want. You're paying for it anyway."

His attitude and that comment infuriated me. Looking directly into his eyes, I rebuked him, "You make me feel as if it's an obligation for me to pay for everything, rather than doing something out of the goodness of my heart. Guess what? I am not buying pizza or going into my friend's apartment." Before he could say anything, I walked out of the pizzeria and as I was leaving, I angrily told David, "Go back to your seminary; I am going home." That is how our planned romantic afternoon ended.

He tried to call me that afternoon to apologize, but I refused to take his phone calls. At about 8:00 p.m. that evening, David showed up at my house begging for forgiveness. First, I did not want to listen to anything he had to say, and then I started rationalizing his behavior: "Maybe I was too hard on him; maybe I used that comment as an excuse to not cross the intimacy line. Maybe due to guilt, fear or whatever reason, I was not ready to do that. It was not right to lead him on." By the time I finished telling myself all these things, I broke down and forgave him again.

We made up once more and things were good for a few days; then David would do something that would end up in another argument. It was obvious to everyone who knew us that we were acting like two adolescents in love, but we were not communicating at the same maturity level -- my love for David had blinded me to that fact, and I was trying to make sense out something irrational. I had always considered myself a peacemaker; I hardly or maybe never had I argued with my late husband. Now I was arguing most of the time with David, and I could not understand why.

Looking back, most of our arguments were caused by David's immaturity and jealousy. He was insanely jealous even of my relationship with my spiritual advisor, Father Roy, without reason. Father Roy is one of the holiest of priests I know and a wonderful friend to my whole family. David suspected that Father Roy did not approve of our marriage, and I remember him angrily saying several times, "Father Roy probably thinks no one is good enough to marry you; so why doesn't he marry you himself"?

But probably the most idiotic claim that I foolishly endured from David was that any children that he and I were to have were not going to be loved by me as much as I loved my other children. I do not remember how the argument about that started, but I will never forget when one day he told me, "You are so damn dedicated to your children. I am sure that any children we may have will end up being second-class citizens."

I was not aware of how crazy and foolish I had been to put up with so much nonsense from David. He always ended up apologizing profusely after each argument, and I foolishly believed it would not happen again.

In May of that year (1989), I graduated from Boston College with a Master's Degree in Spanish Literature. When I graduated, I already had a job offer and a signed contract to teach at the Boston Public School system the following school year. I had met the recruiter for the Boston Public Schools bilingual program at a Christmas party. When he heard that I was a teaching fellow at Boston College and about to complete a master's degree program there, the recruiter immediately made me an offer that I could not refuse. The salary was more than I had ever dreamed of ever making. And as an added incentive, I would be working with children with whom I had my native language, culture, and possibly childhood experiences in common.

Just before I graduated from Boston College, David informed me that he had decided to spend the whole summer working in the Navy in San Diego, California. When he first told me about his summer plans, I was sure that I was going to have a summer without sunshine that year because he would not be around. But to my surprise, I had a very pleasant and peaceful summer!

I went to Rome for two weeks with Jane, and that trip was absolutely incredible! We were given a very warm reception from the North American College, where my son was studying. We had the good fortune of getting to meet Pope John Paul II in person. We were also able to do some traveling while we were in Rome. We went to Venice, Assisi, and other fabulous places. I had always wanted to go to Assisi because it was the birthplace of Saint Francis, the founder of my late husband's religious order.

When I returned home from Rome that summer, I had a delightful visit from my mother and sister, who had come all the way from Honduras. My mother had met David in a previous visit, but she did not get to talk to him because of the language barrier. She also had met many of the other seminarians at about the same time, but she distinctly remembered David because of his height and good looks.

When I told my mother about my relationship with David, she was very surprised and asked me a question that helped me think about my future plans with him. With much concern, my mother asked me, "Cándida, do you think that young man you are in love with is ever going to mature?"

I do not remember my answer, but I remember how I felt. My mother's question hit me like a ton of bricks. I finally figured out that if David's immaturity was so obvious to someone who hardly knew him and did not even speak the same language, it had to be really obvious.

My mother's question laid the first stone, but it was Father Ryan, one of the teachers at the seminary, who helped me to fully come to my senses. He and I had become great friends during the five years that my son had been in the seminary. Father Ryan had a special place in his heart for Spanish-speaking people because he felt attracted by the warmth of their culture.

At forty-five years of age, Father Ryan decided to leave his teaching position at Saint John's seminary and become a missionary in South America, which meant that he had to learn Spanish and embrace almost a brand-new vocation.

I had told Father Ryan about David because we were the kind of friends who could share almost anything. He seemed very sad when I told him the news, but he did not offer any feedback at that time. However, the day before leaving for South America, I received an almost urgent telephone call from him. "I need to see you immediately," Father Ryan told me with a sense of urgency in his voice. "I have something very important to tell you."

I met Father Ryan two hours after his telephone call in *El Torito*, a Mexican restaurant two towns away from my house. I was very nervous while driving to meet him. I suspected that Father Ryan was going to tell me not to interfere with the vocation of a potential priest. However, my hunch was completely wrong.

Father Ryan began his talk by asking me to listen carefully not only with my ears, but also with my heart to what he had to tell me. Then he looked me straight in the eyes with a concerned look and said,

> *Cándida, you know that I love you as a friend, and I wish I could sugarcoat the bitter pill that I am going to give you, but I have no time for that. I am leaving for the missions tomorrow, and I have no idea when I will be back. So, I have to be upfront with you. The saddest thing that you have ever told me is about you considering marrying David. If you go through with that marriage, you will be digging your own grave, and you will have an overgrown child to take care of for the rest of your life. I am not referring to his age; find another 28-year-old man to marry if that is what you want, but be sure he is mature, and I will gladly give you my blessing. But I cannot be happy for you if you marry someone who I have seen throw a temper tantrum at the seminary because we didn't have the cookies he wanted.*

I listened to Father Ryan with an open mind and heart and without interrupting him. But at this point I told him, "You do not have to say another word; now I understand everything, and I know what I have to do." I thanked Father Ryan for being a true friend by telling me the truth no matter how painful it was to hear.

I had every intention of ending my relationship with David as soon as he returned from the Navy. Knowing that it was the right thing to do, did not make it any easier or less painful. But probably through divine intervention, the decision was made for me. While David had been away working in the Navy, he made the decision to go back to the seminary.

I imagine that David must have lost sleep over deciding how to break the news to me as gently as he could. He had no idea about my own decision. When he came to my house that day, he seemed to have reverted to his old disposition. As we made small talk, his mood seemed to soften. Then after a while with a soft and nervous voice, he delivered what seemed to me a well-rehearsed speech. "I finally figured out," he said, "that I must have a vocation for the religious life. I love you like I never loved anyone before. You are so kind, beautiful and exotic. Any man has to be out of his freaking mind to break up a marriage engagement with you, but I have decided to return to the seminary."

A wave of conflicting emotions rushed through my head as David was breaking up with me. Mostly I was very sad, but somewhat relieved that the decision had been made for me. I accepted David's decision with an air of dignity. I gave him my blessing and wished him well. I never told David that I had planned to break up with him too. I felt that under the circumstances, there was not need to share that information with him.

Doing the right thing and having full knowledge that it is the right thing to do, does not spare one the pain of a lost love and a crushed dream. It was hard to keep David out my life. He made things even harder for me by keeping in touch and asking me to continue providing emotional support to him while he remained in the seminary. He even asked me, "Please do not move on with your life until I become a priest. I do not think that I could bear knowing you are dating another man." David was crying when he made that supplication.

However, by this time, his tears did not affect me in the same way as before. I flatly told him, "I cannot do that. And as far as providing you with emotional support while you are at the seminary, I cannot do that either. You have God, your family, your teachers, and fellow seminarians who can provide you with all of the support you want. You don't need me!" I emphasized.

While I was going through this emotional turmoil with David, I received terribly sad and disturbing news. My dear friend Father Ryan, who had left for South America only a few months before, was now dead. He did fulfill his calling of being a missionary in South America the short time he was there by passionately working on defending human rights. But regretfully by doing so, it cost him his life. He was found dead in the ocean somewhere in Perú. After our meeting at the Mexican restaurant, I only saw him one more time, at his wake when his body was brought back to the United States.

The saying "When it rains it pours," was particularly true at this time in my life. In addition to the grief I still felt for the death of my husband, the pain of losing a friend dear to my heart, Father Ryan, and the sadness of getting David out of my life, I also had to witness my children's growing pains, which was even more difficult. This was especially true in the case of Francis, my oldest son. It was around this time that he left the seminary and came home from Rome. He was so thrilled to be home! One whole school year waiting to see Rachel, his girlfriend, probably had seemed like an eternity to him. He had no idea then that he was in for the greatest disappointment and heartbreak of his life.

I was completely supportive of my son's decision to leave the seminary. He had kept his end of the agreement we had made in Spain, which was for him to go back to Rome for another year, and then make the decision about his future after much prayer and meditation.

During that year, Rachel and Francis stayed in touch through letters and telephone calls. My son was sure that their love could only be compared with that of Romeo and Juliet, but hoped for a happier ending for him and Rachel. He was also convinced that the girl he had fallen madly in love with was completely faithful and sincere.

I had my doubts about Rachel's sincerity. There was a rumor that she had a live-in boyfriend. I tried very gently to prepare my son for the fall, but he became very upset and made the comment, "Rachel is as pure as the Blessed Mother." I knew then that he had to find out for himself the reality of the situation. I also realized that no matter how much we want to protect our children from growing pains, it is impossible to do so. As parents, all we can do is to be there for our children to help pick up the pieces when their hearts get broken and their dreams get crushed.

While Francis was in Rome, he had become somewhat of a celebrity in our hometown. He had been on local television on several occasions for different reasons. He was shown with Pope John Paul II a couple times and he was interviewed for being the first American runner to cross the finish line during the 1989 Rome marathon.

Rachel seemed to be very impressed with the positive publicity that her boyfriend had received. When Francis returned from Rome, she had a wonderful homecoming party for him. During the party, Rachel kept on showing the segments of Francis on television to her numerous guests, and she was obviously beaming with pride. I had the impression that more than giving a warm welcome home to her boyfriend, she was using the opportunity to impress her friends.

His homecoming was everything Francis had hoped for and dreamed of, but unfortunately his happiness was short-lived. After only a couple weeks after being back home, he experienced the cold shoulder not only from his girlfriend, but also from some people in our parish who were supposed to be his friends. These people were no longer interested in his friendship since he had decided not to become a priest.

Rachel played the off-and-on-again girlfriend game for several months. She would break up with Francis, and a couple of weeks later, she would call him to get back together. Francis would jump at the chance, of course, and would go from pure devastation to absolute joy! This emotional rollercoaster ride went on for at least four times.

I will never forget the last time Rachel called Francis to get back together, about the fourth time she had broken up with him. I had gone to the movies with my friend Keith, and he was still at my house when Francis returned home all smiles because that night Rachel and he had gotten back together once again. Francis cheerfully announced to the both of us what he thought it was a fabulous news. Keith did not say anything, and I only gave my son a sad look. Then he asked, "Isn't anybody going to congratulate me because Rachel and I are together again?"

Neither Keith nor I said anything. Then I saw a side of my son that I had not seen before. He got very angry and shouted, "Whoever is not happy for me can go to hell!"

Keith got up from his chair, gave Francis a stern look and said, "Don't you dare talk to your mother that way! Every time that girl has stomped on and crushed your heart, she has picked up the pieces. The next time that girl breaks your heart, your mother should leave the pieces on the ground."

Francis realized then that he had been completely out line and apologized to the both of us.

Finally, around the fifth time that Rachel had broken up with him, Francis decided he had endured enough emotional beating and decided that it was time to quit the game. When Rachel wanted to get back together one more time, he did not take the bait and he finally ended the relationship.

Later on, Francis found out through a mutual friend that his supposedly wonderful girlfriend had been involved in another relationship. He also confirmed the rumors that she had a live-in boyfriend almost the entire time he had been in Rome missing her and hoping for a future together.

Not only did Francis go through the agonizing pain of being betrayed, but it took him years to heal and the experience left him with emotional scars. He never went back to the seminary and found his life's mission working with underprivileged young people in the educational field. Most of these young people already had messed-up lives and criminal records before attending the program my son was directing. Giving these young men and women the chance to straighten out their lives and getting educated was my son's way of making a difference in the world and dealing with his own pain by focusing on others.

I believe that a dimension of the human condition is to experience all kinds of emotions including heartbreaks, some from which we never fully recover. I also believe that another element of the human condition is to be blinded by the presence of love. Obviously, that is what happened to me with David, but after much reflection I have concluded that other factors were also involved. In addition to truly loving this young man, I was able to live the adolescence I never had through my experience with him. Years later, I came to understand that unconsciously I was trying to pay a debt, which I felt I owed life or the world, to do for another human being what my late husband had done for me.

Frank made me feel as someone very special when I felt like a nobody. He loved me unconditionally when I considered myself unlovable. He believed in me when I did not believe in myself. He unclipped my wings so I could soar through life and become the woman that I am today.

Some people who know about my life have asked me, "Are you bitter at all about the hardships in your life?" My answer is always the same: "Not at all."

In spite of my miserable childhood, the persecution I experienced for marrying a man of the cloth, the severe financial hardship I endured when I first came to the United States, the sacrifice of spending twenty years of my life caring for a demanding and cranky mother-in-law, and the pain of losing some of the people most dear to my heart, I still consider myself one of the luckiest women in the world.

I have experienced the sweetness of love to the fullest, the peace of forgiveness, the joy and pride of having four great children, the blessing of being a grandmother, the privilege of having a loving extended family and cherished friends, the good fortune of living in a country where women and men have the same rights and opportunities, the success that comes from hard work and the satisfaction of a fulfilling career. And yet, my biggest dream still is to continue soaring through life with the boldness of an eagle, with an open heart and unclipped wings.

I owe all of these blessings to a loving God and to a true Franciscan missionary who was able to see—with the eyes of the soul—the goodness, the inner beauty, and the potential of a humble peasant girl from Honduras.

AFTERWORD

I am an agnostic (almost atheist), a hater of mankind, and a believer that anyone without dogs as companions is not to be trusted. My friend Cándida is a devout Catholic, a lover of mankind, and has no particular connection to canines. How can it be that of the two people I trust in this world, she is one of them?

Her story, an interesting one to be sure, cannot fully capture her in spite of her descriptive discourse. She is part angel, but not ethereal. She is an earth angel. I love her brown hands, working hands—hands that have never stopped, hands that can make everything special and delicious and perfect.

How can a cynic like I am be so enamored with this sentimental romantic? For years, she has tried to find me my Principe Azul (literally Blue Prince, meaning knight in shining armor). She fixed me up with countless men . . . drunks, chronic gamblers, and even some who were quite physically unattractive. Even her womanizing brother was on the list after she was convinced he had "changed." It is not that she thinks little of me, but that she sees well of everyone else. She does not see or dwell on defect. She sees beauty. She is beauty.

I asked her a while ago if she had forgiven her mother. Of course, she had. She does things that most humans would find impossible. She lives on earth, but she has evolved from someplace else.

Her family and present-day husband appear as normal and typical Americans. Everyone is fairly well-adjusted and faces the usual daily challenges of life. She too leads a quiet suburban existence in the

Boston area. The drama of her youth seems long gone, but kindness still oozes out of her. She is loved by all who meet her, and she is always helping someone . . . always.

Carolann D'Arcangelo

About the Author

Cándida Rosa DeVito was born in 1949 in Las Limas, a remote village located in Olancho, Honduras. She was only able to obtain an elementary school education in her own country because of the lack of opportunities for women during that time.

Her journey from the remote village of Las Limas to Boston, Massachusetts, U.S.A. in the early 1960s, gave Cándida a hope for a newfound freedom. However, she soon discovered that she had to face countless challenges and obstacles in her new homeland, including language and cultural barriers. Nevertheless, she was able to thrive both professionally and personally despite these struggles.

Cándida's family and friends proudly witnessed her transformation from a timid young lady with very minimal education to a highly educated and confident professional. After spending five years getting her high school diploma, she obtained a teaching degree from Salem State University and graduated Summa Cum Laude. She then went on to acquire a Master's Degree in Spanish literature from Boston College and had an accomplished career as a teacher for the Boston Public Schools. She received numerous awards for her excellence and dedication and has been featured in several newspapers, including the *New York Times*.

The writing of her life story, Sacred Vows: A True Story of Forbidden Love, is the fulfillment of a personal dream and an inspiration to all. Cándida's first edition of this book is titled "Secrets of Forbidden Love." At the request of many readers, the book was translated into Spanish by the author under the title "Secretos de un Amor Prohibido."

Cándida currently works as an education consultant and writer. She lives in the Boston-area with her husband Paul and Rudy, their Chihuahua.

CPSIA information can be obtained
at www.ICGtesting.com
Printed in the USA
BVHW071038290320
576275BV00001B/102

9 781648 030581